Journey Along the Andes

Christopher Portway

i

impact books

This edition first published in Great Britain 1993 by
Impact Books, 112 Bolingbroke Grove, London SW11 1DA

First published in Great Britain 1984 by
The Oxford Illustrated Press, Sparkford, YEovil,
Somerset BA22 7JJ

ISBN 1-874687-12-9

Books by the same author:

Non-fiction
Journey to Dana (Kimber)
The Pregnant Unicorn (Dalton)
Corner Seat (Hale)
Double Circuit (Hale)
The Great Railway Adventure (Oxford Illustrated Press/Coronet Books)
Czechmate (John Murray)
Indian Odyssey (Impact Books)

Fiction
All Exits Barred (Hale)
Lost Vengeance (Hale)
The Tirana Assignment (Hale)
The Anarchy Pedlars (Hale)

Printed and bound by The Guernsey Press, Guernsey

CONTENTS

Acknowledgements

For unstinting help given before, during and after my journey I would like to single out for very special thanks the following:

Bill Harding, H.E. the then British Ambassador, Peru.
Brian McCauley, the then Principal of the American School of Lima, and Helen McCauley.
The South American Explorers Club, Lima.
The staff of the National Library, Lima.
The staff of the Military Geographical Institute, Lima.
Eduardo Jansen, Lima.
Nick Asheshov, *The Lima Times.*
Valentine Inga Castro, schoolmaster of Haurautambo, Peru.
The Peruvian Police Force and, in particular, the Chief of Police in Pomabamba, Peru, and his wife.
Senior Enrique Veloz, President of the Association de Andinismo de la Federación Deportiva de Chimborazo, Riobamba, Ecuador.
Brian and Jo Hanson, London.
The Times.
Time Life Books
John Brooks, Editor of the *South American Handbook.*
British Caledonian Airways.

Also my thanks go to Curtis Brown Ltd for permission to publish excerpts from *Highway of the Sun* by Victor von Hagen (Victor Gollancz).

Prelude

Inca history has its origins in myth and continues in legend. As Victor von Hagen pronounces in his *Realm of The Incas* we know no more about the origins of the Incas than that which they tell us of themselves in their own version of history and mythology. The original Inca people are reputed to have come out of, or about, Lake Titicaca, wandered north between the double barrier of the Andes, come to the valley of Cuzco and there laid the beginnings of their empire. And that the Incas and their empire *did* evolve within the valley of Cuzco has been confirmed by archaeology — as has the spread of that empire by the more recent discovery of their exclusively designed and constructed edifices and roads, many of which I was to see on my own journey.

The *Encyclopaedia Britannica* defines 'Inca' as

> 'a Peruvian tribe, speaking the Quichua dialect, who, at the time of the Spanish expedition under Francisco Pizarro in 1533, exercised paramount rule over a region extending west of the Atlantic slope of South America between Quito in Ecuador and the Maule river in Chile. They were a highland people and organised a renaissance of the earlier 'civilisation', characterized by megalithic, polygonal structures of stone, which appears to have prevailed in the uplands of Bolivia and Peru at an anterior date (known as the Tiahuanaco period). The earliest traditional records of the people are mythological...'

A cautious definition indeed, and one reflecting the combination of fact and fiction that, perhaps, is the chief attraction of the Inca story.

The first Inca ruler is the legendary Manco (c. AD 1100) who, in all probability, *was* a legendary character of the Tiahuanaco period. His successor appears to be Sinchi Roca and it is probable that his accession heralded the epoch associated with Inca domination. In fact he may be regarded as the first actual Inca ruler. The Incas enjoyed four centuries of unbroken rule until it was abruptly terminated by the execution of Lord-Inca Atahualpa by the Spaniard Francisco Pizarro in 1533.

The Incas were adept at the working of gold, silver and precious stones; they made pottery and wove fabrics of cotton and vicuna wool. They were proficient farmers, irrigating their fields by means of aqueducts, manuring them with guano, and introducing a kind of coulter, after the manner of the plough. But it was their building and road making in which they really excelled. Their buildings were simple though massive, being seldom more than one storey high, and roofed with thatch; the arch was not employed. Their highways, however, are the greatest memorials to the Incas, the one supreme accomplishment for which the world will always remember them.

Chronology

c.2500 BC: Coastal Indians engaged in agriculture.
1200-400 BC: Chavín de Huantar culture, central Andes.
400 BC-AD 800: Paracas culture, south coast of Peru.
400 BC-AD 1000: Nazca, south coastal culture.
272 BC-AD 1000: Mochica coastal culture.
400 BC-AD 1000: Tiahuanaco Andean Empire.
c. AD 1100: Cuzco founded by legendary historical figure of Manco Capac, first Lord-Inca.
1250: Inca culture in and about Cuzco valley.
1300: Tiahuanaco coast invasion collapses. Other cultures emerge from its ruin. Chimú, Mochic-speaking people as were the Mochicas, rise and form an immense empire; rivals of the Incas.
1350: Incas begin expansion. Inca Roca, 6th Inca, builds bridge across the Apurimac river.
1390: Kingdom of Chimor completes capital, Chan-Chan.
1437: Viracocha, 8th Inca. Cuzco is besieged by Chanca tribe.
1438: Inca troops under Yupanqui, son of Viracocha, defeat Chancas. Proclaimed 9th Inca, he takes name of Pachacuti.
1450: Pachacuti enlarges Inca Empire.
1466: Chimú Empire is overun by Incas who now control all of Peru.
1471: Topa Inca, 10th Lord-Inca. Era of road-building.
1492: Topa Inca conquers all of Chile to the Maule river.
1493: Huayna Capac, 11th Lord-Inca. Completes coastal road from Chile to Tumbes.
1498: Huana Capac extends conquest into Colombia. Completes Andean highway, Quito into Chile.
1513: Vasco Nunez de Balboa discovers the Pacific. The Incas become aware of white man's presence.
1519: Atahualpa becomes Lord-Inca.

1522: The Spanish explorers become aware of the Kingdom of Gold (Peru).

1527: Francisco Pizarro makes first landing.

1527: Death of Huayna Capac.

1527: Civil war between Huáscar, crowned 12th Inca, and Atahualpa, who dominates the north.

1532: Huáscar defeated.

1532 (Nov 16): Atahualpa captured by Pizarro in Cajamarca, held captive, agrees to ransom himself.

1533 (Aug 29): His ransom completed, Atahualpa is executed by the Spaniards.

1533 (Aug): Coronation of Huallpa at Cajamarca. Spaniards march south.

1533 (Oct): Death of Huallpa at Jauja.

1533 (Nov 8): Battle of Vilcaconga between Quisquais and Hernando de Soto.

1533 (Nov): Entry of Pizarro's force into Cuzco.

1533 (Dec): Coronation of Manco Inca at Cuzco.

1534 (mid-Feb): Riquelme repulses Quisquais's attack at Jauja.

1534 (Feb): Pedro de Alvarado lands in Ecuador at Puerto Viejo.

1534 (March): Sebastián de Benalcazar leaves San Miguel for Quito.

1534 (May 3): Battle of Teocajas between Benalcazar and Ruminavi.

1534 (mid-June): Quito occupied by Benalcazar.

Introduction

We all have our pet interests and mine is travel. Travel using the railways in particular, or failing that, travel by any means and for any reason that presents itself to me. Thus, whilst I have ridden the railways in most countries of the world, I have also driven the Alaskan Highway, followed the Karakoram Highway in Pakistan and the silk routes of China's Sinkiang, walked a Roman road in Britain as well as the ghost Canol Road in Canada's North-West Territory and rafted the full length of an African river. The arteries, historic and current, of this earth invariably provide the oft-stoney path for my journeys.

But there was one journey that I hadn't done and which I very much wanted to do. Ever since my turbulent school-days the subject of the Inca roads and the Incas themselves had intrigued me, so here, in my more mature years, was an obvious destination towards which to set my ageing mind and feet, should an opportunity arise. Yet the eventual accomplishment of this venture was to come about almost by accident.

The path that led me to the Inca trail was a devious one full of frustrations, false leads and dead ends. Let me explain.

I suppose it had to come. Yachts-people sail it, landlubbers walk, cycle or drive round it. The world was simply crying out for someone to ride a horse around it. And came the time when someone arrived on the scene to do just that. His name was Jack Bailey, a young farmhand from Buckinghamshire who had written to an expeditionary magazine asking for help to make just such a journey. I became involved when I rashly answered his cry for help and found myself given the task of organising what was somewhat grandly titled 'The Round The World Horse Expedition'. I had no particular desire to make that particular journey myself but I was only too pleased to help young Jack.

Jack already held the *Guinness Book of Records* record for the ride from Land's End to John O'Groats on horseback so I suppose he imagined himself to be all set for a world circuit. His innocence of the restrictions likely to be imposed both by nature and man on such a venture was monumental to the point of disbelief. His enthusiasm for his project had already cost him his wife, and when I met him, a partner of his enterprise had just dropped out. That left just Jack and nine-year-old Jason, his sturdy Welsh cob/Clydesdale bay gelding against the world, with me attempting to smooth their path and agreeing to join them for the more difficult parts.

The initial route chosen had been the direct one, eastwards via Siberia, across the Bering Sea and southwards through North, Central and South America. In my capacity as 'project manager' I made the contacts with the London embassy of the Soviet Union and its ambassador, a socialist Lord (Fenner Brockway, a friend of mine) and HRH The Duke of Edinburgh who, about this time, was accompanying his daughter to the Kiev horse trials. I also contacted, with some success, various newspapers, magazines, television, food and equipment companies for sponsorship and promotion.

But things started to go wrong — problems in dealing with the Russians meant we had to re-route the initial path of the journey to include east and west Europe, Asia and the Far East and the Americas. Then we fell into the hands of a professional promoter and film producer who rushed off to the United States to announce our impending project and was never seen again. With him had gone our hopes, and with his non-return, they quickly faded. It was Jack who cracked first. He suddenly decided to throw in the sponge and so died an escapade on which we had expended a lot of effort.

That should have been the end of the matter and for Jack it was. But for me, my interest was reawakened when a second horseman entered my life, in the guise of one Gordon Roddick. He had heard of our aborted venture and had written to suggest that the intercontinental hack that *he* had dreamed up might well fit into the scheme of things. Stung by defeat and disappointment I replied that my years of experience in managing unsuccessful horse rides were at anyone's disposal. The new venture was less ambitious than Jack's circumnavigation of the globe but still formidable enough to raise my interest. Additionally I recognized in the new rider a kindred spirit and a character as stubborn as my own. Under the emergent colours of 'The Intercontinental Horse Trek' I began anew the dreary search for recognition, sponsorship and knowledge.

Sebastian Snow, the global hiker, walked it. A.F. Tschiffely, renowned travel author of the early twentieth century, rode it. Here we go again, I thought. For a hiker or a horseman the long-distance marathon between the bottom and the top of South America had all been done before; it's what might be termed 'old sombrero'. But Tschiffely and his two mounts undertook *their* hack sixty years ago and things have changed for the worse since then. Politics have poisoned the frontiers and traffic has contaminated the ways between them. Nobody has repeated Tschiffely's epic ride for the stumbling blocks of modern 'civilization' have multiplied making it a re-issue of an old challenge. World-traveller Roddick, however, a very unlikely resident of staid Littlehampton, decided to take it up. And this time things did get off the ground.

I sat at home champing at the bit — for again my initial role was that of manager — while Gordon spent two months fighting corrupt authority in Buenos Aires, acquiring two Creole horses (Tupé and Bajador) and the sheaf of documents necessary to ride them northwards. The deed accomplished, man and beasts trudged towards the Paraguayan border. The authorities in Paraguay were co-operative, not only inviting Gordon to a reception attended by President Stroessner's cousin, but putting out a national radio announcement to the effect that the good citizens of Paraguay were to look after the intrepid rider. Paperwork was not to be avoided even here, though, carried out over a month on a Brook Bond *estancia* (ranch), the chore was made quite palatable. With a donated mule to keep Tupé and Bajador company, Gordon made for the pitiless and waterless Chaco Plain.

The military were helpful too. Soldiers warned him of the dangers of riding too close to the Paraguay-Argentina border and left the corpse of their dead officer outside his bedroom one night to emphasize the point. Smuggling is a major industry in the area and law and order a lesser-known commodity.

In spite of dire warnings Gordon managed to survive on the parched and awful plain though horses and mule became sick and a five-week rest at an army post was deemed necessary to heal and recuperate the beasts.

An emotional crossing of the Paraguay-Bolivian border was heightened by first glimpses of hills and the distant Andes. But Bolivia had some unpleasant surprises in store. While resting one day Tupé escaped into thick jungle and scrub and a whole week was lost in tracing him down. Weakened himself with fatigue and disease Gordon carried on into the Camari where one, Ché Guevara had met his end. Here Tupé teetered on the edge of death after an overdose of Algorobba pods, a bean-like tree fruit, but was saved by drastic application of a hypodermic needle and frequent drenches.

Then, nearing Sucre, tragedy struck. The one occasion when Gordon accepted the services of a self-appointed guide he was led the wrong way and both horses, bolting suddenly, plunged to their deaths over a cliff. Gordon, horseless and dejected, was forced to abort the project and sent me a telegram accordingly. Yet another of my undertakings had bitten the dust.

But one can't just stand by and let a venture like this die like the unfortunate Tupé and Bajador. Into the vacuum came the notion of continuing northwards myself from Bolivia along the historic mountain route of that most famous of Inca highways — the royal road. It was a chance that, assuredly, would never come my way again and fate was handing it to me on a plate from which had already fallen two aborted missions and two dead horses. Additionally, time and a flight ticket to Lima — the latter donated by British Caledonian Airways — were to hand, the former allotted for my intended joining up with Gordon just two months hence. Straightaway I launched into a fever of preparation with the aim of replacing the old journey with the new one.

I also had to find a new companion since Gordon was not only a sick and disillusioned man but one whose thwarted amibition revolved around the single purpose of the follow-up of Tschiffely's ride. My search for a colleague was brief. It produced David Taylor, of Bletchley, who not only spoke Spanish but had travelled in the Andean countries so could be of inestimable help as a counter to my own ignorance. A dark-haired, slight youth in his early twenties, David was as plainly ambitious as he was enthusiastic. I was a little concerned about the difference in our ages but this seemed a small price for a companion well versed in Inca lore.

We had met earlier in London at one of the monthly meetings of the Globetrotters Club, an association of travellers and aspiring travellers that is a breeding ground for volunteers for travel ventures of this sort. He was at the stage in life when he had just put university behind him yet a future nine-to-five job was deemed a horrible obligation to be postponed for as long as possible. A sojourn in South America of three to four months offered a worthwhile method of delaying the inevitable.

However David's enthusiasm for the proposed journey went deeper than that. South America and the Andean countries in particular, together with his continued Incain studies, were, so he reckoned, to feature large in his profession and aspirations. A burning ambition was to deliver a paper before a distinguished audience of fellows of the Royal Geographical Society — which, with a little help from me, he subsequently did — while his personal god was John Hemming, not only director of that august body but a world-authority on the Inca civilisation. Even at this early stage of our acquaintanceship it was plain that I had become no more than a prop for David's endeavours — though I could conceive of no evil in the fact. His quest for knowledge and fame would only enhance the chances of success in our own forthcoming mission.

To carry this out I had little more than three months at my disposal; the distance we proposed to cover was well in excess of 3,000 miles — much of it (particularly the 1,700-odd miles between Cuzco and Quito) on foot. Furthermore it was not going to be simply a case of following the remnants of a road but also of searching for those remnants. I alone held a strong compulsion to keep faith with Gordon and parallel his planned route in

Bolivia, Peru, Ecuador and Colombia; even returning to it when possible.

Neither of us held any illusions as to the difficulty of the task we had set ourselves. Northern Peru contains some of the remotest territory on earth, the altitude would rarely be less than 12,000 feet and we would be subjected to the most savage of mountain weathers. We could expect no assistance should we run into trouble and we would have to carry everything for prolonged existence in this inhospitable wilderness upon our shoulders.

Becoming lost in so vast a territory was another possibility since not only were maps of the supposed route of the royal road rare in the extreme but those we possessed or were likely to acquire contradicted one another to a bewildering degree. It was hoped to clarify some of these disparities upon arrival at Lima.

The peoples we would meet deep in the Andes provided another question mark. Neither of us could be at all certain of the sort of reception we might expect from the more primitive communities astride our path. Communication, too, would be a problem for we were aware that only in the urban regions was the Spanish tongue understood and spoken. We would carry some basic foodstuffs but would still have to rely on local villages for more substantial fare.

On the credit side I was as fit as anyone could be for my age — 54 — and David held the advantage of youth. But our optimism and inspiration sprang largely from the written words of the fourteenth-century Spanish chronicler, Pedro Cieza de León, whose diary records:

> 'I believe since the history of man, there has been no other account of such grandeur as is to be seen on this road which passes over deep valleys and lofty mountains, by snowy heights, over falls of water, through the living rock and along the edges of tortuous torrents. In all these places, the road is well constructed, on the inclining mountains well terraced, through the living rock cut along the riverbanks supported by retaining walls, in the snowy heights built with steps and resting places, and along its entire length swept cleanly and cleared of debris — with post stations and storehouses and

Temples of the Sun at appointed intervals along its length.'

As expeditionary journeys go this one was absurdly unprepared. But if de León wrote the truth and the ravages of time and the elements had not been unduly harsh it was to be hoped that the route of the royal road would still be clear enough to provide, if not a banister, at least an indication of the way to go. With two of my previously managed expeditionary journeys in ruins, another ingredient for success could have lain within the adage of being third time lucky.

1

LIMA–AREQUIPA–PUNO –LA PAZ–CUZCO

The coast of Venezuela stood sideways like a wallpaper with no repeating motif: red earth, cubic brown houses, silver oil tanks. The Boeing 747 banked again and we descended to Caracas Airport, small and unsophisticated but in a flurry of reconstruction through new-found oil wealth. Outside, it was abruptly midsummer and for an hour I had to suffer the heat in my winter woollies while fuel was pumped into the drooping wings of the plane. Then we were off once more and flying over the city of Caracas which showed itself to be compressed between mountain foothills and relentless sea. The big aircraft was nearly empty with just nine of us scattered amongst its regiment of seats. I begged my fifth iced water from a group of idling hostesses as we continued over the seemingly eternal ocean and into a long-overdue night.

Arrival at Lima on the coast of Peru, was scheduled for 20.40 hours and we bounced along the main runway of Jorge Chavez International on the dot. Contrary to expectations the immigration formalities were swift and painless and David Taylor, who had arrived at the Peruvian capital ahead of me, was in reception. Within seconds I was bathed in sweat as we lugged my framed rucksack and our combined camping gear to a *collectivo* (private taxi) and stowed everything away in the voluminous boot. Unfortunately the beer I downed at the first bar we found in the city centre simply made things worse.

I had managed to arrange a *pied à terre* in the Peruvian capital. Helena McCauley was a close friend of my Czech-born wife's sister and had, very kindly, offered us her home as a base for initial operations. Czech herself, she was married to an American doing a stint as principal of the American School of Lima. They lived in the pleasant suburb of Chaclycayo some fifty minute's bus ride out of Lima proper and, though David had been staying there for two nights already, he still found the house, shrouded in darkness and wisteria, not at all easy to locate amongst the chequerboard of similar shrub-shaded streets and well-to-do homes.

My companion had left Britain a fortnight before by way of a flight from Luxembourg. At Caracas, on the South American mainland, he had taken to the long-distance buses, reaching Lima ahead of me which was a pretty rugged effort. The reason we hadn't travelled out together was that I had been given my ticket by British Caledonian — a fact that was perhaps quite reasonably resented by David, particularly since travel by South American bus wasn't exactly easy or comfortable.

This, I think, was the first occasion of ill will between us, though in this instance, it never came out into the open. That David didn't find making friends easy and was apt to be impatient with older people (like myself) I discovered very soon after I had got to know him. Perhaps we were being optimistic in thinking that such a newly formed partnership between two people who were so different in age, temperament and interests could survive such a rigorous expedition.

But if that was the first, the second occasion of ill feeling was to come from me. Right from the moment of arrival in Peru a disturbing emotion had developed within me. Though twice his age I had succumbed to a rarely-expressed inferiority complex that intruded into my relationship with him. His awesome superiority of knowledge of both local conditions and historical fact — not to mention his command of Spanish — left me strangely deflated. It was not as if this proficiency was flaunted in my face. Not at all. It was, I think, a simple matter of our being born of different generations coupled to the prospect of the two of us having to live together in close proximity for months on end and in the most trying circumstances. All the while I was painfully aware that, without his capabilities, I would have been hopelessly lost.

Arriving late, our hosts had wisely retired to bed leaving two vociferous dogs to greet us. David had been entrusted with the front door key so we were able to let ourselves in. On my first night in Peru, and one of the very few in a Peruvian bed, I slept like a log.

I met Helena and Brian over the breakfast table. David was already one of the family and, again, I was the new boy. It came to me, idiotically, that they were *my* friends and that if it hadn't been for me, David would not have been sitting so pretty as he was. (My mother was jealous of her friendships and I thought, O God, I'm getting like her). But my childish resentment died within minutes of meeting the McCauleys as straightaway I was made to feel at home.

Brian was very much the all-American boy and was almost childishly enthusiastic about everything: his home, his job, his hobbies and, most of all his own physical fitness, about which he was obsessive. His accustomed recreational routine included cold baths, running sessions and horse-riding at the Chosica Country Club.

Our days in Lima were put to vital use. Though David and I had undertaken much research and preparatory work in Britain there was still much to be done in the Peruvian capital. Preliminary contacts were made with the aid of the Peruvian telephone system, surely the most inefficient in the world, but it was through Helena that we finally got our first really helpful introduction. This was to one Edy Jansen, a senior industrial bank employee whose knowledge and collection of maps of the Inca realm and culture were invaluable and who bore enough seniority, it seemed, to be able to delegate his office chores while he dealt contentedly with our frequent intrusion and questions. He helped us fill the many gaps as to our likely route — particularly in the Peruvian-Ecuadoran border area for which we were expressly forbidden map coverage owing to it being a restricted zone. Even within Ecuador Edy was able to pinpoint landmarks that we should look out for. A close friend of Edy's, a *La Prensa* journalist called Louis Enrique Tori, who also spoke good English, often joined us at the bank and likewise provided much information. We also met Nick Asheshov of the *Lima Times* (who was also the Lima correspondent of the *Daily Telegraph* and *Daily Mail)*, who was reputed to be a source of useful connections. We ran him to earth in his office off the Plaza de Armas where he listened to our plans with interest and asked that we maintain contact with him. In return he divulged some of his connections. Next we called at the British Embassy there to meet Bill Harding, the ambassador, with whom I had corresponded prior to his appointment to Lima. This most kindly gentleman was to give us an official letter, well embellished with stamps and seals, that was to play a not inconsiderable part in smoothing the path both inside and outside Peruvian borders.

We visited all manner of institutions during those four days in the sweltering city, the longest period being spent at the Military Geographic Institute on the outskirts of town. Here we pored for hours over large-scale maps of Peru attempting to equate sixteenth-century details of a mystical road against modern Ordnance Survey sheets. This, we found to be a well-nigh impossible imposition not least because of the divided opinions as to the route of the original artery. However we struck one singular piece of luck with the discovery that on three of the modern Peruvian map sheets — those covering the Yanahuanca and La Unión regions — the old route was actually marked by a dotted line and titled *camino Incaico* (Inca road). Later we were to become aware that accuracy was not the strongest feature of these maps; an unkind comment, perhaps, against cartographers attempting to chart so remote and difficult territory as that of the central Andes.

The Inca empire at the zenith of its power stretched over much of western South America. In order to hold the huge realm together and convert great territories of mountain, desert and jungle into the close-knit empire it became (not to mention the continued waging of war to further expand it), communications had to be of the highest order. This was where the system of roads came in, the hub of the great complex being the Inca capital, Cuzco.

The complex was based upon two chief highways the first of which followed the coast and second which was loosely parallel to it, ran through the mountains. The coastal road stretched from Tumbes (the frontier town which marked the coastal end of the Inca empire and which is now close to the Ecuadoran border),

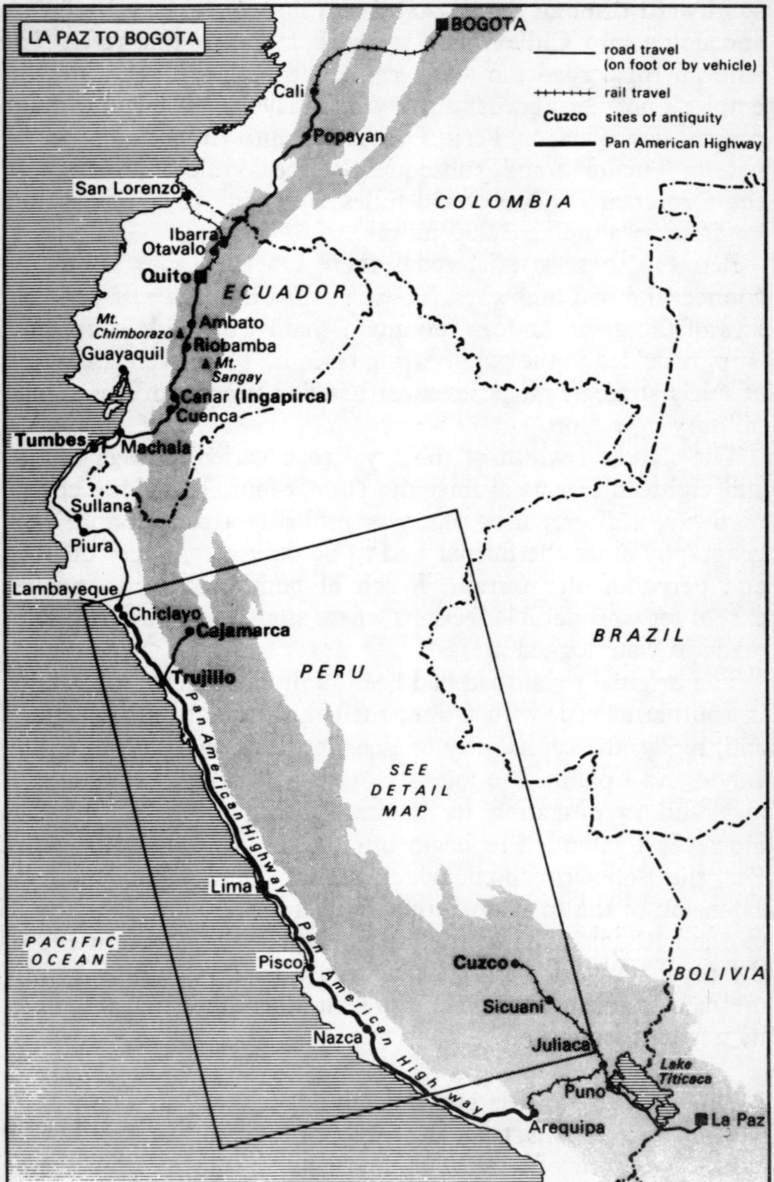
LA PAZ TO BOGOTA
road travel
(on foot or by vehicle)
rail travel
Cuzco
sites of antiquity
Pan American Highway
BOGOTA
Cali
Popayan
COLOMBIA
San Lorenzo
Ibarra
Otavalo
Quito
ECUADOR
Mt. Chimborazo
Ambato
Riobamba
Guayaquil
Mt. Sangay
Canar (Ingapirca)
Cuenca
Tumbes
Machala
Sullana
Piura
Lambayeque
Chiclayo
Cajamarca
Trujillo
PERU
BRAZIL
Pan American Highway
SEE DETAIL MAP
Lima
PACIFIC OCEAN
Pisco
Cuzco
Sicuani
BOLIVIA
Nazca
Juliaca
Lake Titicaca
Puno
La Paz
Arequipa

southward through the coastal desert and entire length of Peru and down into Chile where it ended at the Maule river. The Andean royal road ran along the spine of the Andes from the empire's northern border at the Ancasmayo river, down through present-day Ecuador, Peru, Bolivia and into Argentina to terminate at Tucumán and, subsequently, the Maule. The length of the former artery was 2,520 miles while the royal road could boast an astounding 3,250 miles.

Between these arterial roads there ran numerous laterals to connect the two highways. These pushed into the east-west valleys of the great Andean mountain chain while side routes and 'slip roads' led to the gold-bearing regions. There were also roads of solely strategic purposes constructed in support of a particular military operation.

The standard width of the royal road varied between fifteen and eighteen feet as against the twenty-four feet of the coastal highway, a discrepancy that was probably a compromise with geography since the former had to be built across very difficult and perpendicular terrain. Much of both roads was unpaved except for considerable sections where stone causeways had to be made in waterlogged areas.

The original royal road had been built to connect Cuzco, now in southern Peru, with Quito, then the Inca's northern capital and, today, the capital city of Ecuador. This was the route that David and I planned to follow closely — locating it when necessary and investigating its landmarks and points of interest. However I intended to begin our journey further south at La Paz, the Bolivian capital, which was not only on the southern extension of the royal road into Bolivia but also on the route of Gordon Roddick's broken odyssey. And at the northern end of the royal route, at Quito, David and I would continue by any means of transport available into Colombia following, this time, its northern extension.

Lima in late April is hot and humid. Our urban wanderings were effected by bus, tram and on foot but mainly on foot for the city is a warren of narrow back streets. It also lacks in scenic splendour and its pavements, let there be no doubt, are unkempt, hard and crowded. The citizens sigh for the sun at this time. Lima has a strange climate which precipitates, through the winter months, an overcast sky when fog and humidity make it feel colder than it is. Our first visit coincided with the onset of winter though the local mist had not yet materialised.

Nobody in Peru imagines that her Indian heritage could be greater than that of her Spanish conquerors and most certainly Lima feels herself to be a Spanish city and continues to honour her Spanish founder who, legend has it, was suckled by a sow. The remains of Francisco Pizarro lie in a chapel of the twin-towered cathedral in the Plaza de Armas. The Incas completed their conquest of Peru and Ecuador in about 1450, after centuries of fighting, but Pizarro, helped by his own treachery and a civil war simmering between his enemies, managed *his* subsequent conquest in less than a year after landing on the coast at Tumbes in May 1532 and working his way south to effect the capture of Cuzco, the Inca capital. But an inland capital high in the mountains was useless to the sea-going Spaniards and in 1535 Lima, close to the ocean, was founded, by Pizarro, on a site that had once held Rimac, city of the pre-Inca Chimus. It is said that the Indians suggested the site to the hated Spanish occupiers as being particularly suitable for building their capital, merely because they thought they would all be bound to die in its miserable climate.

The city's power was at its zenith during the eighteenth century. It held some of the best colonial buildings in South America and there were few cities in the old world which could rival the wealth of its men or the luxury of its women. Today its influence has waned and Lima has become just another South American metropolis of shabby opulence amidst vibrant slums.

After a hectic day in such an environment it was pleasant to escape to our temporary home at Chaclycayo and the Andean foothills. Usually we got there in time to join Brian for his daily run. Devid declined to participate but I felt it expedient to do so and enjoyed the jog into the hills, the dogs running excitedly ahead. It might have set my old heart beating faster but it made for a ravenous appetite for dinner and was certainly good training.

Our final day we spent at Chaclycayo packing equipment; not too onerous a task because, with an envisaged return to the city a few weeks hence, on our way back northwards from La Paz, we deemed it desirable to leave some of the heavier gear behind. David saw no purpose in, nor reason for, a detour to the Bolivian capital and was all for making straight for Cuzco but I was determined to commence our journey from the point from where Gordon, defeated and horseless, had to fly home. I am a tidy-minded traveller, abhorring loose ends, and, for me, there remained a strong connection between my former colleague's abruptly terminated progress and the imminent start of my own, on a parallel course if differing theme. I told David I would meet him in Cuzco if he wanted to go straight there but he was spirited enough to accede to my wishes and agreed to accompany me. That evening we caught an uncomfortable long-distance bus from one of Lima's down-at-heel coach stations bound for Arequipa, second city of Peru in the south of the country, and prepared ourselves for a seventeen-hour confinement.

For seventeen substitute twenty-seven, for that was the number of hours we spent in that unlovely vehicle. The Pan-American Highway, in spite of its evocative sounding name, is a beast of a road frequently poorly-surfaced, invariably ragged-edged and ill-used. Hugging the coast for hundreds of miles it is a desert highway with the attendant aggravations of heat, wind and desolate scenery. Its traffic is ruthless. In place of kilometre stones are the multiple graves of its victims.

Darkness fell long before we reached Pisco — named after the celebrated brandy — while Ica was no more than a glimpse of pleasant white houses and a luminous church that draws pilgrims in thousands. A full moon gave beauty to arid highlands and a rugged coast and, near Nazca, the bus gave up the ghost at the bottom of a hill. After hours in close proximity to the toilet, to alight into a cool crisp night was a pleasure indeed even if it was but for the utilitarian purpose of pushing the vehicle up the gradient. Lying twenty kilometres inland were those mysterious markings, the Nazca Lines, alleged to be some sort of enormous astronomical pre-Inca calendar.

Daybreak found us stranded in a decrepit coastal village where, by order of the police, we were obliged to await the whims of competitors in the Arequipa-Lima car rally who, because it was a Sunday, had been permitted to turn the Pan-American into a race track. The heat sent me to the sea but hopes of a swim were dashed by the sheer size of the breakers and a beach transformed into a particularly obnoxious refuse dump. It took hours for the first competitor to hurtle himself through the village and hours more for the last. No driver fortuitously broke his neck in my sight but at least one was to kill himself that sun-blasted Sabbath day. I could raise scant sympathy.

Arequipa, it is said, has the most beautiful situation of any town in Peru. We had caught this particular bus so as to give ourselves a whole afternoon in this much-praised city but, instead, arrived there after midnight. It was my first lesson on taking things for granted in South America. A taxi whirled us round the less salubrious hotels and dumped us at an establishment that lacked everything except a closed door.

We did, however, manage to see something of Arequipa before catching our east-bound train to Puno, on account of the fact that the earlier service we had aimed for proved to be but a figment of the timetable-compilor's imagination. It is the volcano El Misti that makes Arequipa; El Misti and its two fiery neighbours, Chachani and Pichu-Pichu. But in its own right the city is worth seeing for the many quaint old Spanish houses and hefty churches. The place was re-established by an emissary of Pizarro's though even in 1540 it was an old Inca city.

In spite of erratic schedules the trains are better at time-keeping than the buses and ours, additionally, offered fine views of the trio of volcanos, their snow-capped peaks looking magical in a haze of morning mist as we wound out of the valley towards Juliaca. Curcero Alto is the highest point on the line and one knows that, east of this point, all water from the myriad mountain streams flows into the Atlantic thousands of miles away the other side of the continent. Two lakes, Lagunillas and Saracocha, came into sight the same time from opposite sides of the train activating our heads like those of a Wimbledon tennis audience as we crept along their shores. Green pastures were dotted with flocks of sheep, llamas and alpacas as the horizon changed from dry peaks to fertile pampa.

The Andes are great humblers of men. They stretch the length of South America, forming a wall 4,500 miles long, draped at the northern end with vegetation, and at the southern end with ice and snow. Only the Himalayas and Karakorams of Asia boast peaks that are higher. And down the length of this range, and on its slopes, lie wild regions of snow, ice and fire, of dripping jungle and seared desert, of cloud cover and merciless sun, of intense heat and bitter cold, of warm moist air and air so thin that breathing becomes a gasp for life. Sitting in my secure corner seat as we ground into Juliaca a stab of something akin to terror pierced me as the reality of what we inexperienced hikers had set out to accomplish began to dawn upon me.

Three thousand miles to the north, at the lusher end of that titanic range, stood Bogota, capital of Colombia. It was from here that we were to return home. In between were all the hazards and extremes of the elements that the great Andes could generate from their cauldron. Along the spine of this awesome climax of geography lay our path, a slender, broken thread in the grip of mighty chasms and peaks of ice and flame, that we had optimistically planned to follow, occasionally by village bus and antiquated lorry but mostly our own feet.

What kind of road or track would we find to accompany us across this desolation? We harboured no illusions of a signposted way leading us by the hand over hill and dale for not even our maps could agree on the exact location of the royal road except for limited sections. And even when on the route the chances of our always being able to recognize the *agger* of an ancient road were likely to be slim. Only its lonely landmarks — the ruins of temples, forts and posthouses we knew lay athwart the path as eternal beacons of stone, would provide any form of guidance.

I contemplated again some other giant road systems that mankind had produced: the Persian royal road over what is now Turkey, Iraq and Iran is one, and the Roman complex in Europe and North Africa is another. Yet when Pedro Cieza wrote, in 1548, 'Accordingly the Incas constructed the grandest road that there is in the world as well as the longest', he was correct in his assumption, for the longest Roman road — that from Britain's Hadrian Wall to Jerusalem — fell far short of the span traversed by the royal Inca road.

Nobody knows the date of the building of either this or the other Inca roads. Certainly earlier Peruvian cultures possessed a highway system, and it was the techniques of the Mochicas, the Tiahuanacans, and the Chimús that were taken over and improved upon by the Incas. As with the Romans, the Incas looked upon the construction of a road as something of which to be immensely proud and named stretches of their highways after their rulers. Each province of the empire built and maintained the section of road within its boundary which, when completed, was taken on by neighbouring provinces though, when the need was urgent, all worked at the same time. That there was a master plan is evident from the standard design of bridges, step-roads and drainage systems and the general uniformity of the road system throughout the land.

Had Gordon Roddick's odyssey not been terminated by disaster the onward route through Peru would have led uncomfortably along that of the old Inca coastal road now lost beneath the worn and rutted tarmac of the Pan-American Highway which was built on top of it. We would have been plagued with incessant traffic and intense heat but the way would have at least remained reasonably flat. The route David and I had chosen held the bigger challenge, leading through some of the greatest barriers with which any landscape could harass a road. The odds against us and our little enterprise completing our journey were high and preoccupied my thoughts as the train rattled cheerfully into an increasingly bucking countryside.

I glanced at David to see if he was similarly engrossed in contemplation but my colleague was deeply immersed in his file of Inca mythology. The ever-practical young man was David. His task was clear. The royal road ran from Cuzco to Quito and it was our duty to locate, observe and traverse it. The fact that we should be travelling a historic route unwalked for hundreds of years was immaterial. That it could lose us in that holocaust of mountains made no apparent impression on his mind. Hastily I fastened mine upon what had gone before, blocking out the doubts and fears with mental pictures of a battered Gordon Roddick plodding through the dusty hell of the Paraguayan Chaco. I might be a little older but if he could do that and if David could do this then I could do it too. For Gordon the challenge of the Andes had not materialised but he had watched their approach as he moved deeper into the Bolivian Altiplano urging on his flagging horses. Though Gordon had fallen I had caught the relay baton and was continuing the contest into this land of a different savagery we had hoped to negotiate together. It was a baton I could not lay down until the Colombian capital stood before me.

Juliaco is a road and rail junction. One way goes east to Puno on Lake Titicaca; the other northwards to Cuzco, the original southern terminal of the royal road and the place from where David and I planned to commence the first trekking portion of our journey. As David had pointed out, it would have been logical to have turned northwards at this point but I stuck to my guns and we remained steadfastly on the Puno-bound train en route towards Bolivia.

We drew into Puno after dark having followed the sombre shores of Lake Titicaca for miles. A seething crowd at the station greeted the train and through this we battled our way to our modest hotel. Basic but reasonably clean, it could produce, at times, hot water though this commodity had yet to register as the singular asset it was.

Though, according to some maps, we were now on the southern extension to the royal road, the town of Puno made hardly an auspicious introduction. Cheerful but decrepit, it is a terminus for ferries and a tourist departure-point for excursions to the famous 'floating islands' of the Uru Indians. Its lakeside beach is a disgrace with dead dogs, inexplicably, the most common item of refuse. But there is attraction within its markets; in fact Puno could be described as a complex of market-places with the largest providing the drama of the day. Here, jousting is part of buying. Food is abundant. Vegetables range from prune-size purple potatoes to artichokes. There are bananas and avocados at give-away prices, shrimps from the coast and enormous salmon trout. The butchers are women, shrouded in white and wearing high-crowned trilbies. In the open market, outside the concrete walls, is the traditional market. Within it Indian women sit with much dignity before their offerings: cooking pots, painted clay bowls, glazed clay figures, talismans, *oca*, sweet potatoes, *chuno* (dehydrated potatoes) and seaweed. There are no hucksters — the women merely wait, expressionless in their patience. The market is almost a place of reverence.

Titicaca stretched away into the distance and if you raise your eyes above the inshore scum — from which women are happily drawing water — the lake is sensationally beautiful. It has the distinction of being the highest navigable lake in the world, 110 miles long by 35 miles wide. The Aymara Indians who farm its harsh shores believe that their white-bearded god, Viracocha, rose from the water's chilly depths to establish their culture. There's something about Titicaca. Only the near-bottomless Siberian lake, Baikal, has affected me as much.

I looked long upon the water, immense, shimmering and threatening. Over it a fleet of grass-balsa boats, hurrying before a following wind, was gliding without disturbing its polished surface. Titicaca is sustained by numerous icy streams yet only one river flows out of this gargantuan lake winding about the grass-bound puna, the barren savannah of the wind-swept Altiplano. Geographical fact and the mysticism of legends merge in the mind to release the triggers of imagination. The lake is of divine origin. Titi, the sacred Mount Puma, offered its name and on an island on the far horizon the sun is said to have given birth to the first Inca ruler. Certainly the waters are feline in nature. It may accept you with an affectionate caress and then, as soon as you are within its power, lash out with foaming claws made devastating by abruptly-raised winds of fury. I looked again at the scum-edged shores and the handsome female water-drawers. Incongruously, a light-hearted observation I heard on the train came through to me 'The titi's better than the caca' and the spell was broken.

David went down with altitude sickness on our first day which gave me time to ponder the lake but we were to come upon it again and again as we rode its full length when we set out in another cramped and airless bus for our destination of La Paz. I must have been feeling the effects of the unaccustomed height too, for I found what is normally considered a colourful drive, with views of the brilliantly blue lake against a background of snow-capped Bolivian peaks, to be no more than tedious. The road was poor and littered with ambushes of Peruvian and, later, Bolivian officials sporting a variety of uniforms and making full use of their right to inflict petty restrictions. And then the lake was lost in the darkness and a bleak Bolivian landscape heralded an arrival at La Paz that was only two hours behind schedule.

At the selection of sites for towns the conquistadors were wizards. These were the men who came upon this crack in the plateau, this gentle, gracious valley, where streams rush through luxuriant undergrowth beneath the arched branches of carob trees. Midway between the Lima of the viceroys and the inexhaustible wealth of Potosi is La Paz and from a town it has grown into a city and become the highest capital in the world.

Its valley really has no physical right to be where it is within the grey cold desert of the Altiplano. The city knows it and resists the lure of the enticing lowlands. The houses of La Paz cling desperately to the slopes so as not to slide down into the valley. It is a city of inclines and through the narrow streets can be glimpsed one of the most picturesque mountains anywhere, Illimani, a white sugar loaf beneath a sky of that lyrical blue which only the purest heights can conjure. Nowhere else are glaciers to be found at the gates of a capital city.

In the far distance the mountains can be picked out, clear in the translucent air, a cluster of peaks towering above the highest desert in the world, a tangle of giants capped by clouds, their feet set in sand, defying through the ages any semblance of geometric order.

Something of what I had sensed of Titicaca I sensed in this uncanny Bolivian city. Perhaps it was not just the city but Bolivia in general: I cannot tell for I was not in Bolivia long enough to learn. But the aura of violence and of indifference beneath the veneer of beauty, tranquility, quaintness and an attractive people struck me from the moment of arrival until the moment of departure. For three days we remained in La Paz searching out information and documents from offices that were closed because of the weekend and later because of a religious holiday.

From time immemorial a Bolivian official has never moved without a bribe. Ministries and state offices are either empty or full of people reading novels. Bolivia is the classic land of revolutions — more than two hundred since its liberation from the Spanish yoke — which adds up to one and a half a year. The adult children (many carrying guns) of La Paz are prone to discharge their weapons in the street for pure joy and occasionally for other reasons, so how can one take these people seriously? Who could really say whether the smiles on these round, apparently good-humoured faces were born of friendliness or brutality? The women no doubt scream *Viva* or *Muera* on such occasions. Their babies with wrinkled faces probably echo their cries. What does it matter? Here it is immaterial, for life is so difficult and to die is too easy.

Again the market place sets the tone. It was filled with ancient splendour and melancholy. People from the arid uplands still hold out their chilled fingers to grasp the warm hands of the lowland men in a kind of mirthless greeting. Here will be heard the language of the pale, almost Mongolian *Quechua,* a sweet, flexible, rhythmic tongue, and that of the *Aymara,* which is insistent, rough and slow. Amongst the motley crowd were mysterious *Urus* from the shores of Titicaca, *Atacamas* from Desaguadero, *Changos* from Poupo, Indians from anywhere along the Andes.

Sitting on the ground the market-women with their lined and serious faces, their bowler hats, plaited hair, tinkling ear-rings and brilliant dresses, offered their precious wares with supreme indifference. Indians, unsmiling, slunk by carrying parrots, cockatoos, iguanas and tortoises. Smoke issued from cookshops like that from a spluttering fuse and flaming orchids contributed shell-bursts of colour. Lively, yet sombre, La Paz is a city of skyscrapers and hovels carved out of rock, that waits for the next inevitable explosion.

Having gained the Bolivian capital and paid silent homage to Gordon's efforts, I was now eager to leave it again. I had been grateful for David's companionship for, more than most, La Paz is a lonely city for a *gringo* Englishman. We left our tenement lodgings near the railway station (that were decidedly the wrong side of the tracks) on a morning crisp with frost. My lethargy had subsided and my footsteps were the springier. We turned about; David to commence an odyssey, I to continue a broken safari.

A confusion of accumulated maps and geographical detail was threatening to detract from our declared task of locating, observing and following the royal road itself or its route. The road, as traced by Victor von Hagen in 1952, traversed both sides of Lake Titicaca from a point south of Ayaviri joining again at the southern end of the lake. The road which ran on the west side was named the Oma-suyu, while that which ran along the eastern shore was the Urco-suyu. This southern extension of the royal road from Cuzco into what is now Bolivia and Chile is, for the most part, buried under five centuries of earth-drift though von Hagen reports* that sections were plain to see running along the puna of the Altiplano. Until Cuzco was reached however neither of us felt constrained to undertake serious observations of the road other than that permitted from the strait-jacket of public transport.

Reverting to the western shore we rejoined the route of Omosuyu at Desaguadero, the coldest and most desolate township on Titicaca made the more unpleasant by the fact of it being the border control centre for the region. In Inca and Spanish times there were no such boundaries. Then the royal road uncluttered by politics, threaded its way through the sandstone cliffs and crossed the Desaguadero River by means of a balsa pontoon bridge. Now, however, it was spanned by a battered wooden structure with iron gates, and was liberally festooned with barbed wire. Somewhere between here and La Paz we had passed close to the famed Tiahuanaco ruins which are, I suppose, meant to strike the tourist all of a heap. Their appeal, no doubt, lies in the mystery of their birth though David was able to tell me that the remains are nothing like so dramatic as those of the Aztec,

***Highway of the Sun* (Gollancz 1956)

Inca or Mayan cultures. In its zenith the city complex of Tiahuanaco is alleged to have contained nearly 150,000 inhabitants in a space of only six acres; assuredly the most densely populated community the world has ever known. Certainly it is the most ancient culture in the Americas; it has no apparent antecedents, and what is more extraordinary, the civilisation vanished as it began — without the slightest trace. Vandals have taken a heavy toll and much of the masonry has been used for 'bedding' the La Paz to Guapui railway line.

Our bus could have been the same vehicle as that on which we had come. It was equally filthy and what it lacked in clients it amply made up for with cargo. An exhaust system exuded black diesel smoke to block out the view and offend our nostrils, and in this manner we came to Zepita. We halted for a while in the village but not long enough to attempt to locate what von Hagen had failed to unearth, the ruins of the old Inca village and its reported *tampu,* or roadhouse. It was the same at Pomata where there was supposed to be a royal variation of such an Incain 'travel-lodge' of which more later. At Juli we managed a quick look at an astonishingly ornately-carved church that could have originated in Valencia, and by nightfall we were back in Puno.

Now and only now could we turn our faces northward and make for Cuzco. Our choice of vehicle rested with the offerings of Peruvian Railways once more for which, as a railway enthusiast, I was truly thankful. Those of South America had till now escaped me but I was not going to let dedication to a road — Inca or otherwise — deflect me from putting right this omission. At Puno station they had a different version of making it more difficult to catch a train by spreading the rumour that none were running today. Of course there *was* one even though it chose to leave at an hour not shown in the timetable. Again we travelled second class declaring a desire to observe the antics of the proletariat but really because of an acute shortage of Peruvian currency.

The coaches were of British manufacture, spartan in the extreme with hard wooden seats and windows jammed shut or unadjustably open. Smoke emitting from the diesel locomotive matched that of our late bus, while our fellow passengers were good solid citizens dressed in their Sunday best though it wasn't

Sunday. Even in our modest grade of accommodation I was aware of a kind of class distinction that encouraged the less rural passengers to keep firmly at arm's length a proletariat of gnarled Indian peasants who spread themselves about the seats as if for permanent residence.

Every now and again the Altiplano would buckle and heave into granite clusters tipped with snow. Herds of llamas and alpacas, grazing contentedly on the rich grassland, were as common as flocks of sheep in Britain. Here and there plots of wheat, barley, potatoes and *quinoa* (a highland grain), which the Aymara Indians produce from every available nook and cranny, had been wrested from the grass. But I was more interested in the llamas. Alpaca husbandry is economically a very important activity in Peru along with other South American countries in the Andean chain. The animal produces valuable fibres and nutritious meat while their coats vary in colour from white to black, with the white topping the commercial charts. Another llama variation is the vicuna teetering on the verge of extinction. In Inca times the animal was protected, the people being conservationists but the brutal conquistadores slaughtered them in thousands, their metaphorical golden fleeces commanding a high price even then. A remote ancestor of the camel, the llama was the closest man got to a domesticated animal since, before the coming of the European, South America was devoid of the horse and other load-carrying beasts. The appearance, in battle, of horses ridden by Spaniards, was said to be one of the factors that caused so much fear and confusion within the Inca ranks. For transport during war and peace the Incas depended on the llama and it has remained a somewhat temperamental but vital beast of burden to this day. The smaller domesticated alpaca is bred solely for its wool as opposed to the vicuna which runs wild.

Alpaca fur hats and scarves were much in evidence as goods for sale by vendors passing down the train. I was tempted to purchase a hat but remembered that everything bought would have to be carried which dampened my enthusiasm. Our only commercial undertaking during that rail journey was the negotiating of an evil-smelling cheese, mistakenly obtained from a woman at Puno station, in exchange for a brass llama souvenir and a clasp knife, a complicated transaction that caused much amusement all round.

The train was in no hurry. Nor were we. It was a delightful trip made the pleasanter by virtue of our being aware of the proximity of the royal road. Though subsequent full-blown expeditions along this route had been unable to prove beyond doubt that the extension road came this way, the stretches of stone paving that were revealed to them along with the fragments of high stone walls and the rounded stone pillars that could only have resulted from the Inca architectural genius, must have been extremely convincing pointers. We dallied long and for no clear reason at Juliaca, through which the old road was presumed to run, and again at Ayaviri, where it apparently bifurcated to run both sides of Lake Titicaca. We likewise stopped nowhere; simply coasted to a quiet halt as if the driver wanted to admire the view. But one enthralling pause was at Sicuani, close to the great Inca temple of Kontiki-Virachoco.

Once the high pass at La Raya was attained we were out of the Titicaca region and at once dropped down into the warmer valley of the Vilcanota, where the air was almost benign. The countryside became purple with the blossom of the potato and *quinoa* while Lake Urcos lay masquerading as an emerald at the bottom of intensely cultivated hills. Eucalyptus trees softened the rock walls of the gorge through which the Vilcanota either glided sedately or pushed in sullen anger.

A blind musician and his family entered our coach and, to the accompaniment of guitar and mouth-organ, the wife sang a haunting Quechua air which has since become a pop tune in Britain. The daughter walked round shyly proferring a collection box into which everybody dropped an offering reasoning, perhaps, that the man's affliction must be the more tragic amongst such idyllic surroundings he would never see.

Abruptly the land flattened out and a glorious sunset transformed distant mountains into walls of mauve. We had arrived at Cuzco, capital of the Incas. Alighting from the train we made our way to the square called Rimac-Pampa that was once the exit place of the great royal road. For David and me it was a beginning.

2

CUZCO–ABANCAY–AYACUCHO –HUANCAYO–LIMA

One fact I noticed right from the moment of stepping off the train. The Indians around me had changed from the lack-lustre, sad-looking ones we had encountered the other side of the La Raya divide to those of the happy beaming faces and laughing eyes of the people surrounding us now. 'Buenos Dias, Caballero', they said with a flourish and though the mindless cry of 'gringo!' still announced our presence, the tone was less derisive.

Cuzco, without doubt, is a friendly city. It is also a tourist centre. All who go to Peru today find their way eventually to Cuzco. It breathes its Inca history as can nowhere else. Founded by Manco Capac it has become a shrine to the Incas, the place where the visitor can do the rounds of its museums, memorials and edifices. David and I felt compelled to make the tour, he with singularly more enthusiasm than I, though he had seen it all before. But the city is emphatically worthy of investigation.

Almost every central street holds a remnant of Incaic wall that has managed to survive the centuries. Much subsequent construction has risen from the ancient stonework which displays the remarkable distinguishing feature that is ever a hallmark of Inca workmanship. Noticeable to the dullest layman is the line of inclination towards the centre of each stone and the rounding of its corners. The edifices of the Lord-Incas and other notables were constructed by professional architects and were the pride of the realm. They were defined by long reaches of stones elaborately cut and fitted with a precision which has never been duplicated anywhere in the world. That which remains in the best state of preservation are those finest buildings and the quality of their planning and construction is plain.

It is legend that records how Manco Capac, the first Inca, came with his four sisters out of the land of the sunrise carrying a wedge of gold. As they travelled, Manco periodically put down the wedge as if in anticipation of some sign being given them. Upon arrival in the valley of the Vilcanota the wedge inexplicably sank out of sight when laid down. Surmising the spot to be the centre of the earth, they halted and with the help of the local Quecha tribes, proceeded to build a city that early in the thirteenth century came to be known as Cuzco.

For at least a century the first Inca and his descendants lived peacefully in the valley. But marauding penetrations by envious neighbouring tribes grew increasingly dangerous and forced the Inca from the defensive to the offensive. About the middle of the fifteenth century the formidable ninth Inca, Pachacuti, began the great militant expansion of the empire. By the end of the reign of his successor, the Incas had either conquered or subjugated all the tribes from near the equator down to the River Maule in Chile, and from the Pacific shore to the edge of the Amazon jungle. Their territory covered nearly a million square miles and they called it 'Tahuantinsuyu', the Four Quarters of the Earth.

This achievement was gained not simply by an ability to wage war; the Inca's strength also lay in the policies they adopted in treating and administering the vanquished peoples. The system was so cunning as to appear benign, a quality that so impressed the defeated that in time they themselves became content to consider themselves loyal Inca subjects; the new regime offered a better life than the one they had had before. So well organised was the pyramid of control by which the laws of the Sun-God, Inti, were transmitted from the god's personal representative, the Lord-Inca, down through the council of state, the judges, the provincial governors, and the local chiefs to each individual in the land, that no dissension or disruptive element was ever able to gain unsuppressible proportions. Yet there was no slavery, no money, no capitalism, no private property beyond a few personal possessions and no taxation other than a form of labour to the state. The system was a near-perfect blend of socialism, communism and monarchy with the right of the Lord-Inca to rule, vested incontrovertibly in the fact that he was an intimate of the sun-god himself.

When a hostile tribe was vanquished, it was common practice for the conquered people to be moved *en masse* to a different part of the empire, there to be taught the Inca language and customs. The land was distributed amongst them and they were totally assimilated into the Inca environment. All land belonged to the state and was divided between people and government. It was the responsibility of the local chief to see that the family communities, or *ayllus,* were allotted according to their own needs and that they provided appropriate labour for working the government land and providing for government projects. It has been suggested that the co-operative working of the land was looked upon by the population as a joyous rather than an onerous undertaking. They contributed voluntarily to enhance the glory of the emperor and the empire. In return they received economic and social security in one of the most successful welfare states in human history.

The vast empire was a model of government and administration. The Inca did not have to be tyrannical in order to control his people because his laws were accepted by all. Disobedience was rare but when it did occur the offenders were punished with severity.

Thus the Incas very efficiently controlled their empire. They understood, furthermore, that the establishment of a system of government was not sufficient in itself. In order that it could be permanently maintained there needed to be a purpose towards which the energy of the people could be directed. It was necessary to canalise the energy in order that neither apathy nor internal pressures could undermine and weaken the structure. One such outlet was the waging of perpetual war. Ostensibly, the reasons for the permanent maintenance of an immense army were to suppress revolts, resist marauding attacks from beyond the frontiers, keep open the lines of communication and to expand the empire to the greater glory of the Lord-Inca and the Sun-God. But in fact the more important reason was the need to occupy the minds of the people. The history of the Inca growth far beyond the confines of their capital, though romanticised by legend, is one that makes stirring reading for it concerns a solid race of determined empire builders not so far removed in spirit and courage from that of our own ancestors.

In spite of my favourable impressions of the citizens of Cuzco it is a sobering fact that whereas the present-day peasant is a poor-class Peruvian, his ancestors four centuries before were the inhabitants of a great and glorious empire, the most powerful and advanced in the American Continent. From the time of Manco Capac, about the beginning of the thirteenth century, there was a continuous line of a dozen or so Incas. They extended their territory a thousand-fold, accumulated vast wealth, created admirable public works, buildings and communications, and devised a highly successful method of government. It was at the peak of his achievement, when Inca Huayna Capac died after quelling revolts in what is now Ecuador, that the first schism appeared to threaten the consistent unified rule of the Incas.

Huayna Capac had two notable sons; one called Huascar and the other, Atahualpa. Before he died, Huayna Capac took the unprecedented step of proposing to divide the empire between the two. Following the demise of Huayna Capac a plague swept the land, disrupted communications and threw everything into confusion. Misunderstandings and rumour gave way to rivalry and civil war. At a great battle at Riobamba in which thousands died, Atahualpa overcame Huascar and claimed the throne. He then made his headquarters at a place called Cajamarca, whilst his armies pursued and exterminated Huascar's remaining forces.

But no sooner had he done so than there came the report of the landing of white men on the coast near Tumbes. The visitors, venturing inland, were courteously invited to Cajamarca and given quarters there. They were small in numbers and seemingly posed no threat to the Inca hierarchy who, additionally, were curious about them. Their leader was the Spaniard, Francisco Pizarro, whose reasons for the visitation were very much more than simple interest and exploration. With Spain embarked upon a mission of conquest in Mexico and Central America, Pizarro's brief from the Spanish throne was one of invasion and development in the name of the Spanish Empire.

Pizarro accepted the proffered hospitality of Atahualpa, flushed with his recent triumph, and it was while the Spanish leader was resting in Cajamarca that he learnt about the Inca's civil war and straightaway began scheming a method by which the disruption could be put to his advantage.

Thus began 'one of the most atrocious acts of perfidy', as the historian, William Prestcott, describes it; a sinister master stroke of double-dealing. Pizarro and his small force of 106 foot-soldiers and 62 cavalrymen approached the rendezvous with the Incas ostensibly as friends and visitors. They had arranged a meeting for dinner on a Saturday evening with Atahualpa who duly arrived accompanied by a retinue of some 6,000 unarmed attendants.

But, with the town deserted by a terrified population who — with commendable perception — imagined an imminent battle would ensue, the Spaniards had been able to lay an ambush around the main square. At the moment of the arrival of the Lord-Inca, Pizarro gave the Spanish war cry 'Santiago!' and his soldiers closed the ring. Guns thundered, bugles blew, horses charged, swords slashed and the terrified Incas attempted to flee. The Spaniards pursued them and many hundreds died. With Atahualpa captured and used as a bargaining counter not only had Pizarro gained for Spain a fortune in Inca gold but was well on the way to winning an empire. The gold ransom — enough to fill a small room — was the initial demand, the captive Lord-Inca agreeing to its collection and delivery to Cajamarca by his bewildered subjects in return for his life. Neither he nor they were to know that, the ransom duly paid, the treacherous Spaniards would go back on their word and execute their distinguished prisoner anyway. Thus the stage was set for the acquisition of not only their gold but the whole of the Inca domain.

The subsequent, almost incredible conquest of the mighty Inca empire by an expedition of 180 Spaniards is surely the most bizarre accomplishment of all. Excuses are legion and the historians have totted up their reasonings and explanations. But the question, why? continues to hang on the lips of those who come to Cuzco where the massiveness and sheer ingeniousness of the military fortifications of the city but add to the enigma.

Cuzco, as a city, emerged in its existing form about 1400. Its mean houses were one-storied but those of the richer citizens were two or even three storeys high. The principal buildings were located about the huge plaza, the towering Sun Temple occupying the most prominent position. To retain its purity, water was conveyed with enormous care through stone conduits laid in the middle of the street.

From the principal plaza, called Huaycapata, spread the wards of the city divided into four sections, created to represent the four principal quarters of the Inca world which gave the realm its name: Tahuantinsuyu. Thus Cuzco is actually a microcosm of their domain; in it lived people drawn from many parts and all quartered in their local sections. Many of the edifices were once sheathed in gold (before the Spaniards removed it) and the city, with all these gold-spangled walls, was surely no less spectacular than those which Marco Polo looked upon in Cathay. Certainly the Inca capital was a most magnificently planned city of which there have been few counterparts in the world.

One of its group of edifices was the Curi-cancha, or 'Golden Enclosure', said to be the first temple complex to be erected by the Incas. Archaeologists are still trying to piece together this most sacred of Inca shrines. But firmly standing today, hardly changed in more than five hundred years, is the great fortress of Cuzco, Sacsahuaman. This amazing structure is a third of a mile long and contains three terraced walls of monolithic blocks, some weighing up to a hundred tons, yet, without prior benefit of the wheel or mortar, each fits together so perfectly that even a razor blade cannot be inserted between them. It could only have been built according to a well-advanced military technique; the blocks look as if they have grown together over the centuries. Each is, however, an entity, quite different in size and shape from its neighbour. I stared at the massive walls and wondered how men alone were able to quarry, shape and transport such monstrous burdens which would have presented a problem to a modern builder with all his mechanical aids. They are today almost immovable, having defied earthquakes and sieges through the ages.

There are other substantial fortress remains in and around Cuzco. Ollantaytambo and Pisac are, likewise, well-known but for sheer brilliance of situation Machu Picchu, the 'Lost City of the Incas' has no rival. Machu Picchu is a word constantly heard the moment you set foot on Peruvian soil. 'Have you been to Machu Picchu?' Though I shy from tourist haunts I was not going to be the only visitor to Cuzco not to visit this most miraculous of ruined cities. Though seventy miles away it was easy to get to, so, leaving David to his researches, I utilised our third day in Cuzco to take the railway down through the dramatic ravine of the Urubamba River to see it.

Today there is nothing remarkable about the journey to Machu Picchu. It was a different matter centuries ago when nuns, or virgins of the Sun as they were known, were forced to flee the ogres of the Spanish authorities in Cuzco along giddy mountain paths to the solitude of this rocky fastness. The conquistadores never discovered this sanctuary. They never considered it worthwhile exploring the depths of the gorge because the likelihood of gold — for which they were invariably searching — being hidden there was small. So, with the passing years, that which was fact became the legend of the lost city to remain alive among the Indians of the neighbourhood until the American archaeologist, Hiram Bingham, re-discovered it at the beginning of this century.

Many Incain peoples had been to Machu Picchu before the Spaniards entered Cuzco, and here others fled, fighting a rear-guard action after Cuzco fell. The valley became an Inca stronghold, and long after the Spaniards believed they had wiped out or subdued this highly civilized empire, the Incas continued to live on in the fastness of these canyons. For centuries the valleys slept and were not penetrated by more than a few friars and a motley band of Indian converts until Bingham discovered the hidden place to promptly announce that he had found the lost city of the Incas.

The Vilcanota Valley through which the river and railway — but no road — makes its way is a worthy train ride. Ahead, through a black gateway of pinnacles, I looked upon a wide gorge filled with sunlight with the mountains beyond. In the centre of the valley, coursing beside fuchsias and white orchids, was a turbulent brown river. This was the Vilcanota, running north to Machu Picchu where it becomes the Urubamba and continues north-east to join a tributary of the Amazon. The river flowed from Sicuani, past the glaciers above the crumbling town of Pisac, and here in a culvert where my train was impatiently tooting — waiting for another to pass — had formed the sacred valley of the Incas. Everyone had left our train to sit and stroll along the track thus giving me the opportunity to see why the shape and size of this valley in such a towering place had first attracted the Incas.

It was part of the Inca genius to seal themselves into concealed valleys. Their grasp of advanced masonry allowed them to build secure fortresses and posting stations out of these natural battlements. A few miles after we had entered the Vilcanota Valley on the way to the ruins we came to Ollantaytambo which offers a lesson on how to site the perfect fortress. Neither the terraces nor the temple walls can be seen until one is virtually on top of them which means that they are hidden from the railway tracks and the river and from an attacking army.

The site has been heavily excavated and contains a great number of half-worked stones but the flights of terraces leading up above the remains of the town are superb as are the curving terraces following the contours of the rocks that overhang the river. The Inca grasp of advanced masonry allowed them to build such secure fortresses out of these natural battlements and, in Ollantaytambo's case, this was put to the test when a regiment of Spanish soldiers led by Hernando Pizarro (a relative of Francisco) attacked the town, and were defeated. 'When we reached "Tambo," their chronicler wrote, 'we found it so well fortified that it was a horrifying sight.' The battle was savage and the Spanish troops were beaten off by the Inca slingers, bowmen and defenders wielding Spanish weapons captured in earlier engagements.

There is little to see from the bottom of the gorge of Machu Picchu likewise and the tropical heat has you in a lather of sweat as soon as the first footsteps are taken up the steep winding path. But the reward for the climb is great. Set 10,000 feet up in a topographical saddle, the remains of this fortress or temple, former town or barracks (nobody knows for sure what the stone foundations held) vie with nature for pure drama.

Machu Picchu is, without qualification, the single most dramatically beautiful setting for a city on the entire face of the globe. The roofless ruins of two hundred and fifty stone buildings were spread out before me across the site. Built on terraces hewn from the mountainside, it has been estimated that this, the ultimate self-sustaining fortified city, was lived in by about a thousand people. Three thousand steps incorporated into a hundred staircases interconnect the separate districts and edifices such as the Palace of the Princess, the Temple of the Sun and the Temple of the Three Windows. The ruins are pure glory but nature, I declare, finally steals the show. However the sight of these extensive ruins against the mighty backdrop of jungle-coated mountains is awe-inspiring beyond belief.

Far below, the river foams through its ravines and before your eyes the towering bulk of Huayna Picchu raises its restless snowy peaks to the sky. On a lower plateau stands Machu Picchu with its terraces clinging to the rocks; the walls growing so naturally that they seem to be part of them. An air of mystery pervades those who now flock here and on the walk back down the path my own mind was far, far away; five centuries away.

The three days we remained in the Cuzco region were inadequate to appreciate to the full its treasures of antiquity but made an inspiring introduction to the royal way that we would now be following in earnest. Our frenzied sightseeing drove us constantly into cafés for liquid refreshment wherein David discovered that a handful of pre-decimalisation British coins held more wonder to the locals than that of their own historic environment and currency. Thus we were able to satisfy our needs for a penny a time which seemed a satisfactory arrangement all round. When the pennies gave out we deemed it appropriate to move on.

For all its Incain wonders Cuzco unaccountably neglects its founder's greatest accomplishment. A shabby track, which we were assured was the royal road, crept out of the backside of the city. Its departure was marked by nothing more permanent than a refuse dump. Clear of the tightly-packed slum dwellings of the suburbs the trail, sprinkled with a few dislodged curb stones that

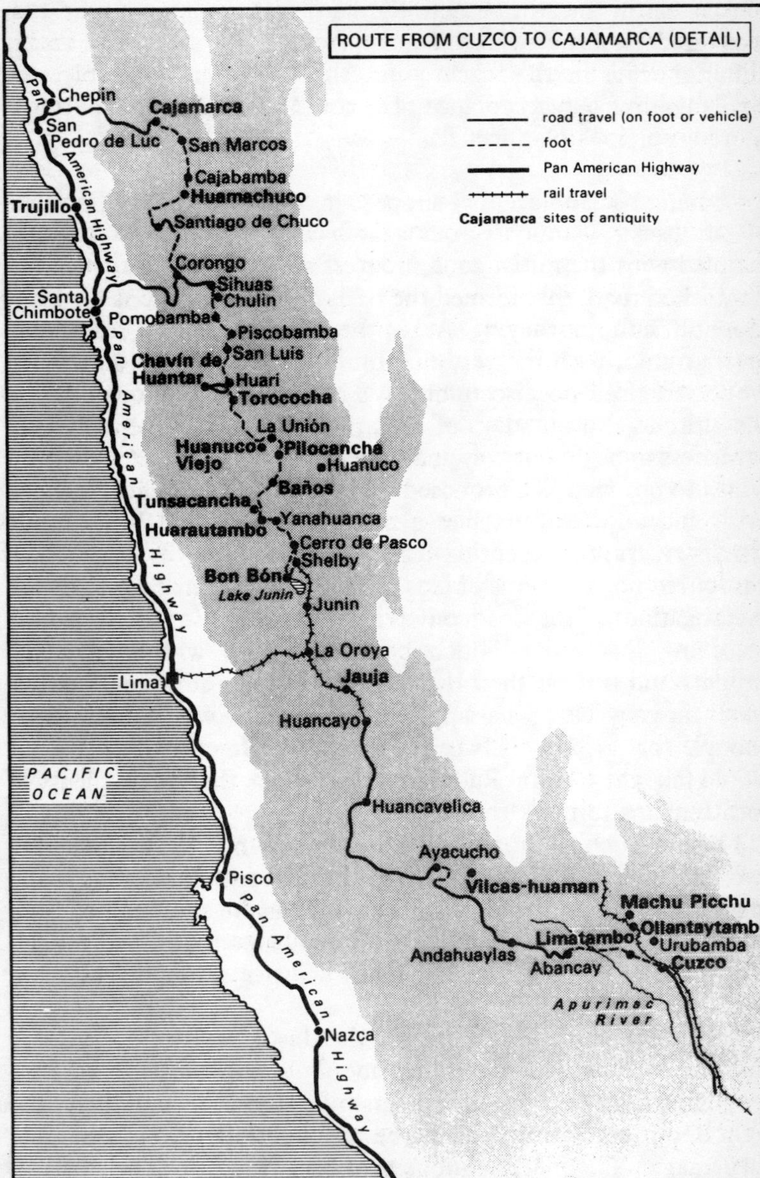
ROUTE FROM CUZCO TO CAJAMARCA (DETAIL)
road travel (on foot or vehicle)
foot
Pan American Highway
rail travel
Cajamarca sites of antiquity
Chepin
San
Pedro de Luc
Cajamarca
San Marcos
Cajabamba
Huamachuco
Trujillo
Santiago de Chuco
Corongo
Sihuas
Chulin
Santa
Chimbote
Pomobamba
Piscobamba
San Luis
Chavín de
Huantar
Huari
Torococha
La Unión
Huanuco
Viejo
Pilocancha
Huanuco
Baños
Tunsacancha
Yanahuanca
Huarautambo
Cerro de Pasco
Shelby
Bon Bón
Lake Junin
Junin
La Oroya
Lima
Jauja
Huancayo
PACIFIC
OCEAN
Huancavelica
Ayacucho
Pisco
Vilcas-huaman
Machu Picchu
Ollantaytambo
Limatambo
Urubamba
Andahuaylas
Abancay
Cuzco
Apurimac
River
Nazca
Pan American Highway
Pan American Highway
Pan American Highway
Pan American Highway

looked hardly Incain, became the hard core for a dust road that wandered lamely towards a great panoply of mountain ranges shining white in the warm sun. Ahead lay, unmistakably, the challenge but our acceptance of it could have been made from a more auspicious platform.

Looking back on events I suppose it was the deceptive lightness of our packs — much of our gear having remained in Lima — coupled with the initial good progress we made along that undistinguished road, that formed the basis of miscalculations for later, more difficult, journeying. At ten thousand feet and on reasonably level ground, with the very minimum of cargo on our shoulders, we experienced no discomfort. We had acclimatised ourselves to the altitude and our days of urban sightseeing had generated an eagerness to be on our way and under our own power. All this lent wings to our feet. We proposed to break ourselves in gently, however, and allowed ourselves a mixture of foot and local public transport travel, accepting each as circumstances arose. We harboured no intentions of closely identifying or making a precise investigation of the road on this southern section of its route, reasoning that others much better equipped with knowledge, support and time at their disposal had already done so. That we were moving along its approximate course was, again, good enough for us and, between Cuzco and Huancayo, where we would take the Central Railway back to Lima, there were plenty of Inca remains to mark the way.

The first such landmark was Limatambo which we calculated as two days march. Our road, though ill-surfaced, made good walking and our rate of progress slowed only as the sun climbed high in the sky. We carried with us but a small amount of food expecting to replenish stocks at the many villages through which we would be passing.

Traffic was surprisingly heavy, the dust clouds of every lorry and ancient bus hanging almost motionless in the clear still air long after they had passed. Passers-by stared at us curiously, the sight of our binoculars drawing bevies of children eager to sample their magic. The more cautious held back, repeating their parrot-cries of 'gringo! gringo!' as if to reassure themselves that this, in fact, was what we were.

The road ambled over a plateau bearing vividly-coloured vegetation. A gorse-like shrub clashed discordantly with plots of what an Englishman would identify as lupin but is, in fact, the flower of a crop called *quinoa.* My eyes were, however, on the road for its casual air struck me as alien to my notions of a no-nonsense Inca road that took the shortest possible distance between A and B. I remembered a walk I had made with my son the previous year. It was a Roman road and we were hiking Dere Street between York and Melrose. It was the long straight stretch from Catterick to Bishop Auckland that had impressed me, for the original road crossed the River Tees without a dent in the line while the modern highway, that followed it, funked the direct crossing to sheer away to shallower waters. Romans and Incas. I felt these two peoples had much in common when it came to road-building. But as for this apology of a road... Could it be that we had got off course somewhere?

We entered a hamlet of what looked like a group of derelict houses. These rural properties had changed little over the centuries when, in the Inca days, the Indian peasant, with the mutual aid of his kin within the commune, built his own house. This was, as it was here, a rectangular windowless room, built of stone plastered with adobe mud. In the remoter north the houses were made entirely of sun-dried adobe bricks. They had one entrance draped by a woollen curtain and the roof, supported by gnarled poles, was thickly thatched with *ichu* grass though the ones we were seeing now could rise only to rusty corrugated iron sheets. No chimneys were in evidence; the smoke issuing from the cooking fire was left to find its own way out.

The village contained a bar, medieval but not derelict. It had rough wooden tables, moist walls and a dirt floor with dogs and chickens scratching about amongst the few clients. Under the hard scrutiny of both animal and human eyes we sat down and ordered a Coke. I don't particularly like Coca Cola but, ice-cold, it makes a good thirst quencher even if it is supposed to rot your teeth. There was no Coke and instead we received a soupy broth in a plastic beaker which, we were told, was the local beer and it came with the compliments of the house. The fermented brew tasted nothing like any beer I know but, trying to look grateful, we forced it down only to be ladled out a fresh dose. This we played with, sipping it gingerly, fearing further supplies.

'You tourists?' asked the donor of the dubious nectar from his battered chair behind the counter.

'Yes and no,' I replied, only confusing the issue.

'No,' put in David with vigour. And, presuming some explanation was desirable, added, 'we're walking.'

'Where to — Cuzco?' enquired the barman making threatening gestures with the jug of maize beer.

To a Peruvian in the south of the country every foreigner in transit *must* be in transit towards Cuzco. They could conceive of no other destination that would draw him. I said that we were going the other way to Huancayo and reinforced my explanation by pointing in the opposite direction.

'Huancayo's a long way,' mused the barman dubiously. He changed the subject abruptly as if he hadn't understood. 'Plenty tourists in Cuzco.'

We agreed and left it at that.

On this trip I refused to look upon myself as a tourist. Or at least not any longer. We had emerged from the well beaten track and were now travellers. Our tourist classification we had left behind at Cuzco. I have nothing against tourists whatsoever. As a travel writer it is my job to be not only a tourist but a professional tourist; to report on the world to those who will follow in my footsteps and to, possibly, smooth their way. I am aware that sometimes my reportage spoils a place but spoils it for whom? Possibly for the pioneer tourists who have discovered it and want it to remain free of their fellows. But tourism brings money to regions desperately in need of this commodity. It also brings greed and ugliness. My job is all pros and cons but at least I'm aware of my responsibilities and make the effort to observe the off-beat corners of the world with a certain compassion and without rose-tinted spectacles. This way there is the hope that the right sort of visitors, those with no notions of selfish exploitation, can come and marvel where others would only mope. But now I was a traveller and we were *not* going to Cuzco.

We finished our drinks with barely-concealed grimaces and

stood up to go. Had they anything to eat asked David. Our stomachs rumbled audibly, crying out in hunger and pain.

Our purchases included four overcooked corn-on-the-cobs that had been simmering on a stove and a couple of tins of luke-warm lemonade. These came from a refrigerator long-since defunct.

'You speak Quechua?' enquired the barman as we turned to leave.

'Spanish but not Quechua,' explained David.

'Then you won't get far.' The man laughed and we shrugged and everyone in the room smiled and nodded. Even the dogs wagged their tails. Out of sight we devoured the corn and the lemonade.

I gave some thought to the remark about our lack of the Quechua tongue. The language derives from a particular tribe who lived around the Apurimac River which we would soon be crossing. It was pronounced the 'official' language by Inca Pachacuti after 1438 and it had to be learnt by every official in the administration. It is now spoken by whites and Indians alike in highland Peru and there are variants of it in Ecuador and the other Andean countries. However the more educated of the rural people could raise a smattering of Spanish as we had learnt from this encounter.

The plateau narrowed to a valley and the mountain panorama, temporarily lost from view behind low sullen hills, opened up again, closer and shimmering through the heat haze. As we strode down the slight incline I could hear the clatter of horses and clink of metal and almost expected to see Francisco Pizarro passing the other way. Round the corner came a trio of horsemen riding out of the sun. As they overtook us each rider raised a hand to his wide-brimmed hat in old-world salute.

We pitched camp at dusk just as we were beginning to feel damp fingers of cold. Our tent was a two-man bivouac of nylon; light yet adequate. I had brought from Britain a couple of inexpensive sleeping bags to use one inside the other so as to produce a layer of air in between. But I had left the second bag in Lima so, to compensate, went to bed fully dressed. Before doing so however we cooked ourselves a wholesome meal of tinned soup and stew over the Primus stove which we coaxed into operation with the greatest difficulty, both of us being new to the idiosyncrasies of paraffin cookers.

Our first Andean night in the open was not, perhaps, as idyllic as we would have wished. We were not actually shivering with cold but nor were we warm enough for uninterrupted sleep. For higher, more northerly, climes I pinned my hopes on the second bag keeping me warm, but David was unable to bask in such reassurance, and we were both a little subdued as we got up the next day.

Porridge oats are one of the universal stock items of Peruvian shops and we were to become masters at judging the quantity needed for a substance of the correct consistency. But that first camp breakfast was a washout. I managed to swallow the thin lumpy gruel but David discarded his in disgust.

Inexplicably the traffic had dried up though where it had diverted to I could not imagine for we had passed no junction. The deficiency only served to increase my feelings that we were on the wrong road. An occasional lorry, luridly painted with prancing llamas and blue roses, trundled by, its driver invariably reducing speed to enquire if we wanted a lift. Our valley widened and became veined with lively streams bounding joyfully over rocks. They were a natural means of irrigation and, to judge by the increase in size and number of cultivated plots embroidering the landscape, full advantage was taken of them. Villages slowed our progress for there were, inevitably, diversions while the local populace satisfied their curiosity as to our nationality, age, place of birth, marital status, income, profession, where we had come from and where we were going. My feet and size eleven boots were a final source of wonder.

Limatambo appeared early in the afternoon. The village lay in the frigid shadow of Mount Salcantay and, at first, we could see no sign of the Inca temple and royal rest station. I came upon it, however, when I nipped behind a hedge to relieve myself and felt a little as Hiram Bingham must have felt on discovering Machu Picchu. At least I knew now we were back on course. The edifice, or what little there was left of it, lay spread out, on open grassland, the few large irregularly-shaped stones faced according to natural contours and, even in ruin, with the usual startling accuracy.

Tarahuasi was a rest station, or *tampu,* par excellence. As with all the world's extensive road systems a series of post houses was deemed a necessity both for upkeep of the road as well as for its travellers. As an Inca chronicler of the times wrote: '. . . there were buildings and store-houses at every four to six leagues (twelve to eighteen miles), with great abundance of all provisions that the surrounding districts could supply'. I suppose, today, we would call them road houses though the *tampus* held, additionally, the means of maintaining the road, a task then controlled by the local *ayllu,* roughly equivalent now to a parish council. There were various types of *tampus.* The royal variety, of some substance and usually forming part of a temple complex, were reserved for the Lord-Inca or his governors when they made their inspection tours of the empire. Others were more utilitarian and built of rough field stone or adobe opening onto a corral where the llamas and beasts of burden were kept.

But for us it was a second night in our lightweight nylon tent. We were a little more successful with our sleeping arrangements than the previous night, though the elements of fatigue might have had something to do with it. David piled on every item of clothing he could find only to end up complaining about the heat. But we were learning and even our breakfast porridge was edible.

Though we were only walking, the geographical changes were noticeable but we were still unprepared for the intense dryness that came upon us as we neared the Apurimac river. Suddenly the land was parched and baked and bare. The day was endless and our sole topic of conversation centred upon what we were going to eat and drink at the village near the bridge.

The 'bridge', of course, was that which crossed the Apurimac and the 'village' a few dots on the map at the southern approaches. The original Apurimac bridge has a firm place in history as well as being immortalised in Thornton Wilder's novel *The Bridge of San Luis Rey.* When the Incas broke out of their traditional territory they first had to traverse this formidable river for it formed the boundary of their northward conquests. To cross the stream they constructed a 'hanging bridge' from cables of braided straw and over this — probably the world's first suspension bridge — many an Inca army poured as did the

Spaniards in the other direction. The old bridge remained in position until quite recent years thanks to the efforts of local villagers who, annually, restrung the cables.

David and I crossed the rushing waters by way of a modern steel structure. Nearby were the supports of a previous Colonial bridge but there were no signs of the famous Inca original. Dotted with cactus, the vertical walls of the gorge through which the river ran echoed its roar. The 'voice' of the Apurimac is well-known, and has earned the river the label of the 'Great Speaker'. Water, as well as the lack of it, here is feared. Too little rainfall and the whole valley is burnt to a crisp from the heat of the sun; too much and the level of the river can rise forty feet in a single day. Conditions appeared to be erring on the dry side while we were there.

Bridges form an integral part of any road system and such structures were amongst the proudest of Inca achievements. In fact they were considered so vital that they were pronounced sacred, and death was decreed for anyone who tampered with one. Many types were built: suspension, pontoon, cantilever and other more simple affairs of stone slabs. The bridge was known as *chaca* and the greatest and most famous was the one here over the Apurimac. With no wood available the only material the Incas could raise for bridge-building was stone and a fleshy-leafed plant called *cabuya* which, when plaited and twisted, formed a cable more endurable than rope. The Spaniards and their mules and horses crossed these swinging suspension bridges with understandable trepidation but the Incas, with their llamas, seemed impervious to their shortcomings.

The usual scattering of houses formed the village of our hopes. One, optimistically titled 'bar' produced the staple luke-warm mineral water and some packets of stale biscuits plus a ladle of potato soup. This uninspiring fare refreshed us nevertheless, though it fell a long way short of our combined anticipation.

Emerging from the dingy room we made for the bridge to be brought to a halt by a chain stretched across the road. A posse of police, reclining by the wayside, struggled reluctantly to their feet to rustle through our passports with more curiosity than any idea as to what they were looking for. The stock questions followed and our life-histories painstakingly laid bare though we felt rather resentful about giving them since the men were only being officious and weren't really interested.

To be *walking* — and for the pleasure of it — plainly constituted a breach of regulations, though which one none of our trio of cowboys seemed able to discover. They conversed long and animatedly with David in quick bursts of Spanish as flights of red and green parakeets wheeled overhead. That authority was unhappy about the likes of us doing what no self-respecting Peruvian would do came through loud and clear but eventually, with much shrugging of shoulders, they processed us onward.

Age has a lot to do with respectability in the Andean countries and I was glad at least to be able to make one contribution to the project. Youngsters, and particularly those flaunting long hair, are invariably classed as hippies — another word for undesirables — and treated as such by authority, particularly at frontiers. But more elderly travellers — and a beard emphasized my vintage — are given the benefit of the doubt.

David had enquired of the policemen the whereabouts of the site of the Inca bridge but either they didn't know or didn't want us to know so, out of sight, we returned to the river and scrambled along the side of the gorge in an effort to find it. I was all for moving on but my companion was adamant. He thought he knew where it was situated though our searching drew a blank and dusk confounded further efforts.

That night we went supperless to bed having spent a frustrating hour attempting to ram tent-pegs into granite. In the morning we pandered to our appetites with a double ration of porridge together with a clutch of boiled eggs bought at an inflated price in the village. The blow-out bolstered our strength for the uphill grind that filled the morning.

Possibly it was because of the shelter afforded by the steep sides of the valley up which the road zig-zagged but the heat came on much sooner than it did on the more exposed plateau. It reflected off the surrounding rock and fried us each time we emerged from the shadow. We floundered on with frequent pauses for rest and before mid-day our water-bottles were as dry as our throats.

'If a bus or anything on wheels comes our way I vote we take it,' observed David, his shirt, like mine, stained dark with sweat.

He was echoing my own thoughts. It wasn't as if we had set ourselves a specific mileage to cover on foot but something akin to guilt rose to trouble our minds nevertheless. Nothing had been said but we had unconsciously designated Abancay as the town we would allow ourselves to accept an onward ride.

I attempted to salve a nagging conscience. 'I don't suppose for one moment we're on the royal road now, anyway. Where does it go when it crosses the old bridge?'

David made stabbing motions at his map-case which had swollen into a file of paper plans, diagrams and notes. 'Certainly it doesn't come up *here*, that's for sure,' he replied with a tinge of sarcasm and I detected a reprimand for having wanted to push on so fast when he might have preferred to stay to hunt down the remains of the suspension bridge.

We had been through all this before. Apart from our differing interests it also boiled down to a question of time; my time, for, as a family man, I felt unable to remain away from home indefinitely. My wife, understanding my wanderlust, makes no restrictions upon my travels for which I am eternally grateful. In return I ensure that my periods of absence are held to a minimum. As a travel journalist she appreciates that my job is to travel but the sort of travel projects that provide my bread and butter are usually those of short duration. Only ten months previously I had been in East Africa for more than a quarter of the year participating in an expedition that, strictly speaking, was outside the confines of my job. Additionally, I had run into trouble — and not for the first time — which had inflicted upon her the traumatic experience of seeing hubby plastered all over her television screen and the pages of her newspaper.

David, on the other hand, was footloose and fancy free. He was at a stage in life when he was tied to no job but enthusiastically imbued with the idea that his future lay with the South American continent. His determination to unravel Incain secrets knew no bounds and I could appreciate that everything we uncovered of interest along the Inca trail could benefit his prospects. Already we had clashed over our differing approach to this journey. I was simply continuing a project started by a colleague, the new banister along the way being the royal road. For David the journey was a scientific venture; a refurbishing of an already considerable knowledge of the Inca culture. We had made these facts clear to one-another at the outset of the adventure but occasions were already arising when our objectives met in head-on collision.

He supplemented the answer to my question. 'It goes through Andahuaylas but von Hagen couldn't find it.'

This I knew already. Andahuaylas lay beyond Abancay, about a hundred kilometres beyond. We trudged on in silence.

At the more dramatic corners, where the road widened to allow opposing Peruvian drivers a chance to survive when passing one another, well-maintained shrines stood in tiny crypts and grottos. Candles bore unwavering flames and fresh flowers lay piled at the base of the infant Christ. A lorry free-wheeled by, its passengers in the buck crossing themselves with drill-like fervour at the sight of the holy statue. At one such roadside temple we discovered a trickle of water descending from beneath the tableau and managed to top up our waterbottles. The liquid was brackish and tasted the more bitter with the addition of purifying tablets and our own act of sacrilege.

The village at the lip of the gorge took us by surprise. It was not marked on our maps but could have been Curahuasi though none of its gawking citizens seemed to know. The houses lay squat and squalid against hills of pale velvet, streaked with the colour wash of a puffball of a sun set in humid cloud. At the local bar-restaurant, that also doubled as shop, meeting place and public lavatory, we drank coke enlivened with a shot of *pisco* and tackled a plate of what was probably elderly goat to judge from the texture and flavour. A group of ancient ladies with lined, unsmiling faces shadowed by black trilbies, solemnly watched us eat as if the spectacle had been specifically laid on for their entertainment. Others joined them as the meal proceeded until the cobwebbed room became the amphitheatre for an enthralled audience.

The unfolding of the map produced a ripple of excitement and twenty sinewy hands traced mythical journeys across the sheet.

'If this is Curahuasi we're 125 kilometres from Cuzco,' said

David and straightaway twenty arms lifted off the map to point the way we had come.

'Ayocucho?' he asked and the forest of arms swung the other way.

I was not in an optimistic frame of mind. 'I doubt if we've got that far. We made pretty slow progress up the gorge,' I said gloomily. 'I doubt if we made fifteen K's today.'

Ahead the road eloquently displayed at least ten kilometres of itself coiling across a dry valley to disappear into a heat haze.

'I'd give my right arm for a bus.' David sounded as exhausted as I felt and certainly we were equally overjoyed as well as amazed when the big Volvo coach lumbered into the village to halt, wheezing gently, in the central square watched over by an anonymous gentleman of stone-hewed countenance. The destination board at the front of the vivid orange vehicle proclaimed Ayacucho and this was good enough for us.

Ensconced in two of the three remaining seats we were content to make the corkscrew miles the easy way. The road was rough and the bus made heavy weather of it. For so surprisingly a modern vehicle the interior was like an oven with not even a fan to stir the heat. Abancay held a statue, a non-operative fountain, a petrol pump (likewise non-operative) and a square. We picked up a lot more passengers than we put down and the stench of stale garlic and cheap rum increased. Two police checks at both ends of the town were our hello and goodbye to Abancay.

The verdant land that surrounded Andahuaylas was wonderfully inviting after the long miles of naked, parched soil that we had endured since the Apurimac river. All around had been a desolate void and we had begun to lose hope of ever seeing green countryside again. Then from the highest point in the winding road we saw in the distance an immense lush plateau and, in the centre, perched on a high ridge, was Andahuaylas.

Once upon a time Andahuaylas had been an Inca city and an important stop on the royal road. A royal *tampu* stood there. 'In the centre of the province of Andahuaylas, were large lodgings and storehouses of the Incas' wrote the Spanish chronicler Ciezo de León. Now there is no road, no *tampu* and those on the bus, who David questioned long and diligently, knew nothing about it either. The decrepit township of today — a broken promise of its distant image — is another disturbing decline from a more distinguised past.

David was good at questioning the locals. Not only was his Spanish very adequate but he displayed no qualms at all when it came to ferreting information or necessities out of strangers. He suffered from neither shyness nor self-consciousness.

Whatever the shortcomings of travel by foot I would happily have got out of the bus and returned to them had it been possible. Fresh air was plainly a commodity scorned by Peruvians and every window remained sealed throughout the night. A girl passenger was repeatedly sick and a big peasant woman — made bigger by a multitude of petticoats — used me as a pillow. In the morning I could feel her fleas sliding about on my own sweaty body.

At least the darkness hid the lethality of that road. Precipitous edges were unguarded; corners were such that they had to be taken in two bites. At the worst zig-zags the driver crossed himself with the rest of us and the good Lord allowed us to live.

Dawn found us in a countryside that reminded me of the Northumberland National Park but colder and marshier. And that's where we broke down. Looking at things with the benefit of hindsight I can only be surprised that we had not broken down earlier for no vehicle on earth can stand the punishment of Peruvian mountain roads for long. Not, I hasten to add, that this road was half as bad as those we were to experience in the north.

Among the catalogue of faults requiring rectification was a multiple puncture and a broken spring. Obviously we were in for a long wait so everyone emerged from the bus to stand around in small cold groups awaiting the approach of another vehicle that might possess the right tools. Ours adequately blocked the road so that when a lorry *did* arrive it had no alternative but to halt and surrender its repair kit. And with that job done we found ourselves with another — and one we could all join in; that of widening the road over the marshy shoulder so that our benefactor could pass and so get out of our way.

For David and I the breakdown was a blessing in disguise. While humping and tossing ballast onto the spongey turf we learnt that one of our fellow-passengers hailed from a village with a name that sounded like Contay close to a site that bore a name about which we had no doubts whatsoever: Vilcas-huaman, 'The Sanctuary of the Hawk'. Here was a celebrated Inca town and the only one of a thousand and more sun temples to survive through the centuries.

'The bus will be stuck here for hours longer. You can be quite sure it won't start even now,' the man told us with an assurance that bespoke of a knowledge culled from many similar experiences. 'Ayacucho is not a great distance away and the cross-country route to my village would be shorter from here than from the town. Would you like to accompany me?' We accepted with alacrity, the idea of even one more hour on the bus being purgatory, while David was particularly excited about an opportunity of looking upon Vilcas-huaman which *was,* for certain, on the royal road.

The three of us collected our belongings, bade a sailor's farewell to the bus-driver's feet protruding from beneath the vehicle and struck off into the open countryside.

'It's not many miles,' said our friend and I sensed he was trying to assure himself of the fact as much as us. He was a youngster of cheerful disposition, wearing a kind of tuxedo with ear-flaps and a thick alpaca jersey.

No doubt the distance as the crow flies was not 'many miles' but crows don't have to make detours around every swamp. Nor do they mind getting their feet wet which is more than can be said for us as we attempted to negotiate a slurpy mixture of bog and clumps of sharp *ichú* grass. Hillocks of granite stood out prominently on the rolling puna country and I did not at all relish the idea of being lost in such a neighbourhood. Our 'guide' was obviously of the same opinion though he tried to hide his anxiety and occasional changes of direction. Now I knew why he wanted our companionship. Having made no preparations for this sudden transfer to our feet we carried no provisions and thus we were all extremely relieved when we saw a village on the horizon late in the afternoon. Our relief turned to incredulity when we learnt it was, indeed, the village aimed for.

We spent the night in the reed-thatched abode of two elderly crones to whom our companion transferred us. They, it appeared, ran the guesthouse of the community and though its comforts were the very basic that hard mud walls and floors can offer at least it was dry and reasonably warm. A fire in an old bucket ensured this while smoke curled languidly around us to find a way out through a badly-fitting door. By candlelight we devoured a thick vegetable potage and it wasn't long before we turned in to our sleeping bags for a fitful sleep.

Vilcas was but an hour's walk away we were told and, although in the event it was nearly two, the estimation was a pretty accurate one for an Andean. We rose early as everybody did, paid our dues and were away. A wide path — it may have been classed as a road in these parts — led us south and we had Vilcas-huaman in our sights long before we reached it.

The plateau on which this Inca city stands is horseshoe-shaped. The Vischongo River cuts around the high massif that is the city's location to give the reason for its name. People continue to live there but in the squalor of new houses that bear no comparison with the old town. I noticed that some of the walls of the modern dwellings had been strengthened by the addition of fragments of palace stone or were built upon an existing Inca framework.

As the geographical centre of the Inca dominion, Vilcas-huaman takes on a mythical character. The city dating from about 1440 attained its greatest opulence during the reign of Huayna Capac, the last great Lord-Inca who, amongst other things, was a compulsive showman. The royal road, of course, passes through and here it sprouts a number of feed roads, one connecting with the coastal highway.

It was the temple that drew us. A great truncated pyramid, it rose in tiers to a small terrace reached by a flight of cyclopean steps. The massive stone doorway which faces the plaza still stands, dignified and lonely. Framed by the foundations of ancient buildings the immense plaza offered a sombre sight, accentuated by an oppressive silence. Once twenty thousand Indians gave it a spectacle, a colour and a sound that reverberated through the Inca Empire. Now there is only this silence broken by the occasional cry of a child or bark of a dog and the scurrying form of a peasant Indian taking a short cut to a hovel.

Everywhere around us those enormous Incain walls were in evidence, immovable, indestructible. Out from the southern extremes of the plaza went the roads and at our backs rose the rock of Pillucho dotted with the remains of Inca store houses. Among the proud stones were the living; disfigured faces, hunger etched deep in suspicious eyes. Here was another pitiful example of history marching backwards; the living gradually dying in this edifice to the dead.

An hour and I had had enough. Not so David who was happily immersed in his note-taking and the delay cost us another night in the village guesthouse but the road to Ayacucho gave us no anxieties. We met little traffic and it was no more than a long slog over the windswept puna to the one-time third city of Peru.

Ayacucho too is another centre that has come down in the world since the mid-fifteenth century yet this one continues to hang onto the remnants of its charms. It was a Spanish city, not Incain, and the royal road disdains its assembly of sagging moss-covered roofs and thirty-three mouldering churches. Time-worn streets — no longer cobbled — radiate from the square that was once a promenade for ladies of the now-ruined colonial mansions.

In Ayacucho we caught another bus, a great brute of a vehicle going right through to Lima. We aimed to go only as far as Huancayo from whence we intended picking up a train to the capital. There is a rule that all clients of long-distance buses must have a reserved seat but this company ignored it to the detriment of all except the company coffers and the driver who supplemented his income by giving lifts to anyone along the way. Amongst the ticket-holding clients made seatless by this practice was a gimlet-eyed woman up front who, to her credit, stood up to the uncaring attitude of the driver and his mate, gradually rallying the passengers to her side. It did little good but made for some spirited entertainment during the drive.

With Ayacucho behind us the green petered out into a return to more barren landscapes of rock gullies containing rivers reduced to trickles. The sun blazed down arbitrarily giving out heat one moment and none at all the next. Small townships, each a carbon copy of the others with their decrepit squares, nameless statues and waterless fountains were dismal in their repetitive squalor. Listless citizens stood aimlessly in the streets with nothing to do except watch the sparse traffic go by. Only the churches held a certain air of regality brandishing impressive bell-towers to match the ornate cemeteries on the hillsides where most of the local care was lavished.

One of our driver's casual pick-ups was a shaggy-haired deaf-mute who forced his way through our crowded coach making a collection. Everybody obligingly contributed but only the front seat passengers probably heard the man ask the driver to let him off a little later. I suspect the two shared the pickings.

A present-day suspension bridge but of narrow proportions that spanned a dry riverbed brought us to a halt while the driver and his mate went round unscrewing wing-mirrors and other protrusions from the coach sides. Suitably streamlined we inched across the chasm, my neighbour excitedly pointing out to me the dark shape of a condor gliding elegantly overhead. Safely the other side everything had to be screwed back into place again. This road was assuredly not one to be travelled in the rainy season. Its curb, foundations and surface were composed exclusively of compressed mud and, even now, chunks of highway had collapsed into bottomless ravines. Just a deluge or two and the road would cease to exist.

Before nightfall we halted for a communal meal at a wayside restaurant. Plates of soup containing the odd raft of fatty meat were set before us. Its taste was nothing to write home about but since it was possibly the last we would have for a while we made the best of it.

'Where's the toilet?' I enquired afterwards and was directed outside onto the road where both men and women were defecating in shadowy groups. With that business attended to it was left to starving dogs to consume the excreta. Vultures would have a thin time in central Peru.

Huancayo, capital of the Department of Junin, without any doubt whatsoever, lies firmly astride the royal road. The city remains one of the largest in the country as befits its situation in the Jauja-Huancayo Valley in the heart of Peru. Lima beckoned to the west but, in the meantime, the validity of our bus tickets expired and we were unceremoniously tipped out into the darkened streets.

That the royal road runs through Huancayo is emphasised by its main street, Calle Real, which is actually part of it. The Lord-Inca once rode in triumph through the town on a golden litter, preceded by heralds and musicians and attended by Virgins of the Sun who strewed the roads with flowers. Priests guarded the litter and detachments of the army marched behind, each weaving its own insignia, puma skins, woollen shirts and Vicuna hats. Important centre as it was in these Inca days it was only subsequently that Huancayo became a capital city, a status which it was to hold on three separate occasions.

One eventuality we hadn't reckoned with was our arrival there at two in the morning; hardly an inspiring hour to go sightseeing even in an environment that encourages it. Huancayo, alas, did not. The *South American Handbook* describes it as 'an old market town with picturesque architecture and good Sunday markets'. It also warns would-be visitors that the city is notorious for thieves.

We spent what was left of the night among the thieves. The hotels had long since closed their doors so, muffled against the cold, we squatted around a street brazier in company with a cheerful assembly of vendors. Joined at intervals, and between business, by ladies of the oldest profession we observed a slice of Huancayo nightlife omitted by the guide books. Those vendors offering coloured fizzy drinks enjoyed an all-night trade; the others, with laden fruit and trinket trollies, seemed content to await the morning, whiling away the hours with idle chatter.

Daybreak found us at the railway station — and allow me to recommend Huancayo's shunting yards as a steam locomotive enthusiast's paradise — partaking of half a dozen fried eggs at a café situated alongside the main market. We purchased tickets for Lima with no great hassle but I nearly lost the train when taking photographs of a tiny tank engine of unbelievably ancient vintage. To yells of encouragement from the populace I had to run for the Lima-bound 'Tren de la Sierra' slinking off, while my back had been turned, ever faster out of the station.

Night travel — whether by road or by rail — is a mode of

progress I try to avoid when possible since, invariably, a point of interest is lost to the darkness. In the bus we had seen nothing of Huancavelica, a Spanish city built upon an Indian settlement. No great loss here perhaps but I would have liked to have seen Jauja, a little over an hour out of Huancayo, and the annoying thing was that we could have done so as we now passed it in broad daylight.

Where the Mantaro river leaves the valley to begin its passage through its gorge, there, encircled by hills sprinkled with mouldering ruins, lies old Jauja. The ancient fortresses had once belonged to the Wankas Huancas, a fierce little people whose houses resembled miniature castles.

It was this tribe that effectively blocked the Incas' northern conquest for a time until they were fought to extinction. After the great battle, the Incas incorporated the survivors into their kingdom, but permitting them to keep their own culture and language. The royal road is recorded as running through the old town, the outlines and some ruined walls of which are alleged to be still visible.

During the advance of the Spanish army towards Cuzco in 1533, Jauja was the scene of the strongest Inca resistance of the campaign and Lord-Inca Tupac Huallpa died there. Clearly a place of considerable geographical and mental inspiration is Jauja and I was as annoyed as David for losing the opportunity of exploring its relics.

It has been said that the Central Railway from Huancayo to Lima is one of the wonders of Latin America. It reaches its greatest altitude, 4,782 metres, inside a tunnel between Ticlio and Galera which makes the line the highest passenger-serving system in the world. Along its whole length it traverses sixty-six tunnels, fifty-nine bridges and twenty-two zigzags where the steep mountainside permits no other method of ascending or descending it. The views are incomparable. Galera, the world's highest station for a standard gauge railway, is dappled by perpetual snow. White-coated medics with oxygen cylinders and rubber face-masks haunt the corridors and passengers, taken unawares, have a habit of vomitting in their laps.

It is commonly thought that the line was planned by the

American, Henry Meiggs, but it was actually a Peruvian, Ernesto Malinowski, who surveyed the route; Meiggs only supervised and promoted it, from its beginnings in 1870 until his death in 1877. But it was another twenty-seven years before the railway reached Huancayo. A trans-Andean line, from Huancayo to Cuzco, although proposed and surveyed in 1907, remains a dream. Had it been fact ours could have been an easier journey for sure.

At La Oroya, where the line branches — the other goes north to the tin and copper mines of Cerro de Pasco, to whence we would be travelling ourselves in very few days — our train was delayed. Children came onto the platform to beg, and trilby-hatted Indian women brought round knitted goods to sell in addition to fried cakes and burnt portions of meat. The town itself, nestling contentedly amongst its slag heaps and smelting ovens, reminded me of Port Talbot, set as it is in countryside reminiscent of South Wales.

I alighted onto the platform to stretch my legs and a wizened old man sitting with a basket of fruit between his knees caught my eye. The fruit was about the size of an orange but a yellowish-green in colour; I think it was chirimoya. I went over and entered into negotiations to buy some. Seeing my interest there was a mad rush by every other vendor within sight and I was surrounded by eager, beaming faces. My poor old man was edged out of proceedings so I pushed my way through the throng and made my purchase from him. No doubt it cost me more but the great smile and bear hug that was included in the deal made it a bargain. While I was sampling the fruit and spitting out the pips the engine-driver came over, tapped me on the shoulder and said, 'El Ingleesh, we go'. It was one of the few times in Peru I was given a title other than gringo.

We entered *the* tunnel and attained the highest altitude on the line. Some of the passengers further down the coach began to vomit; puking on the floor and out of the window. The malady spread but never reached our row of seats. The white-coated attendants did not materialise but I noticed a number of victims, handkerchiefs to their mouths, stumble off to the neighbouring coach.

Though a rough ride on worn track the train made a better showing than the buses. Out of the Ticlio Tunnel we emerged onto the downhill stretch to zig-zag slowly down the valley, stopping at each dog leg so the driver's mate could switch the points. It was hardly a valley; more a cut in the rock, a slash so narrow that our diesel's hooter hardly echoed; the walls too close to sustain an answering sound.

In this way we came to Chosica, a short bus ride from Chaclycayo. The huge mountain barrier was behind us, its valleys no more than vertical cracks with no evidence of trees or habitations amongst them. Before us was Lima, a desert city hemmed in by a hot plateau on one side and the grey Pacific on the other.

Lima was like coming home. We would stay but a few days, collect the remainder of our gear and be off to the north. From Cuzco the journey so far, along a well-trodden path had taken but a week and had been a warm-up — a 'dry run' in military parlance — following the approximate route of the royal road. For our way to the north thereafter the old Inca stones themselves would guide our progress.

3

LA OROYA—CERRO DE PASCO —YANAHUANCA—HUARAUTAMBO

The steam train that stood in a siding of La Oroya had to be seen to be believed. The locomotive was a kind of demented samovar on wheels with iron patches on its boiler, leaking pipes under its belly and dribbling valves shooting jets of vapour sideways. The coaches were hardly more substantial than packing crates; antiquated, dishevelled, paintless and windowless — and crowded. But there was no doubt as to the contraption's destination unless *everybody* in the two coaches had got it wrong. Cerro de Pasco it was. Or bust. David and I were going only as far as the village of Shelby, close to Lake Junin. Cerro was the end of the track.

We struggled aboard with our clumsy loads, and our combined weight alone ensured us seats. With more than a hundred pounds of pack on our two pairs of shoulders plus an assortment of objects such as tin mugs and plastic bottles dangling about us we literally fell onto benches abruptly made empty. This was no Inofer (Peruvian Railways) train but some privately-owned local, our fare covering the three-hour grind up into the hills absurdly totalling just 15 pence apiece.

Our second sojourn in Lima had been rewarding. We had repeated the rounds of our contacts and had come away with as much additional data as could be crammed into receptive minds inside of six days. Most vital of all we now held large-scale maps obtained from military sources, of the territory through which we expected the route of the royal road to lead us. But this notwithstanding I had become heartily bored with the none too enthusiastic attentions of British Cultural Institutes, Peruvian National Libraries, Military Geographical Institutes and of searching out the way to them through the concrete jungle of a capital city. We had managed to travel first class back to La Oroya on the 'Tren de Sierra' by courtesy of the Inofer Public Relations Department and for most of the way up the Central Valley we had been paced by a convoy of sleek cars belonging to the Japanese Fuega-Alaska rally with a Japanese television camera team photographing them enthusiastically from our train. Fuega to Alaska. Certainly one hell of a distance but, with speed the only criterion, it seemed to me a somewhat pointless exercise. Our proposed trek through central and northern Peru, on the other hand, was going to break no records nor make headlines but the rewards of making a way on foot where few had gone before made a little more sense.

Our Cerro Flyer rattled and scurried across the bucking countryside, the line surreptitiously climbing another thousand feet in the process of attaining the wet and mournful Junin pampa, one of the world's largest high-altitude plains, from the Montaro River valley. The landscape wore a prehistoric look: simple terrible hills and gullies; thorn bushes and rocks; and everything smoothed by the wind and looking as if a great flood had denuded it and washed it of all its particular features. Passengers on the train did not look out of the windows, except at the stations, and then only in the hope of buying something to eat. There were few signboards on the platforms; none were necessary except for strangers like the two of us who kept bleating the question 'Shelby? Shelby?' as we drew into successive halts. In the gathering dusk, bringing with it fierce icy draughts through the non-existent windows, we glimpsed the eastern shore of Lake Junin, an elongated mass of grey-green water, before the view was eclipsed by an abrupt nightfall.

The engine was fuelled by oil so did not belch black smoke so much but it had bronchial trouble, respiring in great gasps and wheezes down the slopes and up the grades. The track was narrow gauge and badly laid so that the whole train bucked, swayed and creaked while, when it was moving fast — which was seldom — it made such a racket of jarring couplings and groaning timber that I had the distinct impression that everything was on the verge of bursting apart.

Shelby lay in complete darkness. We stumbled like drunken astronauts onto an empty station devoid of staff or a single fellow-passenger and looked around intent only upon locating a site for our tent. Chinks of light showed from the darker shadows of ramshackle houses but only barking dogs were aware that Shelby had visitors. The keen wind, edged with frost, gave our search for a camp-site a sense of urgency.

Lake Junin is Peru's second largest lake. Adjoining it an obelisk marks the battlefield where the Peruvians under Bolivar defeated the Spaniards in 1824. But, this notwithstanding, the lake and its bleak surroundings of wind-swept yellow grass make for uninspiring sightseeing. That was my opinion anyway as we emerged from a frost-encrusted tent next morning, though my judgement may have been adversely affected by both altitude sickness and a dose of the 'runs'.

The original inhabitants of these parts were famed for their war-like spirit and to conquer them the Incas had to assault their last-ditch island stronghold in the centre of the lake. Once subdued, however, they showed themselves loyal vassals of the Inca and the region was of such importance that it became 'one of the directions of empire'. And it was here that we were to see, at last, an unblemished section of the royal road. First, however, it was necessary to find a dot on the map called Bonbón denoting the remains of an Inca command centre that enjoyed a certain 'cause célèbre' in Inca research circles.

The river which drains Junin together with the dam that has recently been constructed at the neck of the lake were the keys to our quest. Somewhere close by we should come across another Inca site and a junction of several roads. And once at Bonbón we would be astride the royal road once more.

The flat Pampa de Junin, criss-crossed by foot-tracks and laced with ditches half hidden beneath the thick tufts of sharp grass, was not particularly difficult ground for walking. But what brought me low that freezing morning (that was to turn oven-hot before mid-day), was oxygen deficiency. The pack on my shoulders was punishment enough — indeed the first steps had me progressing backwards — but the rarefied atmosphere of 13,000 feet simply short-circuited my breathing apparatus and had me alternately gasping for air or convulsed in violent retching. Fortunately David was unaffected and though he set a pace I was unable to match, his figure disappearing into the distance gave me the determination to struggle on.

To move at all with this affliction was folly. I could have done myself considerable harm. It took me six kilometres and all day — the time taken to walk that distance — to realize it. By late afternoon we pitched camp again and while David put up the tent I lay down and slept and slept...

I slept all evening and all night and in the morning the worst was over. Diarrhoea plagued me but one can live with that. The day started badly with the discovery that our packet of a breakfast cereal (donated by Helena) had become contaminated by kerosine. So porridge, the old stand-by, returned to the menu, and while we were consuming this an antidote to the catalogue of misfortunes arrived in the form of a pleasant-faced youth with Indian features, on a bicycle. That he had come in friendship as well as curiosity he made clear with an offer of four stale bread rolls. His name, he vouchsafed, was Carlos. Yes he knew where Bonbón was. Yes he would show us the way. He followed our eyes to his bicycle. Yes he would help to carry our baggage.

With our main packs secured across the saddle and handlebars the three of us set off. Within minutes we were doused in sweat beneath our thick outer garments, removal of which only added to the carrying problem. But we were delighted to find ourselves on one of the Inca roads radiating from Bonbón. The fact never registered at first on account of the stinging salt in our eyes and it was only gradually that we became aware that we were walking down a wide grass thoroughfare bordered by familiar-shaped stone. We stopped, David to take measurements, I for more prosaic reasons. The road was eighteen feet wide, the average width for the royal road in the open regions where mountains made no restrictions. From the crown, the line of the road could be seen running diagonally across the pampa, avoiding the steep escarpment to our right.

We wanted to avoid it too but Carlos had other ideas and had us panting after him towards the cockscomb of rocks at the summit. It was a severe test but from the top we obtained a remarkable view of the *agger* of the royal route below and could appreciate the reasoning behind what Carlos intended as a short cut. In the other direction the pampa stretched away as far as the eye could see to a lunar barrier of pinnacles like eye-teeth in a huge jawbone. Midway to it, symmetrically-shaped rocks were scattered amongst the debris of nature. We were looking at Bonbón. The road, skirting our escarpment, disappeared into the river that provided a tadpole-like tail to Lake Junin.

It was now the bicycle that became the hindrance as we all lent a hand in pushing it through the rocky obstructions. The reverse slope offered easier going but a series of streams barred the way to the ruins and never was water so cold. We waded each riverlet rather than trust the rickety stepping stones provided by an unknown hand.

Before we began to explore the remains of Bonbón we sat down to a mid-day meal of onion soup and some dry pancakes conjured up by Carlos. The sun remained warm but scudding clouds periodically obscured it to release sudden bursts of hail. Less than a mile away loomed the dam built by the Cerro de Pasco Mining Corporation whose engineers had torn down much of the ancient site to raise the stones for the dam's foundations. Submerged in the expanse of water beneath it could be seen all that was left of an Inca suspension bridge. A causeway led from its northern end to enter an immense plaza surrounding the dais of a sun temple, and from this fanned the radial roads; one to the coast, the others north and south as feed roads to the nearby royal artery. There were literally hundreds of stone structures within Bonbón and those which had not been entirely denuded revealed their original form.

We spent the rest of the day and much of the following morning searching the ancient foundations for the debris of centuries. Fragments of pottery and pieces of figurines lay everywhere but what was of particular interest were the open sections of wall going deep into five hundred years of soil strata. Carlos left us before nightfall to return to his village, promising to return at daybreak. To our surprise he kept to his word, seemingly eager to continue in his role as mechanical packhorse. The night was a cold one again and, this time, our cooking operations were prolonged by the Primus stove plunger jamming in the narrow-necked kerosine bottle. Comfort-wise our campsite could have been better chosen, the sloping ground precipitating a slide out of the tent every time we turned over in our sleeping bags.

But the new day was clear and cloudless. While striking camp we were visited by three well-wrapped horsemen — Andean cowboys in ponchos and wide-brimmed hats — who were members of an *hacienda,* or ranch, some miles to the south. At first they were distinctly hostile, displaying open suspicion, but upon learning of our intentions, became friendly — even to the extent of inviting us to stay at their ranch-house. We were tempted by the offer but our route led in the opposite direction. Other horsemen, passing in the distance, had spotted the tent and reported our presence. Our visitors were the troubleshooters, the investigators. We noticed the long ugly knives at their belts and were happy not to have raised their anger.

Joined by the faithful Carlos and his iron steed we continued on our way allowing the north-bound road to guide our footsteps. Behind, the lonely stones of Bonbón faded into the fickle heat haze. Somewhere ahead lay Cerro de Pasco, a town to be avoided if possible. According to our intelligence the road despised the place equally fervently, passing to the west. By late afternoon the suburbs had trapped us, however, and we had become the centre of a curiosity by the local citizens that was almost belligerent in its intensity.

Cerro is a mining town of considerable squalor built around the gigantic open-cast zinc mine that is the sole reason for Cerro's existence. Visitors other than Peruvian businessmen are rare. We therefore received the full treatment. Within an enormous throng of squawking people we attempted to answer the multitude of questions flung at us and finally took refuge in a decrepit little café that sold ice-cold Coca Cola. Keeping a firm eye on our packs over which too many wandering hands were passing for my peace of mind we devoured a clutch of fried eggs that arrived unheralded. With us in the darkened room was a group of men well into the second stages of intoxication from the contents of a big flagon of red wine which they passed to us at ever-increasing intervals. Much later, in almost as happy a state as them we staggered from this den of iniquity to search for a camp site out of range of too many eyes. In this endeavour the darkness and cold worked for us.

North of Cerro the royal road simply evaporated. Our efforts to trace its course were of no avail. Victor von Hagen's map showed the route taking in Yanahuanca and Huanuco but we were unable to understand how Huanuco could be on the same road without recourse to a dogs-leg not shown on his or other maps. The modern road, such as it is, from Cerro de Pasco continues north-east to Huanuco and another, very minor road swings north to Yanahuanca. It was this small dirt road we picked up next day while trying to solve the puzzle and, since Yanahuanca — 50 kilometres distant — was the subsequent landmark, we stayed on it. If nothing else it made an escape route from Cerro.

Carlos had left us the previous evening. Either the local reaction to our presence had unnerved him or he felt that he had come far enough, for his shy 'goodnight' had developed into a reluctant 'goodbye'. We presented him with one half of my mess tin set upon which his eyes had sometimes strayed and, contentedly, he had slid into the dusk. We missed the lad.

We missed his strong bike too, for now it was back to carrying with a vengeance. Initially the way led downhill following an ever-widening valley along which the road bounded in a riotous succession of coils and zigzags. And with every step a new vista opened up as the valley walls drew themselves erect into giant cliffs sprinkled with golden cascades of gorse. Here and there the steep hillside became chequered with cultivated terraces and I marvelled at the immense human effort that went into such terracing just for the sake of salvaging a little soil. Some of those plots were, I swear, angled at not less than forty-five degrees and must have been the devil to work.

Occasionally a climb was necessary where the road had dipped too far or a shoulder of rock needed avoidance. Here, above the 10,000-foot mark, the going became tough. We would climb fifty feet, rest five minutes, climb again, rest. In this manner we found we could cope with our loads but with Yanahuanca in sight after three days of such travelling we were nearing the point of exhaustion.

Our entry into the township triggered a minor revolution. Within seconds we were trapped inside a tight knot of upwards of two score of people, mostly children. It was as if they had never seen a foreigner, though few exhibited fear. We pushed through to the central square intent upon replenishing our depleted stocks of food since Yanahuanca was likely to be the last centre of any size for hundreds of miles.

Two young men came to our assistance; managing to bring some order to the chaos of chanting voices and pushing hands. They also understood our need to locate a campsite for the night. We struggled to a piece of waste ground upon which it was indicated we could pitch our tent. But our retinue failed to diminish and stood around in expectant groups as if waiting for us to perform some miracle for their benefit. Grinning Indian faces, alive with mischief, boded ill for a peaceful night.

Our predicament finally got through to one of the two youths who invited us into the grounds of his family's dwelling. At least it possessed a fenced-in plot of land which would be an improvement on common ground. Then with our fan club marshalled twenty yards away behind the fence we graduated to the balcony of the wooden house and finally were installed upon the floor of the communal bedroom. The show at an end, the crowd dispersed, and supper that night was a quiet collaborative affair of fried potatoes and eggs cooked with the help of our stove as well as the family range.

Our hosts were numerous; a family community representing all ages and sexes. The house consisted of no more than two habitable rooms divided by partitions into cubicles containing beds or tables depending upon their function. A pair of toothless old women shared one bed, their grinning faces framed by gigantic pillows and mountains of off-white linen. The kitchen occupied most of the second room and was manned by a team of middle-aged ladies busily kneading flour as if their lives depended on it. As for the man of the house, a pleasant fellow sporting a heavy black moustache, he was well content to settle himself in his chair and prattle to us about world affairs; a world that, for him, spread not so very far outside of Yanahuanca. In addition to the two youths, who disappeared from time to time, the remainder of the household was made up of sundry babies and dogs of varying degrees of friendliness.

We left early the next morning before the younger citizens had an opportunity to besiege us. Even so, we weren't early enough to avoid two truant schoolboys who began to follow us and so we pressed them into service as porters for our side packs. With them we toiled up an inclined track accompanying the white-flecked waters of the Yanahuanca River bubbling through its ravine of rockbound walls. An hour later we stood on the cross-roads, the spot where the presumed royal road, descending from its mysterious route from Cerro de Pasco, crossed the river and our track, to set its face firmly north. We gazed exasperated towards the place it had come from. It was so clear and easy to pick out burrowing through an outcrop of rock and coming down to the river in a series of well-cut steps, that we couldn't understand how we could have missed it. The bridge, if there had been one, no longer survived but the road, so plainly defined, seemed to be laughing at our inability to locate it outside of Cerro de Pasco. Now we *had* located it, however, we would stick firmly to it. So we told one another with feeling as we gazed upon its stonework, rough and loosened by the countless feet of mules and horses, and headed north into the wilderness.

Neither David nor I voiced any doubts about achieving our aim. Such were our loads that the prospect of attempting to carry them ourselves across country likely to be devoid of the simplest of amenities and on ground untrodden except by cattle was daunting indeed. It had been bad enough on the well-defined track between Cerro and Yanahuanca when we had been secure in the knowledge that urban communities existed at both ends. But from now on the ground would be rising all the while and hadn't we already tasted the bitter fruits of altitude sickness? Even without the sickness the thin air of twelve or fourteen thousand feet would drain us of strength. In lower climes we could have taken the weight of our rucksacks in our stride for it is surprising what a man can carry upon his shoulders. Plainly we had over-estimated our carrying capacity in the environment such as the Andes had to offer.

Yet we were reluctant to jettison items of equipment that might come in useful at a later date or even turn out to be vital. And if anything had to go at least we should *give* it away in exchange for some service or act of kindness. I could discern nothing discardable anyway and, though David's stock of Inca text books weighed heavy, he steadfastly refused to consider their abandonment.

One temporary solution stared us in the face as we dithered taking photographs and adjusting the webbing of our carrying frames. The mule stood, aimless and bovine, its ears hanging forward in resignation. Its mate stood in the lee of a wall, munching steadily. A small boy, his eyes transfixed on us, sat on his haunches, finely balanced on a boulder as if he had been there all his life. He appeared to be the keeper of the two beasts.

In his usual no-nonsense manner David approached the boy and asked if the animals were his. The youngster, struck dumb, remained rooted to the spot until a woman from a nearby hovel approached to claim ownership. Plainly she smelt money to be made.

Our subsequent negotiations in support of borrowing the animals to cover the distance to the next village brought the whole family into the deal and by the time all was settled we were a party of five humans and two mules laden with assorted cargo. Being tall I was designated as too lanky for riding a mule and since my pack obstinately refused to remain upon its bony back all I benefitted from was the removal of my side pack. David, on the other hand, won himself a mount, albeit not of the greatest comfort but adequate for negotiating that stony hillside. The woman rode the second mule and with odd males hanging onto sundry tails we progressed towards the escarpment of the new valley.

The Inca road here was not only emphatically in evidence but was doing duty as a farm track to the present day. It had been confined within a more recently-constructed wall and such was its unevenness that new tracks had been worn alongside. An underground stream, moreover, had surfaced to find a convenient course along the road so that water too contributed to the state of disrepair.

Two miles brought us to the first of a number of stone ruins that littered the hillside. An old mill, its millstone intact, was clearly of colonial origin but subsequent relics could only have arisen from Inca and pre-Inca sources. David worked himself into a fever of excitement as he scrambled about the ruins while I, exhausted beyond measure, could only collapse on the ground thankful for the halt. Our retinue showed impatience at the delay, the woman promptly demanding waiting money, a demand that was satisfied by the donation of a ballpoint pen.

Progressing from ruin to ruin we traced a zig-zag course over the hill and so to the hamlet of Huarautambo. The place lay in a saucer of a wide valley, astride a minor river, a community of adobe dwellings roofed with corrugated iron sheets. The centre was the standard square and a collapsing bell-tower of clay and stone.

Our arrival coincided with the release from school of a hundred boistrous children and within seconds we were surrounded by the whole population of Huarautambo whose elders displayed as much aggressive curiosity as their young. We were poked, questioned, gaped at, shouted at, stared at and finally rescued from these attentions by the village schoolmaster who not only invited us to his home for tea but offered us the village schoolroom in lieu of our tent. His name, he informed us courteously, was Valentine Inge.

From Valentine we enquired of the means of continuing the journey and were told, following much consultation in Spanish, that a convoy of horsemen were due through en route to the next village 'many days' to the north and that we would be welcome to join them. They were expected *'manana'*, the next day. In the meantime the good Valentine had much to show us for it was not everyday that 'intelligent beings from the outside world', as he put it, came to Huarautambo.

A mania for gold grips those who live along the royal road. That there are still many caches of buried treasure on the route to Cajamarca is borne out when peasant farmers, hand-ploughing their lonely plots, periodically unearth gold pots and chalices. The gold was buried by the roadside in 1533 when the Incas, who were taking it to Cajamarca to pay the ransom demanded by the Spaniards for the release of the Inca chief Atahualpa, heard that the Spaniards had in fact betrayed them and killed Atahualpa. Inca tombs, too, were filled — not only with the dead recipient — but gold to ease the new life in the Great Beyond.

Most such tombs have long been discovered but there remain lonely caverns that, when probed by ever-hungry men, occasionally throw up a centuries' old secret of riches that can be imagined only in their wildest of dreams.

One such cave-tomb had, only the year before, been discovered by Valentine. He took us to see it. The cave-mouth was high on a cliff face; not at all easy to reach and the entrance was so narrow that we were forced to squeeze ourselves into dark tunnels half-hidden by undergrowth. Inside was a carpet of skulls and bones which crunched underfoot as we gingerly explored the cavern. In this instance no gold had been unearthed and the villagers had thereupon given vent to their disappointment by destroying most of the human remains. A pity this, for many of the skulls bore witness to a deforming process that was obviously a tribal custom of the time. Much of the afternoon we spent examining these relics and, still led by the remarkable Valentine, continued on a tour of inspection of the numerous pre-Inca walls and concealment pits about the village. High on the hillside he showed us some ancient cave-paintings that were jewels of unappreciated antiquity seldom, if ever, observed by foreign eyes.

The purely Inca jewel within Huarautambo lay in the grounds of what might be described as the local 'manor'. A plump lady wearing straining trousers and the air of a Brighton landlady invited us to see for ourselves the familiar stonework of Inca construction which formed two walls of her cowshed and pigsty. Here, plainly, was part of the *tampu* after which the village was named. Additionally there was a stone seat and water well of the same period, still both in use.

A weekend ensured that the school was entirely at our disposal. It was a two-storey building, the first floor attained by a ladder, and here amongst antiquated desks we lay out our bedding. The floor was filthy, and the windows opaque with dirt, and a human skull (probably from the cave-tomb), leered from a ledge. A candle was our only source of light.

We spent the evening with Valentine, his Quechuan-speaking wife and children, in their dark one-room home next to the school. Desperately poor, their furnishings were no more than a rough table, two old school-room chairs, an ancient double bed screened by a curtain, and some cooking implements that lay around a rusty petrol-stove on the floor. By candlelight too we shared their meagre fare of a vegetable stew of maize, carrots, potato with a little *charqui* (sun-dried meat) thickened by the addition of one of our packet soups. The petrol stove emitted a frightful din but at least provided a little warmth to compensate for the wicked draught from the ever-open door. Valentine exhibited a ferocious appetite for reading matter and our maps and David's text books were avidly studied. Though a schoolmaster, he was denied even the rudiments of any cultural literature. For such a man to be locked away in this mountain fastness seemed to me a tragic waste of a human life, but with a hundred children and the affairs of the village vested in his teachings and abilities perhaps it did hold some purpose.

Back in the schoolroom our night was cold and the floor hard. The sole lavatory in the village was a pit inside a cabin overhanging the river. In total darkness I was, on several occasions, to experience its amenities and, the first time, all but followed my offerings into the surging torrent beneath. A few yards downstream was the community laundry, a piece of open ground over which, in daytime, was spread a patchwork of colourful linens to dry under the sun. Trout abounded in the cold clear water to offer the villagers at least one good source of inexpensive nourishment.

We breakfasted with Valentine on our donated oats to which the herb *manzanilla* was added — not, I thought, to any advantage — and since the horse convoy was not expected until 'later' the three of us spent the morning high in the hills observing more cave-paintings all but destroyed by the ignorant villagers. Valentine spoke sorrowfully but not bitterly of the destructive habits of his flock many of them, he alleged, triggered through superstition or an underlying fear of anything they failed to understand. And their obsession with gold invariably led to greed, petty jealousies and an open hatred that turned, in extreme cases, to murder.

Short of breath but wiser, we descended from the heights only to learn that our horsemen were not expected until the next morning. Disappointed we could only mooch about the village.

It was later that same day that we came into the scheming orbit of one, José. José's sole interest in life was gold: he dreamt of it, lived for it, breathed for it. Furthermore he knew where a cache was hidden or so he affirmed. The only trouble was that he also had a superstitious nature and his fear of the gods was stronger than his greed. Now, two gringos — unbelievers — had arrived in the village and, with them, a solution to the problem. His weasel face creased into a crafty smile as he sidled up and put the proposition to us. In fact he put it a number of times creating, with his surreptitious approaches and urgent whisperings, more suspicion among his fellow-villagers than if he had come straight out with it. He had seen the 'money light' — a blue haze that is supposed to hang over a grave containing treasure — and, if we would undertake the actual digging to his instructions, he would go fifty-fifty with us on the proceeds. He reinforced his argument that gold must be present by a reference to his brother who had, allegedly, found a golden war axe nearby. We were sworn to secrecy.

With everyone going to bed at nightfall, our evenings were becoming decidedly lacking in activity so we agreed to make a tryst with him that very night. This 'money light' expression we had heard before. It had its basis in scientific fact whereby the leather of the bags containing gold and valuables buried with the corpse could give off a gas as the substance rotted away — though any rotting process would have long since completed its cycle. But José's request raised more interesting suppositions. What if there *was* gold and we found it? What would we do with it? We could hardly pocket even half a treasure that belonged to the village, yet if we gave it away we would straightaway come under suspicion from a people prone to violent passions. The right thing would be to hand anything discovered to the authorities but this would be tantamount to lining the pockets of some minor and ill-deserving official. However, the likelihood of us finding anything was remote though the fun of trying was not to be denied. As my mind meandered over the possibilities I realized that, I too, had caught the Andean disease of gold fever.

We met, the three of us, in the square. The sky held hazy stars but the darkness was pitch black. José carried two long-handled spades and an unlit candle. Without a word we filed out of the village, meeting not a soul. In silence we climbed upwards, stumbling and cursing and breathing hard. Below, Huarautambo slept.

José knew exactly where he was going. We ascended to the base of a steep escarpment there to watch him count a number of paces that led him to a small pile of stones. Excitement could be heard in his voice as, in a mixture of Spanish and Quechuan, he indicated the spot to dig.

And while he exhorted us to greater efforts over an ever-widening pitch, David and I dug, infected by his enthusiasm. The night was cool but within an hour we had stripped to our singlets. When the second hour passed I began to have uncharitable thoughts about being taken for a ride and long before the third I was sure of it. Of course we found nothing but, at least, we levelled the score a little by 'allowing' José to return the spoil to the hole.

Smarting, we slunk back to the village, two exhausted gringos and a puzzled Peruvian. Just before we parted towards our respective beds José made a whispered suggestion. The only word we caught was 'metal detector' but we were in no mood for more gold-hunting on this or any other night.

All through the next day we waited for the horsemen, impatient and angry at the delay. Three days in Huarautambo was as much as we could take even given the companionship of Valentine. Our interest switched to irritation and depression. We became all the more aware of the less endearing habits of the villagers and felt sickened. That cruelty to animals is an unpleasant characteristic of South America we had already witnessed, but watching a youth kick a defenceless puppy had us up in arms, though our protestations were completely misunderstood and almost provoked a civil war. My size eleven safari boots became a constant source of sniggers that had me itching to give each tormentor a back-hander. And our evening meals with Valentine in his dismal hovel were as thin as the gruel that was our nightly fare. Half-tame rabbits and guinea-pigs and lean, starving dogs would creep into the room through the open door and forage for any scraps so that even the conversation died under a welter of interruptions as the unfortunate animals were noisily ejected.

But the wait also produced some bonuses. Lying stretched out in the sun beside the river, surrounded by youngsters listening enraptured as Valentine translated our tales of Britain, was one. Another was the sight of the village women congregated on their doorsteps for a wool-spinning session spanning five hundred years of history. And all the while, the glorious majesty of the mountains was about us, clasping the village in their gnarled hands.

It was after we had resigned ourselves to, and were preparing for, another night in the dank, bare school that the shouts reached out to us. 'Where are the gringos?' 'Where are the gringos?' Children dashed across the square to deliver the news that our long-awaited horsemen had arrived and were impatient to continue their journey. Hastily we packed our scattered equipment, and having affected a fleeting farewell of Valentine, we joined the knot of men and horses in front of Huarautambo's single shop.

A villainous crowd they were and there was a woman amongst them. She was of indeterminate age, Indian featured, wearing a trilby hat and carrying on her back a sleeping baby. The males of the group ranged in age from about twelve upwards. A thin boy held the horses while the three men, extremely drunk, were shouting at all and sundry as they clumsily loaded and reloaded the horses; poor skinny beasts, hungry and vicious. Neither of us liked the look of our new travelling companions one iota and the bargaining that ensued before we and our rucksacks were accepted was hard and ugly. Like most of their kind the men were obsessed with the possibility of finding gold and the fact that we were equipped with maps and the knowledge to read them offered the notion that we could be persuaded to find it for them. This was evidently in their minds and was probably the reason they accepted us for, without further ado, they strapped our packs to one of the unladen horses. All the while the woman chewed *coca* — a cocaine-based plant that allays hunger — ejecting brown spittle as if to emphasise every point the men-folk raised.

We moved off, an untidy cavalcade, along the cattle path that parallelled the royal route leading towards the head of the valley.

Only the leader was permitted to ride the one unladen horse and how he managed to stay aloft, still swigging mouthfulls of *cana* (a type of rum) from a flagon beat me. The rest of us lesser mortals walked, David and I somewhat deferentially in the rear. One of the other men was a dab hand with a long whip which he intermittently cracked across the horses' backs with a noise that echoed across the valley.

We made for the distant escarpment between two peaks over which we were given to understand it was necessary to be before nightfall — and it was already into afternoon. The river stuck close to us and every now and again we had to cross it, leaping from stone to stone attempting to keep our feet dry. The woman trudged stoically on the flank, her living load never uttering a sound.

With the coming of dusk the path mounted a steeply inclining set of Inca-constructed steps that had been made for the passage of llamas (not horses), and our poor frightened animals were whipped up this uneven stairway without mercy. They slithered and stumbled, their loads frequently slipping sideways round their bellies to frighten them still further. At the top was a rock plateau and the foundations of a stone shepherd's hut which was evidently the destination for here we halted and the horses unloaded and hobbled. Unbidden, the woman made a fire out of handfuls of dry grass over which she heated her menfolk's ready-prepared stew in a blackened cooking pot. David and I, struggling in the dark, managed to coax our temperamental stove into boiling some soup and, to encourage co-operation, offered the others a packet of onion consommé to which they reciprocated with some stale rolls and heavy doses of *cana*. Everyone became all at once more amiable and since they had no compunction about sleeping directly beneath the stars we saw no reason to be different; we wouldn't have been able to erect the tent on the rocky ground anyway.

Face upwards I lay marvelling at the galaxy of stars in the heavens above us. To remain awake and watchful I deemed prudent, reasoning that we might otherwise have our throats cut, though I was already mellowing towards our roughneck companions. Assuredly their appearance made them look more ferocious than they were, and though they whispered furtively amongst themselves for much of the night I don't think they were planning our demise; I wouldn't sleep; only rest I told myself, and awoke in the early hours chilled to the marrow and soaked with frozen dew.

We left with the dawn fortified by a breakfast of boiled eggs and copious draughts of *cana.* The day started with a disaster. The horse carrying David's pack shed its load, panicked and kicked the packframe into a tangle of bent and fractured aluminium. The loss of the frame made for easier carrying by horse or mule but ensured an increased reliance upon this form of transportation.

The offending animal caught, calmed and reloaded we progressed up a long incline, its Inca paving worn and broken by the years and ill-use. But again there was little doubt about it being the royal road; its dimensions and the sheer scale of it was the Inca hallmark. The leader, whose name we discovered to be Ron, sat bareback on his mount, long legs dangling and still swigging *cana* as he talked to himself in a petulant voice. His ragged troops followed, struggling up the uneven steps, each finding his own pace while the horses were kicked and thrashed over every obstacle. Within an hour I was in a state of utter exhaustion, my chest heaving and my breath emerging in great sobs. Every dozen or so steps and I was forced to a halt, there to fight for air, and vomit at the same time as the higher altitude thinned the air still further. Up and up we climbed, the pace relentless, my companions unmerciful. All around was a storm of rock and, above, the sun hovered in the sky, a ball of fire raising the temperature from freezing to burning hot.

A new plateau emerged to allow a rest and Ron insisted that his guests partook of mouthfulls of his firewater; I drank until my brain reeled. Refusal was taken as an insult resulting in a spasm of surly anger and a threatening display of weaponry. So we drank to keep the peace. On again but the path levelled out and became easier, softened by patches of grass and swamp. We had now entered a further valley and the road, grass-surfaced, wide and bordered by stones, swept haughtily into the distance. A pause was made at a lonely hut from which a peasant woman emerged accompanied by a retinue of pigs but her smile of welcome faded as she caught sight of David and me. Here in such aggressively lonely climes the arrival of strangers was reason for suspicion, not welcome.

Oro, the word for gold was pointedly aimed at us. We were passing a complex of caverns, their mouths half buried in the ground beneath a scattering of great boulders. David and I shook our heads but this response only served to infuriate the others who imagined that we were trying to put them off the scent. But our 'no' had meant 'no, we don't know', not 'no, we won't tell you what we know' and everything got progressively more confusing until, arriving at an overgrown pit, Ron reigned in his horse, halted the convoy, dismounted and announced that *oro* was indisputably to be found here. He looked at us as if for confirmation, got none, studied our map in bewilderment and, finally, grabbed a spade from the back of one of the packhorses. To humour the man we offered to help and, within seconds, everyone was crowding round the hole enthusiastically taking it in turns to dig into the peaty soil.

Losing interest as swiftly as he had raised it Ron returned to his horse, gulped down more *cana,* cursed us, patted us on the back, shouted obscenities at everyone and insisted we drink with him. Choking as the stuff seared my throat, I was still hearing his maniacal laughter when we moved off again — with Ron talking to himself as if there had been no interruption.

Another rise and we were at a point called Incapoyo where we came across a magnificent sight. There in the distance, etched against a blue sky, lay the enormous bulk of the, I think, Cordillera Huayhuash range stretching across the horizon in a glorious panorama of snow peaks. The explorer, Colonel Fawcett, might have been standing by my side for I heard his words 'Never had I seen mountains like these, and I was crushed by the grandeur — speechless with the overpowering wonder of it'. The road, now straight as a die, cantered on down into a long downward-sloping valley, a most comforting sight after the gyrations and gradients of the last miles. We halted again on the brow of yet another escarpment and settled down in long *ichú* grass for a hot meal. Ron remained happily drunk while his compatriots grilled pieces of meat strung together over a grass fire and we made some lumpy porridge with the help of the stove. The woman steadfastly ignored Ron's antics and the baby on her back never made so much as a whimper. I attempted to get near enough to see how the little mite was faring for I was having morbid thoughts about its condition but the woman determinedly kept herself to herself and swung away from us with a snarl.

It took all the afternoon to negotiate that new valley that was veined with bogs and streams, and just when I was wondering whether it would ever come to an end we turned into the hillside for another of those heart-stopping, breath-robbing climbs interspersed with the urging of unwilling horses up near-vertical crests peppered with outcrops of granite. The royal road came with us, narrowing and deteriorating in the process and changing gear into more steps, broken and uneven. The way was strewn with delightful wild flowers: blue daisies, alpine crocuses and strange orange dandelions with no stalks that might have been a figment of my fevered imagination as I struggled to fight the nausea of physical weakness. Startled birds, akin to plovers, rose in clusters from underfoot to frighten me out of the remnants of my wits.

The summit of one escarpment only led to another and it all became too much for one unfortunate horse that had been limping for a long time. Suddenly the wretched beast collapsed and rolled down the steep incline thrashing wildly, and taking my rucksack with it. Fortunately my pack parted company from the horse without damage, but when the animal eventually managed to rise to its feet it flatly refused to take another step in spite of multiple beatings. My rucksack was transferred to a second horse and the miscreant was abandoned to fend for itself, though I like to think it was collected by Ron on a subsequent return journey.

Finally we attained a crest that *was* the top only to perceive yet a further valley opening up before us. This one had at its end an incredible skyline of giant white peaks but our emotions were raised the more by the sight of the road leading downhill. Nobody spoke, not even Ron who had relapsed into a sullen silence since the discarding of the packhorse. The other men took it in turns to steal a ride on the remaining already overladen horses but the woman, David and I plodded on with leaden feet. Worse, I was struck down by another attack of diarrhoea which put me well behind the column.

It was dusk again when we reached the hamlet. Composed of only three mud hovels with badly-thatched roofs and situated some way off the road, I would never have noticed it had I been on my own. But it was journey's end so far as this long day was concerned. My water bottle had long been empty and my tongue was sticking to the roof of my mouth. I don't think I could have gone on much further.

Outside one of the hovels we stopped and our companions piled into it. Smoke emerged from the straw roof and while David and I lay spreadeagled on the ground a child hesitatingly brought us a dirty mug of sweet tea that became one of perhaps half a dozen momentous drinks of my lifetime.

We pitched our tent nearby on the brow of the hill not knowing or caring what blessings or horrors the next day might bring but as the moonlight focused the summit of 22,000-foot Nevado Yerupaja amidst the Cordillera Huayhuash it came to me that there could be no other campsite in the world offering a view of such splendour.

4

HUARAUTAMBO–PILCOCANCHA –LA UNIÓN–HUARI

I suppose we must have covered about 30 miles from Huarautambo but it was not so much the distance or the roughness of the route that affected us as the fact that we had been unable to undertake it at our own pace.

This was all too likely to be the continued disadvantage of travel in company with others; we would be tied to the speed of horse or mule and the Andean Peruvians who have greater lung-power than low-altitude Britons. But the best answer lay with the possibility of the acquisition of a pack animal — either on purchase or loan — though the likelihood of purchase seemed slight. Beasts of burden were the means of life to these people, the potato-gathering season was in full swing and so nobody was likely to give up the means of a prolonged source of income for the sort of money we could raise. Simple hire, therefore, offered the only compromise though this would entail the services of an accompanying horseman to effect the return of the animal. David and I were, for once, in agreement on this arrangement though neither of us would rule out the joining of another convoy should the opportunity arise. In the cold light of a new day such matters took on a new importance.

A heavy frost sheathed the tent in clusters of diamonds that flashed and twinkled in the early morning sun. In spite of the bitter cold the tremendous sight on the horizon lured us out of our sleeping bags to watch a procession of clouds like a flock of sheep climb up the ravines between the hills. The air was cool but agreeable and the first streaks of sapphire were appearing behind the peaks. The few villagers were already out milking cows on the hillsides as we performed our ablutions from a water-hole that also served as the only source of drinking water. Fresh it might have been, though a film of green scum bordered the sides of the hole.

Breakfast was baked potatoes obligingly brought by a sober Ron who came over to see how we had fared. In return we gave him some soup powder and opened negotiations on the subject of horsepower and the resumption of the journey. *'Manana'*, was all we could get out of him, hardly an original or comforting statement in the circumstances. Plainly nobody was going anywhere today. But an enforced rest-day provoked little dissention amongst any of us and as the sun got up the idleness proved only beneficial.

If our large scale map of the area could be believed the three hovels had a name: Angoltuto. It overlooked the deep valley of the Lauricocha River across which the royal road made its way. The warmth of the sun lasted very few hours and by early afternoon the chill of the altitude and mountain shadows had us squeezing into the tiny bivouac. The spartan fare of which we were being forced to partake together with an increased appetite had our thoughts firmly switched to the subject of food and not even the inspiration of the breathtaking panorama could persuade them to go away.

The next day there arose the prospect of being isolated at Angoltuto for an indefinite period when negotiations broke down between David and Ron as to the sum payable for onward baggage transportation to Gasacucho which was the village destination of the convoy. According to Ron our money's worth had run out; yet he had known we aimed to reach Banos, a larger village well beyond Gasacucho. The sly leader knew he had us over a barrel and, accordingly, demanded a ridiculously high figure. David halved it and stuck resolutely to the amount even when Ron turned on his heel in high dudgeon. But David had called his bluff and he finally capitulated.

We had been unable to ascertain the exact purpose of the convoy; whether it was a regular shopping and provision-replenishment expedition or one made between Yanahuanco and Gasacucho for a specific reason no one seemed willing to tell us. We were not at all sure even if the Ron entourage had come from Yanahuanco for as we hadn't seen their arrival in Huarautambo we hadn't seen the direction from which they had come. The question was academic but it could have had a bearing upon the likelihood or otherwise of our joining other such convoys in the future.

The party that left Angolotuto after hours of delay was of a different composition than before. Some of the horses too were not those with which we had set out. One of the new ones, a pitiful grey mare had a club foot, and we were horrified to observe that both our packs and a large sack of potatoes were piled onto her. Two small children were strapped to another, fitter beast and, of course, Ron rode the third with a fourth well weighed down with more potatoes. Only one other man came, a lean, morose figure, he of the whip, which left David and me and the unfortunate woman with her ever-silent child, to follow on foot.

A series of steps, easy for us but painful for the horses, led down the steep side of the valley and I shuddered every time the poor grey cripple was whipped and kicked over each rocky knoll which even the fitter beasts found difficult to negotiate. I shuddered too because every stumble and near-fall put at risk our surviving baggage, much of which had already sustained damage as a result of the earlier mishaps. But the mare was more sure-footed than her contorted hoof led us to believe and we gained the river in reasonable order.

The Lauricocha was wide, fast-flowing but not deep. Even so we were glad of and surprised at Ron's offer of a ride over the torrent. My animal had an initial objection to getting its feet wet but once in midstream changed its mind and had to be thrashed out again. The woman never waited to be invited to be carried across the stream and stoically waded it without a murmur. A tiny puppy that had followed us from the hamlet attempted to swim in its eagerness to keep up and was swept downstream for its pains.

One has inevitably to pay for the pleasure of downhill walking in the mountains with the hard currency of an uphill slog. Our settlement of the account involved a zig-zag nightmare of a climb up the opposite wall of a valley that could be better described as a canyon. Traversing an extremely wet portion of the royal road the woman fell into a swollen stream soaking herself in the process but again made no complaint and there emerged not a murmur or wail from the bundle on her back. Seldom have I felt so concerned for a fellow human.

Beyond the summit the road led us, in softer mood, into pampa dotted with boulders, and then to a series of hamlets each of no more than half a dozen adobe huts. One of these communities, slightly larger than the rest, turned out to be Gashapampa which boasted not only a football pitch but a tin-roofed dwelling that was a village shop. The party came to a halt which gave David and I an opportunity to buy the entire stock of stale biscuits — a dozen small packets — which we consumed on the spot. While thus engaged, and surrounded by the entire population including both football teams (whose game had come to an abrupt end with our arrival), Ron appeared with a recharged rum flagon to announce the parting of the ways so far as he and we were concerned. He was now taking his potatoes to San Miguel de Cauri, he explained, which was not on our route. A demand for the balance of the original fee quoted was then made, accompanied by threats, but we resisted this with a vigour that, once more, sent him into retreat to a chorus of derisive laughter and unpleasantness from the crowd. Our victory such as it was, was short lived however, for there were no horses to be hired in the village. Our baggage was unceremoniously dumped at our feet and, when the farewells came to be made, Ron put a good face on it and even effected quite a moving little speech. A fickle lot indeed.

Our immediate goal was the Inca ruin of Tunsacancha, some eight miles ahead. Here David wanted to spend some time investigating the remains of a rarely-seen *tampu* and one-time Inca habitation. The problem was how to get there before dark with our loads, for it was already mid-afternoon and we did not much care for the look of the villagers. The solving of the problem was plainly a case of taking up our beds and walking so we shouldered our packs as best we could and pressed on fatalistically out of Gashapampa. Our departure was watched by two youths who must have seen a source of income to be acquired out of our stumbling gait for they pursued us and offered to carry some of our gear to the next village. A deal was struck and our cargo distributed onto four backs.

These bearers too hardly inspired our trust. They were shifty-eyed and unfriendly and carried sheath-knives which they toyed with lovingly as they walked. One of them enquired if we carried pistols and I was about to shake my head when David, quicker on the uptake, nodded and patted a bulging pocket in which reposed a battered copy of The *South American Handbook.*

A line of quinel trees, rare at this altitude, gave us the first glimpse of vegetation for days. They were windswept and spindly but any trees in a desert of lonely grassland and rock make a comforting sight. The royal road, broad and clearly-defined, offered easy walking but by the time we reached the single mud farmhouse that formed the next 'village' — that of, presumably, Gasacucho — our legs felt like rubber.

We paid off our helpers who departed, still fingering their knives, and pitched camp below the farm and close to a stream. In the evening light we could make out the ruins further down the valley less than a mile away and, more welcome still, any number of horses grazing on the hillside.

Camping in a valley instead of atop a ridge made for a warmer night, but next day, my ideas of a strip-down wash in the inviting stream quickly faded when we sampled the water's temperature. So once more it was the usual lick and a promise; more promise than lick. The banks of the stream were the haunt of snow-white herons and flocks of black and white geese.

Prior to leaving the tent to walk, unladen, to the ruins we made the acquaintance of the household across the way. Most of the building was given over to potato-storage with the inmates living in an out-house close by. The farmer, a jolly portly fellow, had just killed a sheep and he invited us to buy some of the meat which his wife would cook for us that evening. We arranged to purchase a kilo for the equivalent of 40 pence, hardly an exorbitant charge, and arranged to return for the feast at dusk. We also negotiated our onward transportation as far as Pilocancha, some 25 miles distant, then made our easy way to Tunsacancha well satisfied with developments.

The *tampu* of Tunsacancha is not of great drama to the layman but set, as it is, at a point where two valleys join, the ruins wear a jaunty air. Much smaller and more compact than Bonbón the outlines of the Inca dwellings are clearer to see though they merge a little confusingly with the outcrops of rock at the eastern end. In addition to some foundations and walls a small arch survives and the warm stone was ablaze with a carpet of tiny yellow flowers. A second farm stood adjacent to the remains and, glory be, there was a rough and ready shop where we acquired a stock of cheese, biscuits, eggs and a tin of herrings.

David roamed the *tampu* for many hours, allowing me a sleep under the warm mid-day sun as well as a roam up into the gentle hills to provide a vantage point from which to take photographs. However the prospect of meat for supper drove us back to camp earlier than we had anticipated.

By the time the whole household of one woman and eight men together with an indeterminate number of nose-running and exceptionally dirty children had gathered round the perimeter of the communal room that served as kitchen, bedroom and slaughter-house, darkness had fallen. The woman, swaddled in skirts which, judging by her smell, rarely left her body, toiled over an open fire and the aroma of meat overpowered the less-pleasant odours that permeated the place.

The meal commenced with an issue of sweet *manzanilla* 'tea' and a round of potatoes roasted in their jackets. The notion arose that this was to take the edge off our appetite so that we would not eat our full entitlement of meat and, indeed, this was probably the case. I tried to soft-pedal on the spuds but hunger is the very devil and when the portions of meat were circulated it was too dark to perceive from which section of the sheep's anatomy they originated. A recollection came to me of a meal I had in a Bedouin tent in the Sahara Desert for the circumstances were slightly similar. There, in a community as poor as here, the goat carcase was shared out under a system of numbers so that everybody present had a fair chance of receiving some lean meat as well as the more plentiful blobs of fat. On that occasion too, the darkness mercifully hid the blemishes of dirt and unhygienic handling but at least, amongst the Andes, the offerings were not garnished with a layer of clinging, crunchy sand.

The door was left open to permit the escape of smoke and before the heat of the fire could take effect we were chilled to the marrow. As with Valentine, whenever a fragment of food fell to the ground we felt a rush of furry creatures — probably rabbits and guinea-pigs — around our legs. During the feast nobody spoke a word though constant hawking and spitting offered an orchestral accompaniment to the general grunts of satisfaction. In spite of the surroundings I felt much better after the meal and David even managed a desert of more potatoes. We shook hands all round, confirmed the morning's departure and rolled happily into our sleeping bags.

Neither the patter of rain on the flysheet nor the dry, hacking cough I had developed spoilt that night. The cough was to remain with me many weeks and was to have me in constant paroxysms of choking which became most wearing. David's cross to bear was a painful rash on the back of his hands and, later, a worrying bout of fever which he diagnosed as hepatitis.

As we should have expected no person and no horse materialised with the dawn and by the time we had run the farmer to earth it was only to hear his complete denial of acquiescing to any such arrangements made the previous day. David's angry outburst drew no more than shrugs, evasive replies and the usual explanation concerning the demands of the potato harvest. *'Manana'*, he bleated but we had had enough of the *manana* game and pressed the point that we would be going that day even if we had to carry our own gear, in which case he would lose 250 *soles.* To prove the point we shouldered our sacks and staggered off down the road listening for his surrender. It came, of course, but we were nevertheless much relieved to hear it. A miserable-looking nag together with an equally miserable youth were grudgingly produced; all the more able-bodied beasts and humans having left for potato-transportation duties long before we had emerged from the tent.

The morning was a depressing one with low clouds spitting rain and hiding the brows of the low hills. Our spirits, so high the previous day, sank into our boots as we plodded dismally along behind the horse. The pace was dead slow.

The royal road wandered along beside us through broad sweeping valleys of grass and swamp. The stream we were following widened and had to be crossed at intervals while the swamps forced us into detours that, for a while, lost us the route. Large ugly birds soared overhead. They were not condors and were probably buzzards but, to my depressed mind, they were vultures. By mid-day hunger drove us off course to a village where we hoped to find food but there was none. Suspicious eyes followed our disconsolate departure from the miserable collection of dwellings but during the afternoon the sun poked bright fingers through the stained cottonwool of the clouds to cheer things up no end. The way descended gently down the side of the valley containing Banos and the countryside took on a vastly more appetizing aspect with plots of cultivated lands and crops. We stopped to watch a team of peasants hand-ploughing a meadow, working in unison to turn the soil in swift, methodical movements before our presence distracted them. They were cheerful characters who, in spite of the interruption, smiled, laughed and shook our hands warmly.

It is at a point several miles beyond Banos that the royal road drops finally into the valley. It does so by way of a series of finely-cut stairways, wide and regal. The road remains a thoroughfare to this day, marching across the country in arrogant fashion, the only substantial man-made object around. At the bottom of the valley the river Nupe, fast-flowing and deep, barred the way, with no sign of an Inca or any other bridge. We tracked down a modern timber construction a couple of miles upstream, directly beneath the hillside village of Pilcocancha and made our way towards it. Barely had we gained the square when the heavens opened and sent us hastening for shelter in the local bakery.

To a hungry traveller it made a fine refuge and though the bread was stale David and I put away a good dozen rolls each, watched from the doorway by an ever-swelling crowd who seemed oblivious of the rain. The owner, suddenly the centre of attention, made us doubly welcome extending the invitation to an overnight stay at his humble abode. A shifty-eyed little man, he was not unpleasant though not immediately likeable either.

What he was like when he'd been at the bottle we were soon to learn. With the downpour over and dusk falling, he took us a mile down the road to the thermal hot springs after which Banos is named, by way of the local 'pub', where we felt obliged to buy him a beer. He also managed to procure a Coke bottle full of rum at our expense and that was when our host displayed his less attractive side. But he was still sober when he showed us the three bubbling pools of water which, like the stream that fed them, were encased in a cloud of steam. The baths were of Inca origin and were still in fine order. David and I resolved to return in the morning equipped with soap and towels.

By now we had been joined by the baker's son, a more intelligent youngster of pleasant countenance. Through him we arranged for the use of a horse for as far as La Unión and, again, we convinced ourselves that all was well. Another downpour caught us, this time in the open, and the liquor shack being the nearest refuge, we ran for it getting extremely damp in the process. It was the youngster who eventually accompanied us back to Pilcocancha while his father remained behind to sink more rum.

Of course the inevitable happened. The son had no key to the bakery resulting in us having to hang around outside in more rain until Papa, staggering through the darkness, arrived to let us in. He was in an aggressive mood — the more so when he learnt of our efforts to force an entry — and smelt like a brewery. Threatening us with police prosecution for some imagined damage to his property he demanded restitution in the form of a share in the consumption of our frugal supper and even had the cheek to charge us for the stale rolls he ate with our herrings. Finally the man rose unsteadily, belched and left us, locking the shop door behind him. This was awkward because the call of nature had to be answered, the only receptacles being a row of empty lemonade bottles on the shelves behind the counter. Between us we filled more than half a dozen during the night. We slept on the counter, fearful of rolling off it onto the filthy floor.

Being windowless the room remained in darkness at daybreak and so we were still abed when the door was unlocked to admit not only the baker but a great concord of bread-hunting customers. Swept off the counter in the rush we attempted to dress ourselves as best we could and collect our scattered belongings amongst a score or more of customers-turned-gringo-watchers. In the turmoil I lost my hat. Buying eggs from a rival emporium across the road we boiled them on the Primus, a magical piece of equipment that of course drew hordes of new onlookers.

Noticeable was the number of the men of the village who were high on rum even at so early an hour. But with the stuff cheap by any standards I could appreciate that living out a life in such poverty, in damp houses and on a diet of potato, sugar and stale bread rolls would be dismal enough to turn the staunchest tee-totaler to the bottle. The magnificence of the Andes might be just around the corner but mountain panoramas are unable fill empty stomachs.

It goes without saying that the horse and horseman we had arranged with the baker's son never put in an appearance. Once again we had been green enough to imagine that any negotiations made the previous day would be binding the next. The rain had slackened off as we strode round the village in search of the culprit, finally catching up with him on his way to another job. David argued and shouted at the boy until at mid-day with more rain threatening, he finally produced one grumpy old horse and an equally grumpy old man. So bony was the animal's back that it was an almost impossible task to balance our packs each side of its protruding backbone and we were to lose count of the number of times the load slid to the ground. But at least the horse could not raise the strength to be anything but docile and the man, at longer acquaintance, turned out to be a nice old boy with a heart of gold. He wore a stubble beard on his wizened face that was weatherbeaten and deeply lined.

It was a long and almost vertical climb that took us out of the valley and back onto the royal road that now progressed along the ridge giving superb mountain views in all directions. The rain was eased away by sunshine but the sky remained grey and ominous. Except for a brief halt to share our quota of rolls and to assess the distance to our next stop at the town of La Unión, we carried on without a rest, pleased at the prospect of a night in a town: our maps showed it to be a centre of some size; a metropolis among the wilderness.

We must have walked a good twelve miles and were descending into yet another valley when the storm hit us. A junction had deflected us from the royal route which swung away from La Unión to cross the Pampa Huanuco Viejo and down to the Vizcarra Valley ten kilometres west of the town nestling in the same valley. At the onset of the first drops of rain we should undoubtedly have taken the old man's advice and sheltered at a shepherd's hut. But La Unión was, we wrongly estimated, only nine kilometres ahead and its imagined bright lights and culinary expertise beckoned...

What fell out of the sky as we hurried on was more, much more, than a mere downpour. It was a prolonged cascade of water that had us, in spite of our waterproofs, soaked to the skin within seconds. Never have I seen rain like it though I have experienced many a frightening storm in African and Asian jungles. It had the track inches deep in liquid mud and water in minutes and, all around, the grass disappeared under miniature lakes, their surfaces only broken by the impact of hailstones. Above, the grey ogre of mist and low cloud compressed everything in a sodden embrace and the temperature plummeted to zero. My teeth were chattering as splinters of icy liquid ran down my back from sodden clothing unable to absorb it.

A house on the flank of a hill emerged from the murk and we ran towards it intent upon escaping the sweep of water. The doors were locked; nobody was at home but dogs barked and snarled at our ankles as we flattened ourselves against the mud walls for protection. All three of us started to shiver uncontrollably and we became abruptly aware of the very real prospect of hyperthermia in this desolate and suddenly terrible place.

Darkness was less than an hour away but we stubbornly resisted the old man's pleas to remain and take what refuge we could in an adjoining cowshed. A slight slackening of the deluge tempted us back to the flooded track to squelch through the mud in half-crazed desperation. Thoroughly alarmed, the old man had us racing along behind the horse that, likewise, sensed the danger.

The track wound down into a culvert and night merged with the angry black storm clouds. The river, when we came to it, was hidden in darkness. From a hundred yards ahead the man shouted something, mounted his horse and disappeared. This way he must have waded the river for we heard him mounting the opposite bank in a flurry of pounding hoofs and straining girths. For a moment we imagined he was abandoning us.

The river was the Guytoc, normally no more than a brook when not a dried-up water course. Now, swollen by the heavy rains, it had become a roaring torrent flecked with madness. Apprehensively we removed our boots, tied the laces together and hung them round our necks. We entered the ice-cold stream, I leading, and in an instant the water level reached our thighs, pulling at our resisting legs and threatening to topple us into the sullen depths. I took another cautious step, lost my balance and floundered into deep water. Even as I went down into the flow I remembered being near-drowned in a remote but much larger Kenyan river just a year before but in the little Guytoc, with no crocodiles or whirlpools, it all seemed undramatic and rather foolish. But there was no doubt about the power of its water as I threshed wildly, out of my depth, and was dragged forward by a vicious current. A blow against my mouth proved my boots were still with me as I glimpsed foaming water ahead. 'I must keep my boots, I must keep my boots' I told myself over and over again and I heard David shout once but ignored him. The black outline of the other bank showed close so I threw myself sideways, grabbed at some foliage, lost my hold, tried again and scrambled on all fours up a muddy shore. Light-headed with relief I turned to help David but he too was safely across the maelstrom. He was badly shaken and showed it in his desperate grip on my arm.

Our shouts brought back the old man, now leading his horse. He waited, mumbling to himself, as we struggled back into wet socks and boots. 'Keep moving, keep moving' I kept repeating, for the numbing inertia of exposure was paralysing my limbs. Plainly neither of us was in a fit state to reach La Unión but what was the alternative? A pitch dark night made movement almost impossible; yet movement alone could save us. We stumbled on, David suffering from the pain of a burst blister.

Miraculously, the darker outline of a farm rose before us. I perceived we were moving across a plain for the indistinct outline of low hills had receded. In their place, stark against the night sky, was this group of buildings. No lights showed but our noisy arrival drew people from the shadows.

Upon learning of our plight the household swiftly went to work in the rudimentary kitchen to produce a hot meal while an elderly man helped us spread dry hay on the ground beneath a lean-to that partly covered a small courtyard. We peeled off our wet clothes replacing them with items that were merely damp. The stew of potato, vegetable and macaroni soup with *manzanilla* tea was disposed of in record time to the accompaniment of our loud expressions of appreciation. Optimistically we hung out our wet garments before settling down in none-too-dry sleeping bags liberally encased in stale hay. A litter of pigs, some hens and a dog found their way onto our beds but their warm-blooded presence was welcome and sleep came easily.

A cockerel standing on my foot awoke me as it heralded the dawn. We threw things at the wretched bird but this did no good so we rose and dressed gingerly in the clothes that had remained sodden in the damp night air. The household — the man lost some of his years by daylight but his wife seemed to have gained some — were also up and about, having slept with three children all of a heap in an outhouse which appeared to be the only living quarters. The overawed youngsters, each one sucking his or her thumb, watched us pack our strewn belongings and prepare to resume the broken journey to La Unión. The sun shone with vivid intensity, making a mockery of the previous night's fiasco. To the standard infinitesimal charge levied for our accommodation and meal by our hosts we added some small gifts, and were away.

Indeed we were soon on a broad open plain, the Pampa Huanco Viejo, stretching in all directions with just a blur of hills on the horizon. An hour's walking brought us to the edge of a sharp descent leading down into the Vizcarra Valley; more a gorge than a valley at this point. An excruciating path of jagged broken stones took us, over another hour, into the outskirts of the township of La Unión where our ravenous appetites led us to the nearest restaurant. It was filthy dirty and the choice of food was limited but we didn't care. Six fried eggs apiece made a satisfactory start to breakfast, after which we paused just long enough to bid farewell to our companion and pay him off, before returning to another helping of eggs. Then we went in search of a hotel aware that, just occasionally, urban living has its rewards.

La Unión, let it be said, is no metropolis. The little town is split into two halves by the River Vizcarra, the bridge connecting the residential suburb of Ripán having been part swept away by flood. The verdant-walled canyon in which La Unión lies is very much more beautiful than the clustered, paint-lacking dwellings and unpaved streets of the town. The township contains a couple of hotels of the basic variety plus a simple town hall that doubles as a community centre and cinema.

We spent three days in La Unión. Our hotel raised a bed and a communal tap from which issued, if we were lucky, spasmodic, cold, rusty water. By the end of the second day we had run out of restaurants and discovered that none could produce the meat we craved. The market was the place where the action was to be had and its stalls offered the only colour to contrast with the drab brown houses topped by tin roofs that surrounded it. Of the population, half were high on rum much of the time and the rest all the time. When the good citizens of La Unión weren't staring at us, trying to rob us or asking questions, they were hitting the bottle.

Our first day we put to good use for a prolonged cleaning and mending session. The second we retraced our steps to the Inca ruins of Huanuco Viejo.

We had intentionally by-passed the great edifice on the way to La Unión for we wanted a whole day free to examine the priceless structure. The royal road seems to by-pass it too, unaccountably turning west as if to give the complex wide berth before reverting to its northerly alignment and sweeping across the Vizcarra well clear of the site. The great plain of gently swaying grass looked idyllic under a warm sun, the more so after the sweat and toil of the morning climb back to it. Horses and sheep dotted the landscape — the former of particular interest to us — while closer to the lip of the valley, the almost perpendicular sides offered a bird's-eye view of the Vizcarra below. A scattering of houses stood at the top of the mule path to the plain and as soon as we reached them David began soliciting their occupiers on the subject of horse or mule hire. But we were out of luck — the potato harvest was still in full swing and they couldn't spare either.

The ruins of Huanuco Viejo were not immediately apparent even though we assiduously scanned the pampa with our binoculars. But we knew they must be somewhere and stepped out briskly for the horizon. Our way led through cultivated plots of *olloco,* a variety of peppery potato, *oca, chocho* and the lupin-like *quinoa* for the plain was fertile and the farmers of La Unión made the most of it. A couple winnowing corn by hand greeted us with grave courtesy and offered guidance by pointing out the direction of the ruins.

It was a long walk even when we had them in sight. But what the Inca had built in the middle of this open grassland was truly magnificent. A huge fort-like edifice or *isnu* stood intact, its massive stone walls a marvel of construction. From the parapet the whole complex of Huanuco Viejo was spread out before us, each building in a very fair state of preservation since, without interference from subsequent house, dam or bridge builders, the finely-assembled walls had only the elements to withstand. We wandered for hours among the substantial remnants of old temples, storehouses, barrack blocks and dwelling houses marvelling at the grandeur of the stone arches and staircases. We were not alone in Huanuco Viejo. With us were the ghosts of Incain soldiers, priests and the multitude of citizens who once inhabited this lonely, spectacular place.

The royal road itself was nowhere to be seen; nor was there any sign of a feed road to the complex. The well-nourished grass, thick and succulent, that hid all traces may have been thought flat and substantial enough to dispense with the need for a road into the complex – if, indeed the main route *did* pass it by. What we wanted was a convenient high spot from which it might have been possible to make out the *agger* of any old road – but here in the massive pampa there was not so much as a tree that we could climb.

However it was the grandeur within the ruins, more than unsupported supposition of feed roads without, that concentrated our attentions and ignited our combined imagination. The remains of massed dwelling houses filled the region outside the plaza and the low mound adjoining it. In the centre of the square was what had doubtless been the sun temple. At its western end stood the palace containing six stone gateways on the portals of which crouching animal figures had been carved. These led to a series of immense rooms leading, in turn, into what seemed to be a multiple bath chamber probably fed (though by means unknown), from the hot springs of Banos through which we had passed.

Something of the size of the place can be gathered from a Spaniard writing in 1548: 'Huanuco has a fine royal palace... the chief palace in this province of Huamalies with near it a Temple of the Sun with many virgins and priests. It was so grand a place in the time of the Incas that more than 30,000 Indians were set apart solely for its service'.

It was 1539 when the Spaniards seized this Inca stronghold. For two years they maintained a settlement at the 12,000-foot altitude then, unable to bear the icy winds and bleak conditions, they moved north-east to warmer, more hospitable territory: Indians returned to Huanuco Viejo and were known to be living there as recently as 1608. Huanuco Viejo remains important to historians because it was the principal stronghold from which the Inca conquests were launched in several directions — for which its roads were, of course, of major strategic importance.

It was dark before we regained the ragged path down into La Unión but a brilliant moon illuminated its loose ankle-breaking stones and transformed the ugly town into an illusion of a Swiss Alpine village. We dined in the hotel kitchen not much affected by its horrific lack of hygiene and then, in company with the populace, fell to the temptation of the local rum at 10 pence a tumblerful.

Our last day was occupied with stocking up, eating ourselves silly and, most vital of all, attempting to raise some horse transportation. The day was officially decreed a meatless one but we managed to run to earth a substantial *lomo* — a popular dish containing fragments of meat, chips, onions and tomatoes — in a fly-blown establishment masquerading as an art gallery if its display of naked girl calendars was anything to go by. Anyone wearing a stetson, breeches or afflicted with bandy legs was interrogated by David but in vain. 'They're all on the pampa bringing in potatoes...'

Settling any hotel bill in rural Peru invariably involves a hassle. Bank notes are soiled and greasy to the point of non-identification and nobody can ever raise any change — even if they want to. We left under a late afternoon sun, carrying our gear and trying not to show the agony of the load to a small town community of whom we had grown heartily sick. I found it hard to be sympathetic to such poverty of thought and deed though my strictures may well be considered unworthy. But three days in a place like La Unión is something of a penance made the sourer by false hope raised when struggling for survival in the wilderness.

Horseless again, future progress was in doubt. All we could do was to regain the route of the royal road where it crossed the modern dirt road running out of the town along the valley towards Huallanca, and there await our chances. Our subsequent destination along the royal road was Huari, some 80 miles distant. The route was plainly marked on our large-scale map sheets, but no other roads in that direction were in evidence (at least as far as Huancayoc, quite close to Huari), and the dots denoting villages were few. To reach Huari by the modern highway would involve a detour of at least 150 miles and, even by public transport, could take several days. Given a horse and a reasonable chance we estimated that we could make Huari on foot by way of the royal road in five, perhaps six, days. Now, with most of the day spent we decided upon camping close to the spot where the old road came down from the pampa and, in the morning, to wait awhile and see if we couldn't somehow acquire a horse or mule.

We had little more than seven miles to walk to the crossing but with our baggage problems increased by the damage to David's packframe, it was enough. Such a frame is vital when carrying such a heavy load and, without one, carrying capacity is severely reduced. We limped, with frequent halts, along the uneven valley following the river, and counted every kilometre stone as if our lives depended on it. A hot spring, bubbling and steaming, made a tempting site for an overnight camp but the ground nearby was marshy and sloping so we staggered on. The site we found near the crossing was not much better and here we went to bed just off the road to the sound of barking dogs and human footsteps as men passed by us from outlying villages drawn to the bright lights of La Unión.

The new day started singularly devoid of luck. The bridge over the river was a nerve-racking, rickety structure of tree-trunks topped with turf, and there wasn't a horse in sight. But the royal road made clear its presence, bounding down from the southern side of the valley and disappearing over the hills opposite.

Two houses, one a school, marked the crossing and, at the house, a kind old lady cooked sweet corn for us refusing offers of payment. Part of the house was utilised as a diminutive shop and we spent the waiting hours in desultory conversation occasionally breaking off to waylay a likely horse-owner. During this time she never sold a single item from her extremely limited stock until a man came in and ordered a beer which emerged from a dusty collection of oddments. We joined him in another and he listened, sympathetically, to our tale of woe whereupon he then and there offered to accompany us, with his horse, to a hamlet well on the way to Huari. We could hardly believe our luck.

Within the hour we were on our way. The climb out of the valley was steep, but the new horse was the most healthy and energetic specimen that we had seen to date; so much so in fact that our companion was forced to rein it back when we showed signs of lagging. David and I, however, were making a better show of the going, having at last found our second wind and by evening we had reached some scattered adobe dwellings that rejoiced in the name of Chogolagran. The hamlet stood at the head of yet another valley, this one that of the river Taparaco, a tributary of the Vizcarra. It occurred to me that had we come upon our man – Manuel – earlier in the day we might have gained the next habitation but, nevertheless, I felt well satisfied all the same.

It became apparent too that Manuel was a regular commuter of this route and, accordingly, had contacts along the way. His contact in Chogolagran was a farmer family who offered us their roof but, with five children as well as their livestock under it, we felt that we would be straining their resources by accepting. The tent, accordingly, again became our shelter for the night but our supper of sardines and bread was supplemented by soup and potatoes which Manuel and the family pressed upon us. Manuel displayed the flattened features and coloured face of the Red Indian but his eyes were more slanting than usual, giving an eastern appearance whilst his hair was tinged with grey. He gave an impression of agelessness but I guessed he was around 50. The family were born of a younger generation; there was nothing ageless about the young father in his mid-20s wearing jeans, black shirt and black trilby hat though his wife looked older but probably wasn't. Their children sat in a row watching our strange cooking operations their heads cocked on one side like mystified puppies.

We left early and were on the hoof even before dawn tinged the sky. The royal road closed in towards the narrow river leading us easily along the western flank of the valley. The hamlets of Estanque and San Lorenzo de Isco produced their quota of inquisitive citizens plus a garish cemetery, oddly out of place in such poverty-stricken surroundings. At San Lorenzo a friend of Manuel appeared with what I thought was a welcome mug of water but which turned out to be some home-brewed fire-water to provide an eye-watering aperitif for a frugal lunch.

The road, well-defined and engineered, took full advantage of the contours of the land and seldom was it forced to deviate from the level it first selected when entering the valley. Here the great road of conquest had no need to be guessed at. We were walking over low hills, treeless and bare, the wind blowing in, unobstructed from the Amazon jungles to set the *ichú* grass in motion. As we marched we spoke of the epic of this rural highway's construction for only by staggering human effort and endurance could it have been built. And in this particular region, with no rocky outcrops to provide material, the large stone slabs which made up the paved portions of road had to be carried to it over dreary miles of emptiness and natural obstruction.

By late afternoon, weary but jubilant, we reached a scattering of huts called Taparaco, where a relic of some earlier age was alleged to stand. If so we never found it. But ahead lay the *tampu* of Torococha, some 12 miles distant, a relic of Inca durability.

Close, but not too close, to the wretched houses we bedded down, tentless, in a mound of the previous year's hay, strong-smelling, slightly putrid and very prickly. Even here we were invited to share in the evening meal provided by a childless couple to whom Manuel appeared to be related. They were quite young so far as we could make out and were enthusiastically interested in our doings and hopes. The woman wore plaited hair which she modelled into a castle-like structure upon her head; not at all the usual Indian hair style of single or twin pigtails swinging free. The man constantly chewed a substance that produced colourful spit.

Two days of fine weather gave way, on the third, to grey clouds but no rain fell. We were on the right bank of the river and, by mid-day, came to a marshy patch of land that had us dodging about between rocks and dry tufts of *ichú* attempting to keep our feet out of water. We had swung away from the river but the swamp caught us in its slimy maw whichever direction we took. Manuel told us that we were between two lakes atop of each wall of the valley and that the swamp was a result of their overflow. We found a decrepit building in the area called Torococha but its stones were certainly not Incain, even to my inexperienced eyes. Any further investigation was discouraged by the depressing swamp and I wondered why anyone should choose to build a *tampu* at so moist and inhospitable a spot.

I did not have to wonder for long. Further up the valley were definite signs of road-drainage stone formations of obvious Inca origin. No doubt, at some earlier stage, the whole area had been devoid of this morass of liquid mud. The ruin that could only have been that of the *tampu* stood, away from the village, dauntingly exposed to the cyclonic winds. It was a square block of a building of substantial stone and without windows. Even David could find no reason for delaying there for more than ten minutes.

The end of the swamp brought a steady climb out of the valley and, somewhere, we left behind our river which must have risen at the behest of the twin lakes. Come mid-afternoon and it was time for Manuel to part for a hamlet called Manca Peque a mile off to the right, but this generous man suggested instead that we accompany him there to spend the night while, additionally, he would arrange for a replacement horse. He didn't have to ask twice.

A lonelier habitation I have yet to see with everlasting hills bucking away in every direction and not even the drama of a true mountain to quicken the pulse. The night meant a return to the tent and a diet of potatoes moistened with our own uninspiring soup for, all too plainly, the silent remote people of Manca Peque existed at near-starvation level, their pinched faces and suspicious eyes devoid of humour while any human kindness had been drained from them by hardship. Manuel himself was obviously unhappy at our reception and I wondered what could possibly bring him here but I didn't like to ask. A clutch of ragged children to whom we offered some picture postcards had to be urged to accept them and not the vestige of a smile flitted across their solemn features as they gravely made off with their prize.

Manuel was as good as his word and procured both a horse and a youth to accompany us. The boy, unused to the sly bargaining of his more money conscious brethren, was content to let Manuel fix the price while Manuel himself charged us only a one-way 'fee' of 500 *soles.* At our present rate of progress it seemed highly probable that another two days would have us in Huari.

Once more we left bright and early. Socially the lad was not a patch on Manuel though he was willing enough. Communication was difficult as he spoke only Quechuan. The horse was half-mule and the pace was steady as we walked in near-silence at an altitude of about 13,000 feet, the route firmly sticking to the 12,000-13,000 foot contours.

It became noticeable that, as we progressed northward, village dwellings were more substantially constructed from worked stone taken from ancient ruins and, possibly, the royal road. Most were roofed with grass thatch but the living conditions in these hovels were still surely worse than those of the time of the Inca since, in many cases, entire households slept in one room and generally in one bed made of untanned cattle hides. Nevertheless I sensed an improvement. And the enigma that remained was that these people, though living wretchedly, often owned considerable herds of cattle, horses and pigs.

A larger village below some great bastions of rock became the end of the marked 'Camino Incaico', the route of the royal road, as marked on the map. Henceforth our eyes, and any local knowledge gleaned, alone would show the way. The name of the large village was, as we expected, Huancayoc, but it was good to see the fact confirmed. Where the old road ended and the modern track began we never learnt, for the transfer was a gradual process and we had to accept that they were one and the same. Huancayoc was, by past standards, a village of some prosperity for it possessed a couple of shops and our potato lunch was supported by biscuits that might well have been a left-over from a Spanish soldier's haversack to judge from their antiquity.

If the bigger, more prosperous, village indicated a return to civilisation the environment showed otherwise. It fast became more difficult and devious while rock outcrops, steep and black, pushed us from one miniscule hamlet to another. People and houses appeared with increasing frequency, it is true, and David was forever enquiring as to the whereabouts of the Inca road but a certain savagery of countryside pinned us to its bidding. The answers we got from the locals were baffling. Invariably we were given an affirmative — yes we were on the right road — but we were well aware that this might mean nothing. Gradually, however, we evolved a system by which we could gauge whether the answer was sincere or just the simple desire to please.

A leaden sky and an icy wind kept us walking fast for warmth. Our fourth night we camped on a patch of ground out of range of any village. A swiftly-moving stream offered a water supply and another contribution unleashed itself from above. The thunderstorm that struck during the night hit us soon after we had heated our ubiquitous soup.

We persuaded the lad to come into the tent with us rather than depend upon his woollen poncho. This made a tight squeeze but ensured we remained warm and dry while the thunder rolled among the hills and lightning licked the wet rocks with forks of fire. Rain hissed down, forcing its way through the light nylon of the tent, to finally cease with uncanny abruptness. We lay uneasily listening to the drips falling upon us.

A morning's walk brought us down from the hills past immense boulders hoary with wet moss and sections of eroded rock fallen from sheer sections of cliff as if sliced off by a giant cheesecutter. The steep descent led to the village of Pomachaca at the bottom of a three-way ravine where two angry rivers met head on to continue their flow as one. David was delighted when his feverish enquiries elicited the response that, certainly, the royal road honoured Pomachaca with its presence and a villager pointed out the steep escarpment down which we had come adding that there was now a *real* road to Huari. He was referring, of course, to the dusty street that bore the corrugated imprints of tyre tracks.

With only twelve kilometres to go we set off in high spirits, stopping at the shop to buy some eggs. A Peruvian, plainly a cut above the others, promptly engaged us in conversation. He spoke in American English having spent much of his life in Canada, but was unenthusiastic when he heard about our mission and the difficulties we were experiencing with the countrymen of his birth.

'Peru's problem is a race problem,' he said. 'The Indians are lazy; not at all like the American Indians. The only really poor people in Peru are Indians. They're uneducated and unhealthy.'

I thought this singularly unfair comment. 'Why don't you — or at least your country — educate them then? Provide doctors and schools and everything.' I knew why but, even though I had done so myself, it still seemed unfair to criticise the rural people so. Particularly since I was not all that happy with the urban ones.

The Canadian Peruvian gave me a thin smile. 'They don't even know what they're doing here; why they came here; what they are. They're a lost race. They were always lost.'

'Even before the Spanish came?' put in David.

'Most certainly. The Inca Empire was over-rated.'

David snorted. 'You're the only person I've met with that opinion.'

'If you stayed here longer you would find many people who would agree with me — including yourselves. The Incas — who were they? They had no great culture, no literature, nothing. They didn't impress the Spaniards. All those pots and masks we see in the Museums in Lima and elsewhere. Can't anyone see how crude the things are? The Incas weren't even warriors — they didn't fight the Spaniards. They were simply overpowered.'

I said that the Spaniards had arrived at a period of civil war. Atahualpa had usurped the Inca throne from his brother. The people were fatalistic — they thought the Spaniards had been sent to punish them. It wasn't hard to conquer people who believed they were guilty already.

The Peruvian grunted. 'They were a degenerate race,' he insisted.

'The Incas had a system of social security that was a damn sight better than anything the Andean countries have now.' This from David trying a new tack.

But our friend was not to be deflected from his argument. 'They were what you see — lazy, dirty people with a different mentality.'

'Different from yours you mean?'

'And from yours. This talk about Incas in Peru is nonsense — Peruvian history is Spanish history, not Indian history.' Our man was growing impatient. 'Do you know what fetishism is? What is their religion — fetishism. They have to see the statue and touch the cross. They do not believe what they can't see. That is why they touch the holy things and grovel in the churches.'

I thought of the many Indians I had met and seen in North America, both the United States and Canada where I had noted the good and the bad side of their character. But neither David nor I could quite see the point of this last outburst and so left it at that. Anyway it was interesting to hear another's opinion. As we left, the Peruvian from Canada staring after us, I remembered that we'd never asked him why he'd returned from Canada to such a degenerate community as Pomachaco . . .

A patchwork of cultivation mottled the fertile green valley of the Huari River we now followed and the open landscape beyond made a peaceful and cheerful companion after the recent geographical hostility. To the east the gigantic mountain complex of the Cordillera Bianca occasionally offered a tantalising glimpse of its highest peaks, evocative of snow and altitude.

Huari is half the size of La Unión but its position overlooking the Alpine-like valley is a joy. Impatient to continue and delighted by the improvement in our fortunes and progress we had no thoughts of a prolonged stay. Ahead lay another hurdle in the obstacle course of the Andes and though we had a broken banister in the royal road it was all too likely that ahead, added to the exertions of walking it, would be the exasperations of trying to find it.

5

HUARI—CHAVÍN DE HUANTAR —PISCOBAMBA—POMABAMBA —SIHUAS—CHIMBOTE—TRUJILLO

Like the routine of living, the pattern of our journey emerged and became itself a routine. Stumbling endlessly along rough roads or mere tracks behind a plodding horse led by a succession of characters from the tediously cheerful to the depressingly morose our spirits rose and fell accordingly. Rain squalls drenched us, wind scoured our faces, sun drew sweat from our bodies and the bitter mountain cold lay in wait at every nightfall. Our days were not measured in hours but by occurrences that became lowspots or highspots in the tedium of fatigue and, occasionally, despair.

A highspot usually evolved from an evening descent from a mountain track for a night amongst the tiniest kraal of houses, the simplest community. This was not so much in obeyance to a craving for the amenities of urban living as to a longing for the company of fellow humans. Though neither of us would admit the fact, we desperately needed this antidote to a loneliness which, in the remoteness of the northern Peruvian Andes, has you by the throat.

Huari was one such highspot for it offered a solid *'biftec'* for our bellies and an earthen roof over our heads. Our 'bedroom' was no more than the dirty floor of a three-table restaurant but, while there, we became temporary members of the large, cheerful family who, unstintingly, shared with us the treasure of their companionship.

Prolonged stays in such centres were resisted, however, for, as La Unión had showed, their attractions quickly pall. It was from Huari that we made an excursion to Chavín de Huantar, a town off the royal road but a centre made historic by a culture earlier than the Incas and where ruins of that culture still exist.

We got there aboard a grossly-overloaded lorry, squatting in the buck, clutching our belongings so that they would take up less space amongst the assortment of other passengers and cargo. The road was excruciating, an engineer's nightmare of wrongly-cambered bends and a neglected surface, though the scenery put it into a 'Highway to the Sun' class. We corkscrewed up one side of a pass and, near the top, found a mountain barring the way through which a quite respectable concrete tunnel had been expensively bored. Its dripping darkness might have been an omen for the storm that hit us as we emerged the other side but, if so, we were slow on the uptake. Huddled, compacted together under a few square yards of torn canvas, we were thankful for the soft, yielding paper sacks beneath us until swiftly-multiplying tears in them proclaimed their contents to be lard. As we wound slowly into the Mosna Valley, soaked by persistent rivulets of water through the leaking canvas and greasy from fatty lard oozing from the damaged sacks, I was reminded that walking had its compensations. And it was not as if the ride was free. In the mountain districts of Peru any vehicle serves as a public conveyance with fares to match the calibre of comfort. Gringos are, of course, fair game for cash-conscious drivers and tariffs rise with the lightness of one's skin. Thus we had the privilege of paying highly for this murderous drive.

A couple of young boys carried on an interminable conversation with us all the way to Chavín and at the destination we rewarded their amiability with a distribution of old picture postcards from a stock we had brought along for just such a purpose. 'Look, London Bridge,' we exclaimed, displaying the picture for all to see safe in the assumption that no clever-dick was going to point out that, actually, it was the Charles Bridge in Prague.

It was dark by the time we had scraped the lard off our boots and clothing and partaken of a disappointing meal in the one restaurant that Chavín could offer. Humping our gear a mile out of town we pitched the tent blind, close to the ruins for which the town is renowned.

There are many pre-Inca cultures; it is recorded that for two thousand years prior to the Incas there was in Peru a long steady cultural growth but few facts have emerged from the chronicles of time. There are no dated coins such as the Romans conveniently left to posterity and the archaeologists; even the Incas had no money, but there is evidence that people here were involved with weaving and agriculture as early as 1000 BC. But the first culture of prominence to have been unearthed — literally, as you will see in a moment — is that of Chavín around 1200 AD, its leitmotif a ferocious-looking Cat God found on its pottery and stonework. Here at Chavín de Huantar was the centre of this civilisation and, now, the dusty remains of impressive buildings characterised by well-laid stone walls decorated with stone-carved human and animal (mostly cat) heads were exposed for all to see.

Looking at the remains today one is tempted to believe its peoples lived an underground existence for the fragments of the Chavín culture have become buried under layers of those of subsequent civilisations to a depth of many feet. And this impression is given credibility by virtue of the fact that, around 2500 BC, another such civilisation did indeed live in subterranean houses. We of simple non-archaeological minds must accept this uncomprehendingly for, with the existing proof of the Chavín before our eyes, this is as far back into history as our minds will take us.

David was taken ill with stomach cramps during our morning's investigations of the dark tunnels and silent chambers since bored into this layercake of history so, repeatedly, had to return to the comforting sunlight for air. With both torches lost we were forced to rely upon a limited supply of matches for our advances along the dismal labyrinths and catacombs beneath the site and at each bend the flickering flame revealed a ferocious cat's head with an abruptness that had us also suffering from near heart-failure. If our minds were unable to take in what had gone before the Chavín period the fetid atmosphere of a dead culture helped us to recollect the history that had followed after...

With the first century these Chavín peoples had introduced mirrors, body-ornaments, carved stone and, with their development of irrigation in the Virú Valley, corn. The increasing population attracted the inevitable would-be conquerors and, by AD 800, a system of fortifications had been erected on the dry hills. But they were not enough to halt absorption by the

Mochicas, a people from the north with an expertise of governing. This culture produced pottery — which the Chavín never did — and textiles together with temples, fortresses and walled roads, but after AD 1000 the Mochicas were, in turn, overrun by the tribe called Tiahuanacus from Lake Titicaca bringing with them their cult of the Weeping God.

But though the Tiahuancu might have possessed admirable martial qualities their talents did not stretch to good administration of the land they now dominated, and its cultivated territory reverted to desert. It was therefore fortunate that the next conquest was by those of the ancient Chimor Kingdom. Actually it was a re-conquest, since the Chimus had been here before, archaeological evidence showing they spread their influence as far south as Lima and the Rimac Valley and as far north as modern Ecuador until they in turn were defeated by the all-conquering Incas.

For David and me our next task was the more prosaic one of seeing what Chavín 'new town' had to offer and, more to the point, to find a way of getting out of it.

As expected, the shabby township held a minimum of attractions. All afternoon we waited, in the company of three Americans, for conveyance back to Huari. Waiting for horses, waiting for lorries, waiting for buses. Our patience was becoming a virtue with a vengeance. In the evening we arranged with a slightly-intoxicated lorry driver to pick us up when he left with the dawn next day but, of course, he failed us though we spent our second night on the floor of the police station outside of which the lorry stood. Perhaps the driver was not altogether to blame since the big iron door of the police office was locked and barred and there was nobody around at that hour even had he made the effort. Finally we succeeded, crammed in the back of a Datsun van with two substantial women sitting on our feet. The village of San Marcos lessened the crush but I was still glad to leave the vehicle and return to utilising my legs as their designer intended.

The fertile valley that accompanied us out of Huari was well-populated with both people and horses. The royal road ran along the right flank of it but in due course we were forced onto the present-day artery where it crossed from one valley to the next. Our horse and its keeper hailed from a Huari farm and the young man considered the three-day trek to San Luis to be not beyond his capabilities. Our subsequent overnight encampment was by the lake of Huachococha, beneath the mountain peak of the same name, a most inspirational setting.

The sheer ruggedness of the terrain further emphasised the extent of the Incas' achievements for it seemed incredible that any communication system with the means available to them could ever have been established with sufficient efficiency to control and adminster so huge an empire. But the system of roads was not just for the purpose of the passage of armies or, indeed, that of the Lord-Inca, his retinue, officials and traders. With their establishment lay the means of effective communication so vital to a regime that lived by war and conquest. Since the swift transmission of messages was of paramount importance and the distances over which they had to be passed so enormous, a courier system called *chasqui* was developed. It was not new; the Romans relied upon relays of horse-riders, but the *chasquis* could run in relays to better effect than their mounted Roman counterparts.

Impossible though it may appear, records show that the *chasquis* could cover the 1,250 miles between Cuzco and Quito at altitudes ranging from 6,000 to 17,000 feet in five days! This meant that the runners had to run an average of some 250 miles a day which was very considerably faster than the Roman couriers on their metalled roads. It has been chronicled that fresh sea fish was relayed daily to the Lord-Inca, yet the shortest distance to Cuzco from the sea was 130 miles.

Together with the *tampus,* built at regular intervals along the highway, were the *o'kla,* rudely-made huts just large enough to hold two men, with bed and hearth. What we would describe today as a 'corps of runners' was maintained throughout the expanding empire, its rank and file furnished by each village through which a particular section of the road passed, and trained from earliest youth to run at high altitude. Considerable prestige was to be gained by its members who worked on 15-day shifts, their duties including watching the road for the arrival of runners coming from either direction. Verbal messages passed between the spent *chasqui* and the fresh runner who made off at top speed to the next *chasqui* station. For divulging the message to anyone but the next runner the punishment was death.

For us the end of a day of severe plodding brought the reward that for a few blessed hours our feet could remain motionless. Plainly I was not *chasqui* material even had I the lungs to defeat the demands of altitude. The wear and tear of the passing weeks might have been having its physical effect but, at the same time, it was honing David and me into a team; often an irritable one but a team nevertheless. We now knew the ropes and undertook our little tasks and chores in support of our daily existence and survival amongst one of the most terrifying domains in the world. And here, near Huachococha, came the close of yet another day exhaustingly filled. We were asleep before a single star pierced the heavens.

Aldo — as we came to call our latest companion — had not been reluctant to invite himself into the tight confines of the tent or to share in our frugal fare. He was the most talkative of henchmen and would blather on in an unmelodious mixture of Quechuan and Spanish to which David finally gave up responding. He was, however, full of rural wit and confidence, a humorous figure in his baggy trousers, short white Cordova jacket and black poncho together with a battered straw sombrero which he seldom wore on his head. In the morning it was he who had us out of our sleeping bags at an ungodly hour with much chivvying and demonstrations of impatience to be off. There was a long day ahead, he warned, and most of it uphill.

The present valley we were following widened into a featureless plateau and the carcasses of sheep and goats littered the grass in unexplained profusion. Most had been reduced to skeletons by the attentions of condors so that only weathered hooves remained to indicate their origins. We climbed steadily, traversing the broad side of a convex slope, with the horizon in front of us ever receding as if intentionally denying us access to the skyline.

Quite suddenly we made it. We stood on the very crest of the pass with the whole *cordillera* becoming the landscape towards which the still higher passes lay in wait. The air was remarkable for its clarity and the magnificence of the view tempted us to pause awhile until the cold wind drove us on.

It was hard to fathom the path ahead. At our feet was a precipice below which, a seemingly infinite distance away, we could see the foam-flecked course of a sizeable river of melted snow. Unquestionably we followed Aldo, leading his horse, along the ridge towards a point where the precipice gave way to a forty-five degree slope. The horse, exhausted by the climb, fretted under its load which, in consequence, began to shift first to one side and then to the other as if in sympathy. The packs needed reloading and tightening, a task which Aldo carried out with singular efficiency.

While he was so engaged David and I set off on our own, anxious to escape the cold of the wind-swept ridge and because the path manifested itself on a downward gradient. Now it was we who were skidding and 'traversing' like amateur skiers, but every few moments the horse behind, catching up, would miss its footing and start a minor avalanche of small stones which would rattle past us down the slope.

We were almost at the bottom, breathless and aching, with our boots full of pebbles and our eyes full of dust, when we looked back. There behind us, but away over to our right, Aldo and horse were comfortably negotiating the hump of a spur which provided a natural and well-graduated line of descent to the river. With the realization of how disagreeable and unnecessary our descent had been came the reflection upon the folly of hiring guides and then not letting them guide us. Eventually we were reunited on the river bank which we followed for a few miles until it sheered away towards a point of the compass not on our set alignment.

Over supper that night Aldo was unable to resist the temptation to crow over our clumsy trail-blazing and, duly chastened, we promised to allow him the right to be our 'front man' for the remaining miles to San Luis. Both David and I showed off with a degree of warped pride our prize blisters before turning in for the night, having first dipped our feet in the ice-cold water of the river to pacify their throbbing.

Next day, now firmly behind Aldo, we made better progress along a line of switchback hills and a way that our man plainly knew well though, for most of it, there was no sign of a path. But we had chosen the shortest distance between Huari and San Luis, of that there was little doubt, so we could but presume that the royal road too had made the same choice of route. By early evening the habitations of San Luis showed up in the lengthening shadows of the surrounding heights and a small road materialised from nowhere to lead us by well-cultivated small-holdings into the little town.

Almost at once we were taken in hand by a stalwart of the local constabulary. It was as if Aldo had been in league with the law but, on reflection, I think not. More likely it was our appearance that activated the fresh-faced patrolman of the Guardia Civil. The entry into the town of two extremely dirty foreign devils offered the moral obligation of apprehension. Watched by a gaping crowd of citizens we were marched to police headquarters, our escort dramatically fondling his Smith & Weston .38 in its holster. Once inside the door, however, the show of authority was replaced by extreme overtures of friendship and the plain longing for a chat. The unfortunate youngster, it seemed, had only recently been transferred from Lima for a two-year stint at San Luis without his wife and so was, unashamedly, homesick.

For the rest of the day, our baggage safely stowed in a cell, we became the constable's guests and were pressed to endless glasses of beer and then a meal in the local pub. No more than a large village, San Luis lay in the shadow of the great snow peak of 19,000-foot Nydo Huandoy, a sobering sight with the sunset ablaze behind it.

Before we turned in on the clean floor of the headquarter's guardroom, we made the acquaintance of our host's superior, the chief of police. It was in fact his home-made cream cheese — a local speciality — we had just been tucking into but he was not in the least put out by that and he subsequently invited us to have breakfast at his home next morning.

Speaking for myself, the night was not as restful as it could have been for not only did David and the policeman snore at varying pitches but a prisoner in the cell below was given to hawking to an extent I never thought possible in a human. But the breakfast with the inspector and his charming wife compensated.

Hardly normal breakfast fare is a whole bull's heart served with chips, tomatoes and roast potatoes and more of the delectable cheese. This repast took place in the living room — virtually the only room — in the chief's simple house on the fringe of the town. His wife was an attractive dark lady who appeared genuinely pleased to see us, perhaps on account of the opportunity to meet some new people — a rare occasion in such a rural community. In their miniature courtyard we took family photographs, offered our contribution of small gifts and made the right noises to a trio of well-behaved children.

In such circumstances as these the acquisition of horsepower was no problem at all. Hardly had the bull's heart settled when we were on our way once more with a game little Patagonian mare and a would-be cowboy in tow. If both had been pressed into service on the express orders of the Peruvian Police Force no resentment showed.

Our researches indicated that the royal road passed close to the town of Piscobamba, our next landmark, some two days hence. The track out of San Luis grew smaller and rougher and though Ricardo, our new colleague, insisted it was the old Inca route, we were far from convinced. At Yanama we met an American, an agricultural technician, who, with some Peruvians, was unloading furniture from a lorry. We offered a hand thus earning ourselves a beer, or to be more accurate, a whole succession of beers in one of those midget shops that sold everything. By dusk everyone was too far gone to know how to start the lorry let alone drive it, so we slept in the buck amongst bags of cement which I do not recommend as a mattress or pillow. The lorry was destined for Piscobamba where the American had his quarters and we were tempted to accept his offer of a lift. However, we were in a walking frame of mind so, to soften our rejection, we said that we would see him there a day later.

In the event it was another two for, in meandering about attempting to locate definite signs of Inca origins we wasted precious time and increased our mileage among a confusion of low hills and rivers. We camped the second night in a gorge-like cleft through which the Pomabamba river ran and were in town by mid-day. At the first house our horse and its owner left us, the latter clearly bemused by our indecisive wanderings.

Piscobamba's construction would hardly win a prize in a town-planning competition. Built in the standard mould of a row of buildings grouped round a central plaza, the square in this case was an affair of ugly concrete, cracked and flaking. Except for a show of pot-holed tarmac circumnavigating the grandiose centre-piece there were no streets unless you counted a few half-hearted side tracks composed of dust or mud (according to season) that rambled amongst lesser dwellings of similar material. On the patio of someone's house we cooked our mid-day meal by invitation thus having to share it with its many occupants. Released from these activities we went in search of our American friend, eventually running him to earth in his office-cum-batchelor pad. But it contained some out-of-date copies of the *New York Times* which occupied our rapt attention for a full afternoon after which, with the American's help, we raised our porterage to Pomabamba, the neighbouring town on our itinerary. The royal road, we were assured, was on the east side of the valley astride the ridge of the first escarpment parallel to which we had been walking the last couple of days.

Another night in the now empty lorry and we gleefully escaped from Piscobamba, ascending a hill, only to find a track that was muddier and rougher than the 'main road' to Pomabamba. Our horseman pronounced us crazy from the start and made it abundantly clear that he did not suffer fools gladly. He was an older man, reserved and spikey. So sparse were any Inca-like relics that he had us doubting our own sanity on occasions but beyond the valley of the river Vitcabamoa, which forced the modern road into a long detour, we came upon the confirmation we were looking for. Not only did the track take on the authoritative aura possessed of any Inca highway but, here and there, it showed the familiar bordering stone and, at one spot, the remains of a drainage system. A line of ruined forts excited our curiosity but these were plainly pre-Inca.

Close to one collapsed and overgrown specimen we set up

camp; not one of our more successful sojourns. A downpour of rain extinguished the stove, our candle burnt a hole in the tent, 'Old Grumpy', squeezing in with us, insisted on sleeping with his dirty feet in our faces and, finally, we lost the horse, necessitating a morning spent searching the hillsides.

Complete with truant steed we came down from the wilds about mid-day drawn by the magnet that was Pomabamba but holding little hope of it being Valhalla. Approaching the town, I tripped over a stone, sprawled headlong, cut open my leg and knocked myself out. The incident shook me up more than I realized and, with blood seeping into my boot, the lure of a night in Utopia had me in its grip once more.

Our subsequent rest and recuperation extended to three days such was the calibre of the delightful people and environment of Pomabamba. It was the police, yet again, who provided us with accommodation; not a cell this time but a guest room equipped with two beds. Our magic letter given to us by Bill Harding all those weeks ago in Lima, was brought out for inspection and no doubt contributed to the gesture of hospitality but their kindness went beyond common courtesy. The room adjoined the police station, the staff of which not only allowed us to use their primitive washing facilities but even provided an old woman to make our beds. But, again, it was the chief of police who became the real friend.

El Jefe (the Chief) introduced himself to us as we revelled in our new-found luxury. A middle-aged man with a neat moustache and greying hair he showed a keen interest in our journeyings. He spoke Spanish and invited us to dinner at his home on the outskirts of town. His wife spoke English, he told us with ill-suppressed pride, and so would be happy to have the opportunity of airing a language she seldom found reason to use. In the meantime would we care for a hot bath and, if so, he would take us there now. We could hardly believe our ears.

Pomabamba is blessed with hot thermal springs which means that every house can raise piping hot water (though it is the very devil to get hold of any cold). But we were concerned only with the hot variety and found it in full measure down in the valley just behind the town. The huge stone baths were pre-sixteenth century though it is certain the Incas made use of them too, as do the present-day populace of Pomabamba. With constant hot water channelling through the big vats we wallowed happily like hippos at play and the grime of weeks peeled off, our pink boiled bodies emerging.

Regretting only that we had no clean clothes into which to change we accompanied *El Jefe* to his home set on the side of the hill and surrounded by massed ranks of fruit trees edged by a guard of honour of funeral lillies. Here we made the acquaintance of a smiling lady, small, intelligent and vital, who straightaway launched into a monologue of English small-talk for all the world as if she was having the vicar and his wife to afternoon tea.

'We will take tea — just the three of us, as Muneo must return to the office for an hour or two,' she pronounced after telling us how they owned a flat in Lima, a not-quite-complete house in Pomabamba and five children with matching husbands and wives, and multiple grandchildren. Of their property, their favourite was this rambling old place of mud floors and ancient timbers in spite of its visual short-comings. 'We love it here. It is — what you say — natural; so impractical,' she went on as she poured us weak tea from an ornate silver teapot, heavy and equally impractical. We sat on rickety chairs on a kind of verandah, the table laden with plain white china and old-fashioned, heavy cutlery, overlooking the orange, lemon and peach-hung orchard in the overgrown garden. A faint smell of earthy dampness wafted from the open door behind us which led into an untidy kitchen and a small living room that gave an impression of being rarely lived in. 'We spend most of our leisure outside in the summer months when we're here' we were informed as if the good lady had intercepted my thoughts. 'Of course, in the winter, we are in town or in Lima.' Her family and estates explained and apologised for, the conversation turned to a resumé of our current movements and activities.

I never realised how thirsty I was; my body must have been severely dehydrated, and I noticed David too was taking in endless supplies of tea from the delicate but shallow cups that needed constant refill from the monster teapot. It was only when David aired an opinion of an Inca historical matter that our hostess blossomed into something of an expert on the subject.

'I'm always mystified as to the origins of the Incas,' she told us, her head on one side like a puzzled owl. 'It is all so much muddled with myth and history that there is no precise answer from archaeology. We know they came from around Lake Titicaca and wandered north along the mountains to set up shop, so to speak, at Cuzco. Only what happened from there onwards is confirmed by archaeology. These people of the Incas were, of course, American Indians and native to the Andes. Most of the people here and in all the Andean provinces are Quechuas in that they speak Quechuan but by no stretch of the imagination can they be mistaken for Incas either in their actions or their legacies. And yet. . .at what point did our Quechuas stop being Incas?'

'Perhaps a similar phenomenon can be found in Europe,' I suggested. 'Look at Italy. When did Romans become Italians? I know the inhabitants of Rome and the country now called Italy came under many different rulers but they are basically the same peoples, yet how different they have become. It's called 'evolution',' I added rather facetiously.

David entered the argument. Frightened that my bringing Europe into the discussion would deflect a new source of Inca knowledge, he wrenched the subject back to Quechuas. 'Look at the present-day Quechua,' he observed drily. 'He is inclined to be thickset, with large hands and chest, broad-headed with high cheekbones; almost Mongolian in appearance. Isn't that one's idea of what an Inca looked like? And, you know, they still have many Incain characteristics like being able to breathe and exert themselves at high altitudes,' he grinned at me, 'and don't we know it! Except, perhaps, for the Inca efficiency and organisation we hear about, the modern Quechua is *not* so different. Indian or Quechua woman can still be strikingly good-looking as they apparently were in Incain times when Spaniards got hooked on them. And don't the locals still chew *coca* to help make them impervious to the effects of hunger, cold, exhaustion and pain to the extent unequalled anywhere else in the world? No, I submit that the Inca is still with us though, in the course of time, his motivation has become run down or ground away by successive insensitive occupiers, regimes and governments.'

It was now the turn of our hostess to change the subject, perhaps because she saw the controversial theme of politics looming near — and hubby was a chief of police.

'I wonder if you have noticed I'm wearing what could be construed as a garment of Inca origin,' she remarked with a shy smile. Before she could embarrass us with the necessity of a white lie she stood up to display a kind of overall tied at the waist by a woollen belt. The good lady then proceeded to explain in great detail how the dress of the ordinary man in those early days was rather like a nightgown made by folding a piece of cloth down the middle, cutting a slit for the head, and sewing up the edges, leaving a gap in the folds for the arms, and that the everyday garment of the Inca woman was hardly less simple. It seemed they went in for a little number made from a rectangular piece of woven alpaca cloth passed over the head and made wide enough to overlap and be held in place with a sash. It fell to the ankles; almost to the sandals. 'I made this dress some years ago after reading about the subject and I find it *so* practical.' She ended, sitting down abruptly as if conscious of her enthusiasm.

'What did people wear to keep out the Andean cold in those days?' I asked.

'The menfolk sported a variation of this; a woollen cape garment — I think they called it a *yacolla* — which they threw over their shoulders at night or when the day was cold. And, of course, there was the breechclout. This was passed between the legs and the two ends held in place by a colourful woollen belt. Adulthood began when a man started wearing the breechclout. I don't think there was a woman's equivalent; only the same *yacolla* more finely made from alpaca wool which she put over her shoulders when it got cold. And she probably wore a shawl held together by a copper, silver or even gold metal pin, the *topo,* which you can still buy in the shops.' As an afterthought our hostess came up with a titbit of information that had us all laughing. 'You know the Lord Inca himself dressed as did his people except for the quality of the garments but while an ordinary man seldom removed his clothes, the Lord Inca never never wore the same set twice. His garments were destroyed upon changing and you know why?' She answered her own question by quoting from some remnant of Incain chronicle, 'Because everything touched by the Inca-kings, who were the children of the Sun, had to be burnt and made to ashes and scattered to the winds so no one else could touch them.'

Muneo joined us just as the tea in the pot ran dry. He showed us round the garden and orchard, overgrown and neglected, and I was aghast at the amount of fruit scattered and rotting beneath the trees.

'As you see we have far too much for ourselves so don't hesitate to help yourself.' So as we strolled about *El Jefe's* estate we wolfed down as many succulent and easy-to-peel oranges and tangerines as we could manage.

Dinner was at dusk and was a banquet by any standards, the main dish consisting of little roasted guinea pigs. Rich and indigestible as they are, we did ourselves proud while the live brethren scuttled beneath the table and around our chairs. To drink was a hot concoction that had a cherry brandy base, and for dessert we were given great hunks of honeycomb fresh from the beehives down the bottom of the garden. I have a sweet tooth at the best of times but seldom had I felt such a craving for sugar. The oozing combs, similar in shape and size to stilton cheeses, were brought to the table on a tray and we were encouraged to cut chunks off with a knife. More oranges and tangerines quenched a thirst generated by the cherry brandy and the honey.

We experienced some difficulty in finding our way up the steep slope to the town centre and our bedchamber, a state of affairs possibly not entirely induced by the darkness. The beds were hard but not uncomfortable and we slept the sleep of the just — and well-fed — ignoring the scurrying of tiny feet beneath us.

Pomabamba town we discovered next morning to be of considerable attraction; particularly so when measured against others we had encountered. At the end of one of the back streets we discovered a baker supplying the most delicious cakes together with some relevant data concerning the Inca and pre-Inca forts that dotted the hilltops, a most useful shop serving both mind and body. The one and only bank decided they did not like the look of our traveller's cheques so we were unable to replenish our dwindling reserves of Peruvian *soles*. However, all was not lost. The cashier who had refused the transaction followed us out into the street and, when clear of the bank, made surreptitious signs for us to follow him. He led us to his upstairs flat where he offered us a charmingly-executed blackmarket deal by which everyone benefitted except, possibly, the state. Fruit shops were another source of goodwill. Their owners, observing our interest in some of the rarer types, insisted we sample them without commitment.

Our second evening there we tried the cuisine of a plaza-side restaurant and became involved in an exhausting political discussion, initially with the diners at the next table but subsequently with the whole clientele. Alcohol flowed freely, the more consumed the louder and more jovial became the exchanges. Luckily our room was just across the square but, in the dark, not even our enormous brass key would find its way into the cavernous keyhole without the help of the duty constable next door.

We were making use of the station wash basin in the morning when *El Jefe* looked in to invite us, again, to his home for dinner. To occupy the intervening hours we had another hot bath and explored a nearby pre-Inca ruin. As we strolled down the hill in the late afternoon we came upon a funeral procession winding its solemn way along the shore of the river. A beating drum and the wailing of an unidentifiable wind instrument together with the sombre black garb of the retinue of mourners packed around the flower-strewn coffin, contrasted strangely with their animated chattering. I was put in mind of a film set, the mourners being actors relaxing for a moment after the producer had shouted 'cut!'.

El Jefe was absent when we arrived at his house but his wife bade us welcome and then released the shocking news that her uncle had been murdered by bandits; the funeral we had seen being his. Nonplussed, we tried to withdraw leaving her to private grief but she would have none of it. Muneo was, this very moment, leading another search patrol for the killers but would be joining us shortly and the reason why she, herself, was not at the funeral was that we were her invited guests. This, it appeared, took priority over the mere formalities of a funeral.

'Anyway,' she added brightly. 'You two are just the tonic I need.'

We dined on a finely-cooked omelette, pumpkin pie and cream cheese. Over tea we reminisced about the United States where our hostess had lived for some years before her marriage. Muneo joined us at nightfall following a fruitless search in the hills. 'It's those cattle-rustlers again but we'll run them to earth,' he told us confidently and an impish grin crossed the stern face. 'Someone talks — they always do — and we build up a file. Then, all at once, the pieces of the puzzle come together and we go after them.'

'Do they often resist?' I asked.

'We have many a gun-battle in the hills with gangs of desperate men,' was his reply and his heavily-jowled features went stern again. 'I was going to warn you two about such people but I think you have received a more effective warning than I could ever give you. Be very careful when you are up there.' Muneo jerked his head towards the darkness of the night.

Our plan was to leave the following morning and resume our escarpment-top route. The map showed Sihuas to be the next township directly north of Pomabamba. With all her knowledge of Inca history, our hostess was unable to pinpoint the route of the royal road sweeping by above her town. 'It's up there somewhere — as you've discovered' was her only comment.

In spite of the couple's levity we could feel the strains imposed by the recent tragedy so took our leave as soon as we could politely do so. Muneo accompanied us back to town, seeing us safely to our room. He had very obligingly arranged for horse transportation as far as Sihuas and the horseman would be with us in the square prompt and ready for an early start.

I thought a lot about the killers in the hills. We had been warned right from the start of cattle rustlers who shot anyone they suspected might have witnessed their nefarious operations. Bands of them were reported to haunt the northern Peruvian Andes but we had put the idea to the back of our minds. Now the unpleasant facts were catching up with us.

Muneo was as good as his word. He introduced us to the new horseman and saw us off from the plaza. Leaving Pomabamba was an undoubted wrench. For the first time in our journey we felt sad to leave a town that had little enough to offer a visitor other than its kindness. With a strong horse and a burly farmer's lad in tow we returned to the silence of the mountains, climbing each false crest until we had attained the summit of the escarpment and were back onto the royal road. It welcomed us with a display of Incain-shaped curbstones bordering the wide grass artery; a phantom highway not immediately visible unless you were looking for it.

Fearful of missing it, David had enquired of all who passed by, the whereabouts of the road. Few even knew of it, fewer still showed any interest. Children, away from the urban influences, replied not a word to our questions and, sometimes, women on their own shook their heads and hurried away as if they ran the risk of being contaminated. A tiny village school produced a pock-marked schoolmistress of sterner stuff, however, who knew all about it and was as voluble with her information as her class was mute in their wide-eyed dumbness.

Yet, on the flanks of this beautiful valley, the clear air revealing the massive peaks beyond, all life was present. Wild flowers tangled in a riot of colour; peasants on the plots of cultivation below looked like toys as they tilled the soil behind toy buffaloes and, far away, carried by a soft breeze, came the shrill sound of children's voices released from the paralysis of school discipline. Visions of a Bavarian mountain path I once walked kept superimposing itself on the verdant heights as the old road marched on at a constant 16-foot width.

On the occasions it faded from view there were horse tracks to lead us onward since no other way northward was conceivable for either road or path. Each was hemmed in by the valley which gradually narrowed and shallowed, driving us ever upwards back into violent convulsions of rock and desolation.

We camped where the valley too petered out into a horizon full of the magnificence of the Cordillera Blanca. Our replenished stocks of food, including an abundance of oranges and honey, increased the calibre of camp meals, their very consumption giving comfort since it was lightening the load. A bottle of honey we retained as an emergency item though this mainly on account of the substance refusing to emerge from the narrow-necked container.

Our companion saw fit to leave us next day in sight of a hamlet in which his cousin was reputed to live. He had not been a bad lad but his estimate of 'just a few more hours to Sihuas' was an understatement if there ever was one. Most of the day we spent trying to obtain a replacement and by the time we were successful we were lost. Fortunately the new man knew the whereabouts of the dust road that led north though it was late afternoon before we were firmly on the march again. The replacement was a more morose individual, his mule being better company.

There is nothing at all Incaic about the road that runs from near Chullin to Sihuas. Its tortuous course is as nightmarish as its construction and surface. Potholes and bogs lie in wait for the unwary traveller, while every little village across a valley, gorge or ravine, though just a mile or so away, is reached only after a crazed display of spirals and detours around the smallest obstacle. On foot it was often advantageous to take short cuts but, for all its gyrations, the road knew a thing or two and a reduction in mileage had to be paid for in sweat, blood and tears. This we found out the hard way as we floundered through swamps and gasped our way up severe inclines.

It took two more days to reach Sihuas and for much of the second one we had the township on the flank of its hill in sight but, maddeningly, out of grasp. A number of unfordable rivers too confounded our efforts and, twice, the road was not where it was expected to be which meant an exasperating doubling back to go in search of the thing. To be delayed thus or lost even momentarily, became not only a break to progress but a frightening occurrence in so wild and inhospitable a clime. The final miles we accomplished after darkness had fallen, with the sparse lights of Sihuas laughing at us at the end of the corkscrew road.

The place was assuredly no Pomabamba being a village of few obvious amenities though we saw little of it in the dark. But an incident occurred here that was to cause us to change our plans. A cabin that was a restaurant of sorts lured us inside and while David was castigating the proprietor for breaking his fried eggs a lorry driver entered. He was a friendly, garrulous fellow, unshaven and uncouth, but his offer of a night in his lorry was convenient to say the least. His subsequent offer of a lift to Chimbote had us in two minds but we were unable to resist. Chimbote is a large town on the coast and we had evolved a great yearning for the balmy warmth and amenities of the coast. Northwards lay a hundred miles of nothing. The prospect of an excursion to the seaside was unturndownable.

Our 'mattress' in the buck of the lorry turned out, this time, to be crates of empty Coca Cola bottles and our fellow-dossers were a woman given to eternally breast-feeding her baby, a man displaying a permanent leer, and a goat with a weak bladder. Other miscellaneous items included a bag of sweet potatoes and some dirty straw strewn around as a gesture to soften the impact of the bottle-necks. Sleep under such conditions was understandably elusive and the night was the usual cold one.

The twenty-four-hour drive was the most terrifying I have experienced in my life. All was normal — as far as driving an Andean B-road can be described thus — until we were among a gigantic storm of ruptured earth bisected by huge canyons buttressed with enormous granite cliffs. Hugging the sheer walls of the rock face the lorry, moving much too fast, rattled along the narrow unsurfaced track. There was just, and only just, space for a vehicle of our width and the offside wheels were invariably within inches of the edge which meant that, on occasions, the buck overhung a vertical drop of many hundreds of feet. Landslides had swept away much of the road in places while erosion and ominous cracks turned what was left into an obstacle course that not even a tank would have attempted. Yet the driver drove with unconcerned abandon, the decibles of the horn the only safeguard for what just conceivably *might* be coming round each corner in the other direction. The lorry was hardly in tip-top condition either. Its steering was loose, its tyres threadbare, and the brakes had a tendency to pull the vehicle over to the right — towards the drop to oblivion. For much of the way the precipices were of the kind over which a vehicle would plummet, not roll, and I was not the only one in the buck ready for an instantaneous jump for life. Even the woman dried up in alarm whilst the man quickly lost his leer. The effect on the goat, however, was not so beneficial and he just squirted uncontrollably. The countryside turned from desolation to savagery, pouring its gushing streams onto the road to produce yet another hazard. Candelabra cactii hugged the bare rock.

What would happen if we met another vehicle? The question posed itself at each blind corner but nothing was ever there. Until, suddenly, it *was!* We skidded to a halt with everybody crossing themselves. And because, a quarter of a mile back, there had been an infinitesimal widening of the road it was deemed our duty to reverse to the spot. The other lorry followed closely, the two drivers leaning out of their cabs exchanging lewd pleasantries all the while. I noticed that the passengers in that vehicle looked as shaken as we felt.

The passing point selected was no more than a projection of the ledge overhanging the abyss. A thin bush marked the lip. Yet our lorry backed onto this minute shoulder so that, whilst the rear wheels rested on the bush, the buck hung out over eternity. Everyone hastily graduated towards the cab and prepared to leap into the other lorry at the first sign of ours going over. Scraping its sides on the rock wall as well as on our chassis that vehicle inched by without great damage and we breathed again.

In an unending series of hairpin bends the road took us down to less lethal regions and we finally ground to a halt in a village of ramshackle adobe houses that looked as if they had been struck by an earthquake. And indeed they had for we were now in the Huaraz disaster area of 1962. Here our driver nonchalantly informed us that he was, in fact, going to Huaraz and not Chimbote which left us stranded at a tin-roofed snack bar in the wretched place. A meal of *yoca* did little to raise our spirits.

Eight hours later we were still kicking our heels until a further lorry put in an appearance whose driver was able and willing to take us to Chimbote. And, would you believe it, the buck of that one too was paved with bottles. But these were full — and mostly of beer which softened the blow somewhat. Hardly had our new conveyance got underway when it drew up at a lonely tungsten mine where further bottles were piled on board — in addition to four men and four women all loaded with heavy bundles. Some of the beer collected was the unconsumed stock of the mining community so we all helped ourselves as we went along. The mountains slowly flattened out as we neared the coast while another night concealed the extravagances of the road. Everyone spread themselves as best they could in attitudes of sleep but the rutted surface, the effects of the beer and the cacophony of rattling empty bottles, ensured we remained awake to witness shadowy plantations of bananas and sugar cane under a brilliant moon. A pleasant humidity wrapped us in an unearned sweat as we emerged onto the Pan-American Highway and the coast and, at Santa, turned south to Chimbote. But at Santa we were evicted again.

For what remained of the night David and I spent upright but at least stationary, sitting on chairs in a closed café that served a filling station just outside the town. Our heads pillowed on the table we passed the uncomfortable hours watching the nocturnal activities of cockroaches on the oil-begrimed floor.

Chimbote was a dead loss. Highly industrialised, black and dusty as its anthracite plants, it was also squalid and smelt of fish-meal. Northwards, 90 miles along the highway, lay Trujillo which we knew to be, more pleasant. A truck, stopping of its own accord, took us the last leg of the excursion belting along through sweltering coastal desert territory that was ribboned by a sticky tarmac road lined with the grave stones of its victims. Although hard to imagine, this was the famed Inca coastal road. It may have been appropriate to our researches but there was nothing to show for the privilege. This was reserved for Trujillo, third city of Peru.

The place was founded by Pizarro in the mid-1530s and named after his own Spanish hometown. Built within a green and irrigated oasis that, in spite of virtually no rain, supports sugar cane and rice, its modern buildings have been assimilated without discord into the spread of old churches and houses characterised by graceful colonial balconies and windows. I took to the city the moment of arrival and we made our temporary base the 'Lima Hotel', an establishment of basic amenities but adequate for our needs and indeed luxurious by recent standards.

From the base we ventured forth to explore the crumbling ruins of Chan-Chan, imperial city of the Chimú domain. Walking the few miles across sand-blown grassland we were guided there by the two huge Moche pyramids known as the Huaca del Sol and the Huaca de la Luna that jutted starkly skywards like a couple of Lancastrian slag heaps.

There are nine such structures making Chan-Chan a city of pyramids, temples, house-compounds, gardens and stone-lined reservoirs. In its day it must have been the most heavily-populated city of the Americas, the inhabitants packed inside high perimeter walls served by only one or two very few narrow entrances. The Chimús were mostly coastal people, high-precision workers in ceramics, gold and cloth, and worshippers of the sun. Their empire was in existence between 1000 and 1466 BC (later than the cat-loving Chavín peoples), and it extended, indeed initially overlapped, with that of the Incas. These peoples were of the last of the larger cultures to offer opposition to the Incas, the clash occurring in 1461 when the Incas were victorious following a short sharp battle. Until that time, the Lord-Inca had not wished for war with the Chimú, fearing their strength, but following the fall of Cajamarca in the north, his armies laid siege to the kingdom.

But in defeat the Chimú contributed much in the way of their culture to the Incas who willingly accepted it to further the greater glory of their own empire. In a sense the Incas were like the Romans — inheritors of a skein of cultures which became, in the weaving, a complicated tapestry of human progress.

We lingered at Chan-Chan all day, fascinated by the fast-crumbling edifices that, before many years, will be gone. Man and nature have combined to bring the old city to ruin. A rainless coast this may be, but a freak of meteorological fate allows a deluge at this spot every thirty or less years that turn the walls into a substance looking somewhat akin to chocolate left in the noon-day sun. Man too has contributed to the destruction with his incessant search for gold, particularly since the Spaniards found a cache buried in one of the pyramids.

Most of the tunnel entrances had been blocked, either intentionally by authority or through natural collapse, but we succeeded in opening one and David, with a borrowed torch, crawled on his belly into the pitch dark interior. I soon tired of the clammy atmosphere and streams of dried mud running down my neck so returned to the sunshine. From the summit of the pyramids was an astounding view of sea, desert and the brown Andean foothills. From that spot I could see the fertile lushness of what might be termed the Trujillo oasis merging into the desert sand. That there was once a more regular rainfall here is shown by the ancient marks of water visible everywhere in surfaces fretted into abstract patterns by prehistoric downpours, and in snake-like gullies that once frothed with torrents. The sun that now mercilessly bakes the rock and soil, etches them with deep shadows. And across this parched realm blew the sculpturing wind uncovering the delicate grain of rock strata and heaping sand on the enormous dunes of the coast.

A group of well-to-do schoolgirls, more interested in David than me, shared their picnic lunch with us and lured me into a fast-running stream since my swimming trunks were conveniently doubling as underpants. With the girls we walked back to the town and, in the cool of evening, struggled out of Trujillo intent on catching a bus back along the Pan-American Highway.

Instead, learning of a deficiency of public transportation, we spent the night in yet another police station, this one in the suburb of Laredo. At first we met the usual suspicion but The Letter ironed out the difficulties and we spent a tranquil night shut, but not locked, in a cell. The neighbouring apartment was occupied by a couple of more valid residents who showed sympathy and solidarity with us until they discovered our true status.

The return to Santa, Chimbote and subsequent progress back into the mountains was accomplished with the aid of a variety of vehicles. A local bus, a Toyota pickup, a hefty Volvo truck returning empty to the Huansala mineral mines, a private car whose driver refused payment on account of our nationality, and a lorry with such massive unscalable sides that it became a feat of mountaineering just to get ourselves and our packs into it. And this last operation was accomplished as the vehicle pounded along the road at breakneck speed.

Deeming it unnecessary to return precisely from whence we had come we ended the ride near Corongo, parallel with Sihuas but about forty miles west of it. Whatever trails lay ahead we could face them with a lighter heart and, more important, a lighter load. In Trujillo we had taken the decision to ditch a good fifty per cent of our cargo, a soul-searching operation but a vital one. The lesser weight bearing upon our shoulders made for a sensation as strange as it was exhilarating. Life, we felt, would become a lot simpler — and possibly less lethal than that we had sampled on our excursion into civilisation.

6

CORONGO–SANTIAGO DE CHUCO –HUAMACHUCO–CAJAMARCA

Draw a straight line between Pomabamba and Huamachuco and you have, very approximately, the route of the royal road. Here too, like the Romans before them, the Inca road builders aimed their highways straight at an objective with no pussyfooting around. Somewhere over the next hundred miles, where no modern road ventured, we hoped to find it.

They say that 'a change is as good as a holiday' and the fact remained that, though our alarming rides to and from Trujillo and brief dalliance in that city had evolved into anything but a holiday (we had gone nowhere near the beaches, if there were any), and we had indulged in nothing more luxurious than a square meal or two, the mere switch from one mode of locomotion to another had injected new energy into flagging minds and bodies enabling us now to move at a commendable pace. We were almost skipping from one mountain to another and our confidence, in spite of an erratic passage, remained high. The lightness of our loads offered one reason for this new-found energy but our brushes with urban living too had a similar, if lesser, effect; one environment seemingly complementing the other. Too much 'town life' lent an added attraction to the wilderness — and wings to our feet. Too prolonged an incarceration in the wilds, however, produced a strong desire for the benefits — however modest — of town. But over the ensuing hundred and more miles there was likely to be too few urban centres and so we pinned our confidence on the apparent ease of travel as chronicled by one, Miguel Estete, a Spanish notary, who had accompanied Captain Hernando Pizarro and a detachment of his troops on the return leg of a journey from Pachacamac in 1533. They had toiled up the Patavilca Valley to Cajamarca at its head to make their way to Huanuco and Jauja, and over a particularly desolate part of the coastal Andean range, the Cordillera Huayhuash, by way of a 15,000-foot pass. Part of their route had lain athwart our own so this section of the chronicle made topical reading. Where Captain Pizarro could go so could we.

'. . . Next day the captain set out, and, after a march of five leagues, he passed the night at a village called Guacango. Next day he reached the large town of Piscobamba, which is on the side of a mountain. The chief is called Tauquame; and he and his people received the Captain well, and did good service to his followers. Halfway to this town, at Huacacamba, there is another deep river with two bridges of network close together, resting on a foundation of stone rising from the water. From one side to the other there are cables of reed, the size of a man's thigh, and between are woven many stout cords; to which large stones are fastened, for the purpose of steadying the bridge. The horses crossed this bridge without trouble, but it is a nervous thing to pass over it for the first time, though there is no danger, as it is very strong. There are guards at all these bridges, as in Spain. Next day the Captain departed from Piscobamba, and reached some buildings, after a march of five leagues. Next day he came to a village called Agoa, which is subject to Piscobamba. It is a good village among the mountains, and is surrounded by fields of maze. The chief and his people supplied what was required for the night, and next morning provided porters for the baggage. Next day the Captain marched for four leagues over a very rugged road, and passed the night at Conchuco. This village is in a hollow. Half a league before reaching it, there is a wide road cut in steps in the rock, and there are many difficult passes, and places which might easily be defended. Next day they set out, and reached a place called Andamarca, which is the point where they diverged to go to Pachacamba. At this town the two royal roads to Cuzco unite. From Andamarca to Pombo there are three leagues over a very rugged road; and stone steps are cut for the ascents and descents; while on the outer side there is a stone wall, to protect the traveller from the danger of slipping. If any man fell, he would be dashed to pieces; and it is an excellent thing for the horses, as they would fall if there was no flanking wall. In the middle of the road there is a bridge of stone and wood, very well built, between two masses of rock. At one end of the bridge there are well-built lodgings and a paved court, where, according to the Indians, the lords of the land had banquets and feasts when they travelled by that road...'

Corongo village was the terminus of the road that followed the River Santa northward from Chiquian taking in Recuay, Huaraz and Yungay. It was, by Peruvian rural standards, a main road; a highway running parallel but between fifty and a hundred kilometres distant from the apology of a road linking Huari, Piscobamba and Pomabamba that had been with us, fitfully, from the time of our departure from Huari. Highway 3 seemingly ended at Corongo but then slyly continued as a dirt road to a village called Tauca where it joined a lesser artery designated as Highway 30.

Convinced the royal route proceeded on northwards from Sihuas — the village from where we had made our excursion to the coast — we had discussed the merit of taking the modern road back to the place, but the idea of tramping the forty miles in an easterly direction from Corongo to Sihuas offered little attraction. Traffic was rare and the chances of a lift small. By travelling north-east, across country, on the other hand, we felt confident of getting back on at the correct alignment so, following much poring over two overlapping map sheets, this is what we decided to do. A track obligingly took us in hand, gently guiding us the way we wanted to go.

The locals of Corongo displayed genuine ignorance of the presence of any Inca relics — roads included — in the district so we proceeded to put our own calculations to the test. The heavy brown shading on our maps offered mute warning but, encouraged by our improved mobility, we were not too dismayed and took the precaution of topping up on provisions, aware that Corongo could be the last human settlement for a considerable period. We left as the rays of the morning sun dappled the mountainside above the township.

The track made easy walking, rising all the time but offering no feats of physical endurance. Climbing steadily, traversing the broad side of a convex slope, the horizon in front receded while a cool breeze heralded our return to rarer altitudes.

A cleft opened in the perpendicular wall of crags and we stood upon the crest of a pass with a whole *cordillera* rolled out like a rucked carpet, to the north. A number of guanacos — the most timid but also fiercest of Andean animals — looked up from their grazing and froze as if hypnotised by the sight of us. Usually the guanaco's chosen habitat is well out of reach of any one but a mountaineer so we were as surprised to see them as they were us. In the unlikely event of a human managing to approach it, the animal protects itself most effectively by spitting a dark, pungent fluid with sufficient force to knock a man down, leaving a temporary disfigurement on his skin. We had no wish to sample their methods of self-defence so gave them wide berth.

Soon after setting out, we spontaneously burst into expressions of rejoicing at our new-found liberation from the dead-weight on our shoulders. David was even inspired to run down the steep incline to the bottom of the pass pursued by a miniature avalanche of stones that finally tripped him. A broken or sprained ankle in such an environment could have been disastrous and just the thought of it quickly calmed us down. The path now began to ascend the opposite wall of the valley which gave us reason to start paying attention to the peculiarities of altitude. The accustomed exhaustion and shortage of breath set in all too soon and our elation soon evaporated. Our reward on the summit was spectacular scenery that could be seen in every direction.

Even within this lone valley the colours of the surroundings were everywhere different; slopes of slag-heap grey flanked by others of coral-red rock; peaks of black and blue granite above emerald-green foundations. Only at eventide did the land merge into a single hue when the last rays of the evening sun transformed the *cordillera* into a rose-red corrugation that would have earned an artist the accolade of surrealist.

We had eaten little all day; no more than a bar of chocolate, a packet of dry biscuits and some over-ripe cheese washed down by cold clear water from shimmering pools among the rocks. Setting up camp close to, but below the new ridge we made ourselves a substantial supper of macaroni and, because it was a heavy item to carry, a tin of some unidentifiable meat. A kind of blancmange followed but by a misreading of the instructions, it became a drink. All was peaceful; the calm before the storm.

It started with a row; one of those bitter dissentions that breaks out between humans for no real rhyme or reason. I cannot even remember how the fuse was lit — and it matters less — but I suspect it was a lofty remark of David's touching the raw nerve of my imagined humiliation. We shouted at one another, blew our tops, then smiled sheepishly. But it triggered the weather into bigger things. The darkness of the night was the more intense with the addition of a belt of storm clouds blown in our direction by a wind that, minutes before, was no more than a breeze. We fussed around the tent placing small boulders on pegs and adjusting guy ropes, then crawled into our bags to ride out nature's display of tantrums, still aware of our own. About midnight we found ourselves struggling in the folds of the collapsed tent but, in both gale and darkness, we could do little about re-erecting it. We settled down again with the material around us and prepared for sleep. But not for long.

'All we want now is for it to rain,' I grumbled and the heavens promptly obliged with a stinging torrent. We lay miserably listening to the hail stones striking the rocks, feeling the cold wetness seeping through the nylon and wondering how long the storm would last. I tried putting on more clothes but was unable to find them as rivulets of water leaked their way through those I wore.

Duplicating the form of our row, the rain squall ceased as abruptly as it had started allowing us to re-erect the tent and crawl back into damp sleeping bags, wearing all the clothes we possessed. But sleep had fled.

Morning was a relief and we celebrated its dawning with a breakfast of egg powder and beans; its warmth being of more value than the taste. Glad to be away after a prolonged study of the compass and map, we strode off at high speed, intent on re-galvanising stiff, damp limbs.

Rain clouds still dominated the sky, scudding and changing shape as they headed the way we had come. No more rain fell but what did descend around our ears was a gale-force wind that swept up the valley to engulf us in a cloud of powdered grit. I struggled to don my balaclava, soggy from the night's damping, and promptly lost it to the violent gusts.

We pressed on, collars up and heads down into the gale. Patches of hard, off-white snow lay strewn along the sheltered spots of the mountainside above us, not unlike the clusters of whitened bones of sheep we had passed a while earlier. The new valley into which we descended widened, the walls became less steep and two rounded peaks soared above our heads. As we neared the bottom, the wind dropped to a whisper and rents in the clouds showed a petticoat of blue sky.

The pattern of the subsequent two days changed little. Our switchback progress made clear we were moving against the 'grain' of the mountains; crossing the valleys and not following them. The path had petered out the second day and what we were following became no more than a succession of ridge saddles, each selected by the demand of the compass. The weather remained dry, more by good luck than due to any skill of ours in avoiding the showers for we frequently observed rain falling elsewhere; heavy squalls deluging the peaks within grey mantles of waterlogged cotton wool. Not another living soul or animal did we come across; it was as if we were alone and fortuitously alive in a dead world. Only the great condors, gliding effortlessly overhead, assured us that life still breathed in the universe.

It was while we were on top of one of the interminable crests on the third afternoon that we spotted our first fellow human beings. There were five of them; five men riding horses or mules, leading pack animals. They were a good mile away, had not seen us, but were coming across our path. There was something about them that prompted caution; a suspicion that these fellow-humans might not be so glad to see us as we had, initially, been to see them. I voiced my feelings to David and he agreed with me. I remembered Pomabamba and the warning we had been given about cattle rustlers. A grassy dip offered cover so we crouched down in it and watched the band as they moved nearer. Two of them appeared to have rifles slung over their shoulders and, from the direction they were riding, we judged they would pass no nearer than five hundred yards. We remained silent, thoughtful and concealed.

As soon as men and beasts were out of sight we moved on again feeling a little foolish. Maybe they were perfectly innocent riders on legitimate business between villages and we had acted stupidly and missed an opportunity to confirm our whereabouts and obtain directions. Alternatively, we may have avoided having our throats cut. Discretion seemed the better part of valour.

A while later we came upon some isolated sheep; a sure sign of an approach to some sort of habitation. And not a false sign either since a ragged, poverty-stricken little community came into view with the onset of evening. We camped well away from and out of sight of the place, our suspicions unabated.

We entered the village, warily, next morning but the suspicions now belonged to the villagers. The first of them took hasty refuge in their houses and even the children took to their heels. It was impossible to get near enough to any of them to attempt a conversation and again it was up to the schoolmaster to come to the rescue.

He was awaiting the arrival of his young charges at the corrugated-iron-roofed schoolhouse when we appeared. He spoke a little Spanish and, after a few words of greeting, David probed his knowledge of Incain matters.

I watched as the man pointed to a low range of grass-covered hills, not unlike the Sussex Downs, marking the royal road's alignment we had been seeking. This showed we had not gone too far to the east as David had feared. We thanked him and shook his hand with exaggerated fervour as we left.

Two hours later we stood on the new crest, our eyes searching the rolling land. And, sure enough, a grass track of familiar straightness, softened by a few nature-formed indentations and clusters of flowers, materialised disappearing into the distance. We followed it for many miles until the clarity weakened and the route veered to the west. Faced with a choice, rightly or wrongly we swung off where a junction offered a more northerly alignment.

We were reminded again how distances in these parts are deceptive. Sihuas to Huamachuco may have been a hundred miles as the crow flies but as two hikers slogged it — weaving about looking for landmarks and avoiding the more impossible walls of granite — it must have been in the region of two. At times we could see the great Cordillera Blanca with its twenty-two peaks of more than 19,500 feet, one of them — Huascaran — at 22,205 feet, the country's highest. Even at our average altitude of around 12-13,000 feet we were buffetted and half frozen by a succession of high winds, bitter cold nights and stinging downpours in the days that followed. Only in the late morning was the sun warm, yet the ground in the shadows remained firmly frozen. The thin, stony soil gave a minimum of sustenance to the defiant clumps of coarse yellowing grasses and alpine plants — often bearing minute, delicate flowers — hugging the ground. There were no trees; only tall ferns of the slow-growing, cactus-like puyas.

In such a milieu animals are rare. Most are rodents, lizards or tiny birds that can find cover in the low vegetation, among rocks or in burrows. Yet there are others. We never saw a puma but they existed here as do the guanaco, the fast-running vicuna and the condor, the largest bird of prey in the world. The bird's great wingspan, which has been known to reach ten feet, enables it to glide effortlessly to 18,000 feet on up-currents of air, covering large distances with little exertion.

How we envied them the freedom of the sky. Our way ahead stretched apparently into infinity, a horrific, yet stirring panorama of mountain ranges and escarpments that, we were all too aware, would give us no respite even after we had conquered those we could make out in the far distance. But there was beauty too; beauty on a gigantic scale coupled with the compelling drama of isolation. Together they offered us a combination that, on occasions, reduced us to a condition of suppressed terror and near-panic; a kind of agoraphobia.

Food, or the lack of it, was an ever-present concern. Our luxury items, purchased at Trujillo, ran out inside of a week as did our basic provisions. Whenever we came across the smallest hamlet we would top up with potatoes, the staple diet of the Andean peasant as indeed it became our own. Our emergency foods — oatmeal cake and tins of sardines — were well nigh spent by the time Huamachuco began dotting the hillsides with villages of more prosperous communities and a chequerboard of cultivation. In their usual sly way the Andes began quietly pitching us into a different environment.

Before Huamachuco, however, we were deflected off our route by the proximity and promise of a smaller but no less an attractive-sounding town, Santiago de Chuco. Our map indicated only a short detour and we located the place with no great difficulty, having emerged onto a small road near the hamlet of Mollepata. Hardly had we set out to tramp the twenty-odd miles on the sheer luxury of a road that seemed to know where it was going when, incongruously, a smart Toyota Land Cruiser, driven by an equally smart young man in a city suit, came to a halt beside us.

'I am going to Santiago de Chuco,' he announced and opened his nearside door. It took me a moment to take in that he had spoken in English.

In our unkept state we had all but given up the idea of a lift in anything less down-to-earth than a lorry so our surprise and delight must have shown.

'I recognized you as *Inglés,'* the man explained. 'We do not have many round here.' I could well believe it.

As we drove to Santiago de Chuco it was explained that he was an agricultural executive and had an office in the town which we could use instead of our tent for as long as we remained there. We accepted gratefully and, on arrival in the small town, were taken to a local restaurant as if as a matter of course. We must have looked as hungry as we were dirty and certainly did justice to the meal by reordering it twice. The Ministry of Agriculture building, a substantial block near the centre of town, was composed of a series of run-down office rooms, our friend's amongst them. It lacked everything but the barest furnishings, but a hard floor held no fears for us. Unfortunately, what it lacked in comfort was enthusiastically made up for by bugs that nightfall encouraged out of the cracked plaster.

The countryside held more charm than the town. The one redeeming feature was the plethora of heavy, warm-toned roof slates under which the houses sheltered but away from the mean streets there was a delightful landscape of cultivated valleys, meadows of yellow cereal and an artist's palette of shades of green — including trees, real trees. A warm sun framed in a cloudless blue sky persuaded us to relax on the lip of a gentle canyon and listen to the vague sounds of toil as peasants tilled their plots and scythed their corn. We designated the morning as a holiday and revelled in an unaccustomed idleness, only returning to 'Chuco at the insistence of our appetites.

And then something rather unpleasant happened. Walking along a street we were accosted by a mean-faced individual who flashed a cellophane-covered card in our faces. 'Special Criminal Police,' he added in Spanish to reinforce his status. 'You will come with me.' Not even a 'by your leave' or a 'please' accompanied the order.

So this was the dreaded PIP we had heard about; the Peruvian equivalent of the KGB. With ill-grace we followed the stranger to an office off the main street, speaking not a word. I was more interested than alarmed for, in my travels over the years, I have raised as a side-hobby, a collection of interrogations. In World War Two, as a captive of the Germans, I escaped from my prison camp in Poland only to land up at Gestapo headquarters in Cracow. In the post-war years I made a forbidden errand across the minefields of the Iron Curtain which put me behind bars as an unwilling guest of the STB, the Czech Secret Police. I had since met similar inconveniences in the Soviet Union, Albania, Yugoslavia, East Germany and the Middle East, and only that previous year, found myself in Idi Amin's dismal police headquarters of Uganda's capital, Kampala. I began to assess the likely variance in interrogatory methods the PIP could conjure up.

This latest member of the species had his office in the miniature barrack block that was Santiago de Chuco's law centre. It was as bare as that of our accommodation and probably the only reason the bugs couldn't get out of the wall was for the number of 'wanted' notices stuck over them. The venue, I decided, fitted Kampala. Prague had boasted an anglepoise lamp but then communist methods of extracting information sometimes did border on the James Bond. We were not invited to sit down on account of there being only one chair which our interrogator now occupied.

The tone of the questioning made very plain that he disliked us intensely. Nor did our nationality cut the slightest ice. His interrogation showed a marked lack of skill, led nowhere and was seemingly prompted purely by personal hostility.

'Why have you come to Santiago de Chuco?' was the gist of his enquiry, offering the intimation that to have gone anywhere else would have been wiser. We replied as politely as we could but when he indicated a desire to see the contents of our wallets I told him to get stuffed. Perhaps it was fortunate my words were not understood but he got the message that I was not going to stand for bribery or blackmail.

David, thoroughly alarmed, kept whispering to me to display our ambassadorial missive but my blood was up and I was determined to see how far the little thug would go. Repeatedly we explained our presence in 'Chuco, our unkept appearance, and our intentions; we had broken no law and were minding our own business. I put this forcibly to David who, undoubtedly, translated it into more diplomatic prose.

An hour, two hours went by and abruptly we were let off the hook, though this only after I had demanded to see his superior. Late for lunch we were surprised to find our agricultural friend, Alberto, waiting for us. He was genuinely shocked when told of our encounter with PIP. Cursing them under his breath, he took pains to remind us that they in no way represented the ordinary police, a fact of which we were well aware.

I asked Alberto how his predecessors, the Incas, upheld and coped with law and order. To my surprise, and David's, his answer revealed a considerable knowledge.

Parental authority was strict in those days, he told us, but they had the respect of their children. Learning was by doing; education and 'growing up' were by mimicry and seeing; there was no strong contrasting line of conduct between child and adult. Out of this continuity of parent and child grew the mores which formed the base of Inca justice, though, actually, this process had existed before the Incas advent. Murder, violence, theft, lying, adultery and laziness were, of course, present in Inca society; all were punishable. Murder, unless in self-defence, was dealt with by hanging, stoning or by being pushed over a cliff. Stealing, since one pilfered from a God, also rated the death penalty as did destroying bridges (thus severing the empire's communications) and entering the precincts of the Chosen Women. However stealing was rare since there was virtually no want and thus no temptation to steal; there was simply no incentive for the common man to accumulate possessions.

Theft was regarded as an aberration, and when such a crime *did* occur justice was administered by accused and accusers telling their sides of the story before a *curaca,* or local governor. Laziness was initially punishable by public rebuke; repeated examples by stoning and death — for this was a crime that deprived the Lord-Inca of his subject's services. Drunkenness was permitted so long as it did not encourage laziness or affect the culprit's work. Conservation of animals too formed part of the Inca code of justice and the unauthorised killing of a female vicuna resulted in a similar, but authorised, fate.

In addition to the death penalty, which was usually rapid, ruthless and impartial, there were other forms of punishment: exile to the mines or the cocoa plantations; a kind of penal servitude where the transgresser paid for his sins with toil. The Incas systemised the moral code of the Andean people, and since these codes of conduct were based on the collective conscience of the *ayllu,* therein lay its strength. There was, it appeared, no need for an organisation of the sort that PIP represented.

These explanations continued well into the early evening and were elaborated upon by a couple of older men, acquaintances of Alberto, who joined us at the table. One was a wizened character wearing, unseasonably, a winter cap with ear flaps, and smoking a long, old-fashioned pipe. With his accentuated Indian features he put me in mind of the Lord-Inca himself, a comparison which, I am certain, would have pleased him.

From Alberto we learnt of a farmer who was making a journey to Huanachuco the following morning and he promised to make arrangements for us to join him. He would be glad of our company, we were assured, since the distance was all of a hundred kilometres.

Another night in the bug-infested Ministry of Agriculture and we were on the move once more. The farmer and his four horses arrived at the door in the morning, together with the first batch of Ministry employees — we could hardly believe our good fortune. We had all but given up the idea of equestrian transportation, and here we were being presented with four horses and a guide. What was more we were actually expected to *ride* the horses.

'Call me Pedro,' was the farmer's greeting in English — the only three words he knew — so Pedro he became. About 35, stocky, he had the flattened features and face-colouring of the Red-Indian but with slanting eyes. The horses were sturdy, bad-tempered brutes, not the least affected by our friendly overtures or clumsy riding techniques resulting from long absence from the saddle. With our rucksacks piled awkwardly upon the back of the fourth animal we clip-clopped through 'Chuco for the last time, feeling like cowboy extras in an amateur production of 'High Noon'. For the last time too we passed by the weed-sprouting, broken bell-tower of the church, with all around us a knot of children who acted as if they had never seen anything so funny in their lives.

The journey to Huanachuco was a pleasure. We did no more than follow the modern road, hardly a highway but utilised quite extensively by local traffic. It was a two-day hack taken at no great pace, the intervening night spent in the cowshed of a friend of Pedro. Both he and the host made every effort to give us their beds in the two-room shack that was the latter's home but we would have none of it though we were happy to share their modest supper. The second day we followed the course of the Yomobamba river and it could well have been the original route of the royal road though, of this, Pedro could raise no opinion. Unlike Alberto, our new friend bore not the slightest curiosity about his ancestors. David remained sceptical that we were now riding the royal route though our older maps indicated that we could have been on a link road from the coast. What was certain, however, was that the distance between 'Chuco and Huamachuco was considerably less than the hundred kilometres estimated by Alberto.

One of those impossible sunsets illuminated our entry into Huamachuco but darkness was complete by the time we reached the flower gardens of the plaza, lit by a necklace of electric bulbs.

Without any doubt whatever we were now back astride the royal artery. The town is mentioned frequently in the chronicles of the Incain conquest, Pizarro's Spanish army having rested here for four days after leaving Cajamarca for their south-bound march of conquest in August 1533. Two ruins survive on the outskirts of Huamachuco, both of pre-Inca origin, but one of which probably served as an Inca army barracks. This is Marca Huamachuco, a citadel high on a ridge above the town.

On our own again, and as yet untiring of urban living, we repaired to the best restaurant in town, a sizeable Colonial building of large rooms and wooden balconies inward-looking round an internal patio. Most of the rooms were locked and deserted but seemed to form part of some sort of hotel or hostel, a superior one at that, equipped with ornate doors and gilded mirrors. The meal was a friendly affair with the few guests and staff joining us at a big table, and everyone helping themselves from an enormous tureen of stew. Invited to lay out our sleeping bags on the floor we were to pass yet a third night without the necessity of having to erect the tent.

Before taking to the floorboards, however, we took ourselves for an evening stroll in Huamachuco's few but pleasant streets and had entered a store with the object of acquiring a toilet roll apiece to replenish exhausted stocks when PIP struck again. The representative of the breed on this occasion was a viciously drunk moron who demanded our credentials and openly accused us of being vagabonds. He produced no warrant card or proof of his calling so, initially, we ignored him though some sixth sense told me he was a *'politico'*. The chap followed us around, weaving a slightly erratic course, then disappeared to return later with a saner colleague just as we were enjoying a hot rum punch at a street-side bar. The atmosphere in the establishment, all chat and gaiety one moment, abruptly froze into silent hostility the next as the two men scrutinised our passports and insultingly went through the contents of our pockets. All the while a barrage of questions directed at David had to be coped with as best he could. Only when the ambassadorial letter came to light did the atmosphere change. Hardly had we, with ill-grace, acknowledged receipt of the order to report first thing in the morning to their office when the order was rescinded to a mealy-mouthed request that we might *like* to call there so that assistance could be rendered. Both of us made a mental note to go nowhere near the place.

Celebrating our second deliverance with further drafts of rum punch, we returned back across the square, toilet rolls in hand, to our accommodation. Huamachuco had suddenly gone sour. As we went it dawned on me that other evening strollers were clasping toilet rolls as ladies do handbags. The rum, I thought, but it wasn't. I'd noticed the habit in other towns. The flaunting of toilet rolls was obviously a social obligation in this part of Peru.

Heavy blasts of Latin American music awoke us in the morning and, well breakfasted, we made our way back to the plaza dominated by its substantial bell-tower that lacked a church. Here we joined a school outing in the back of a lorry to the ruins of Marco Huamachuco on the off-chance of it teaching us something about the precise site of the royal road. We were not actually *invited* to go on the excursion; the children simply pushed us good-naturedly aboard and nobody seemed to mind. The ruin of the citadel gave nothing away, however, and when we suggested to the young schoolmistress in charge that it might have been the one-time Inca military camp, she shook her head in a knowledgeable manner. 'No, that's the other one' we were told firmly. We returned baffled.

Back in Huamachuco town we restocked at the market, satisfying a craving for fruit by stuffing ourselves and our rucksacks with bananas. I also purchased a *sombrero* to replace my lost balaclava on the assumption that heat, not cold, would be our next antagonist. In the afternoon we walked north, taking a resurrected Highway 3 towards Cajamarca in the knowledge that it almost certainly was constructed upon its Incain forerunner.

Forty kilometres out lay Cajabamba where Pizarro's men rested for two days before continuing to Huamachuco on their southward march. The road, fairly straight, ran through eucalyptus groves of silvery trunks that became silent sentinels under which we camped for the night. The substance of the road lent itself to the assumption that this, indeed, was the historic route even without the chronicled fact of Pizarro having come this way. Of course his army might not necessarily have kept to the royal road but one can presume that it did.

Like that army we progressed with frequent rests close to or in the townships astride the road to Cajamarca. At Cajabamba we spent a night in a stable which offered yet another change of venue but were served with a meal that was as disgusting as it was original. The little café-bar was filthy into the bargain and, as we waited for the food, the lights went out, a frequent occurrence in rural Peru. We ate by candlelight, and the fact that we were unable to see the dish was probably a saving grace. I would have sworn that the pieces of meat I felt amongst the unidentifiable hash was cat. Certainly we saw plenty of dogs but never a cat in Cajabamba.

It was a dog, however, that initiated another unpleasant incident as we left next day. We had made a diversion to view some presumed traces of the old road up a hillside and, by doing so, aroused the hostile intentions of an exceedingly aggressive hound. Baring its saliva-dripping fangs it came for us, lunging for our legs and calves, to be beaten off with the greatest difficulty with sticks and a hail of stones.

The road took the only practical route by following a wide and ill-defined valley. The imparted morsels of intelligence wrung out of people we came across showed a distinct and encouraging return to awareness of their Inca heritage, the more so the nearer we approached Cajamarca. Alas, the inaccuracy of their statements belied their value with the result that we were continually making forays into the rolling countryside searching for supposed relics that were seldom there.

Ichocán was where we camped out in the plaza close to a water supply of erratic fountains that assured us of a soaking every time we attempted to fill a kettle. No PIP squads here; instead the police were most obliging even to the extent of helping in the erection of the tent on an empty flower bed. Had we arrived a little earlier I am in no doubt that we would have been offered the best cell in the local nick.

The landscape thereafter deteriorated into one of dry and barren appearance made the more disagreeable by our having been spoilt by days of being surrounded by a lush vegetation. At San Marco a kindly lady pressed a cold guinea-pig steak apiece onto us while we were locating a bed — as opposed to a floor — for the night, and the small centres of Matará, Namora and Llacanora became the final stepping stones to Cajamarca. The road now proceeded to unfold into a ribbon of Incain straightness and we camped the last night beside it amongst brown hills above the town.

Marching into Cajamarca at first light emphasized our impatience to notch the halfway point of our journey to Quito and our elation could only have been equalled by that of Francisco Pizarro arriving, the other way, in Cuzco.

7

CAJAMARCA–PIURA–TUMBES–CUENCA

That treachery can become a legend is nowhere shown so eloquently as at Cajamarca. It was in this pleasant town that the biggest double cross of history took place on 16 November 1532 when Spanish exploration turned to Spanish conquest. The astounding audacity of the conquest has tended to obscure and rationalise the crime committed by Francisco Pizarro that November day.

In many ways the Spanish conquest of Peru was similar in pattern, at least superficially, to that of Mexico which was finally subjugated in 1534. The tactical moves were the same with the establishment of a coastal base, the thrust inland, the exploitation of internal divisions, the capture of a ruler in a surprise attack, his elimination when of no further use, and finally the take-over of power by force. This was actually not conscious imitation though some of the strategems employed by both Cortés in Mexico and Pizarro in Peru had become unofficial standard practise in Spanish tactical manoeuvering during exploration and annexation of South American territory.

In the Peruvian instance the small town of Tumbes, in the Gulf of Guayaquil and close to what is now the Peruvian-Ecuadoran border, became the coastal base for the initial explorations. For some months Pizarro's men investigated this arid north-west corner of Peru to eventually establish a Spanish 'city', about a hundred miles south of Tumbes, in the Chiva Valley, and called it San Miguel (since then the town has been moved southward again to the Piura Valley where, as Piura, it stands today). It was while the Spaniards were encamped at San Miguel however that they learnt of the Huascar-Atahualpa conflict — the Inca civil war — and of its outcome, with Atahualpa triumphant. It seems likely that Pizarro's dark schemes crystalized into a plan of campaign at this point.

Additional to Spanish plans for exploration and takeover were those of exploitation built upon the evidence of Peruvian wealth. It was a dream of unlimited gold, as much as the loftier policy of annexation, that, with the blessing of the king of Spain, sent Francisco Pizarro and his soldiers on their brazen mission.

From San Miguel, therefore, he and his force of a hundred and seventy soldiers set out, after some light skirmishing with local tribes not yet absorbed into the Inca empire, for Cajamarca on a visit, ostensibly, of good will.

Atahualpa, meanwhile, rested with his powerful and victorious army at the agreeable hill town of Cajamarca in the course of a leisurely progress towards Cuzco in the wake of his main armies. He had heard of the Spanish landing on the outer perimeter of his empire but was more curious than offended, and anyway, how could so small a force be a threat?

Thus Pizarro and his soldiers duly arrived and despatched their envoys to the Lord-Inca's quarters outside the town. A display of horsemanship was given to Atahualpa who then agreed to a meeting with the Spanish leader in the Plaza. And in that confined space, the Spaniards emerged at a pre-arranged signal, massacred the Inca's retinue and seized Atahualpa.

Spanish chronicles have all remarked upon Atahualpa's shrewdness and the speed with which he reacted to his predicament. Realizing that the Spaniards intended to keep him hostage instead of killing him, he began to reassert himself and used his authority to three main purposes: the discouragement of immediate rescue which could cost his life, the execution of his prisoner, Huascar — to prevent him from taking possible advantage of the situation — and, in the knowledge of the Spaniards' zest for gold, the offering of a ransom of unimaginable quantities.

So, through the first eight months of 1533, Pizarro and his soldiers waited at Cajamarca, with the captured Inca in their charge, while the ransom instalments trickled in from the far-flung regions of the empire. It was a bizarre, unreal situation with Atahualpa ruling from a prison compound in the triangular plaza, keeping his lordly mien, his authority unquestioned by any subject of the empire. Female attendants dressed him in robes of vampire-bat fur, held food to his lips, and ceremoniously burnt everything he discarded. Great chiefs trembled in his presence even though freedom was denied him.

To secure his release, Atahualpa decreed that the realm be ransacked to fill a 17-by 22-foot room with gold and twice with silver. Totally unaware that Pizarro's men spearheaded a massive European invasion of the Tahuatinsuyu, he presumed the bearded ones would go away once they had received their booty.

By July 1533 more than 24 tons of exquisite treasure had been collected: idols and chalices, necklaces and nuggets, accumulated through centuries. Though this was only a fraction of the plunder that awaited the Spaniards elsewhere, Atahualpa's ransom, as duly recorded in the Spanish archives, was worth at least 30 million dollars at today's bullion values for gold and silver.

Nine forges worked for months to reduce the creations of master craftsmen to lumps of gleaming metal. Each horseman's share was 90 pounds of gold and 180 of silver; a foot-soldier got half as much. Pizarro refrained from melting down many magnificent pieces and sent them to Spain as part of the king's share, the 'royal fifth', but the king promptly turned them into coin.

Spaniards newly arrived from Panama, denied an equal share of the ransom, clamoured to get on with the conquest. And only then was the last of the Inca emperors not freed but sentenced to death for treason against the strangers within his own realm.

To avoid the horror of being burnt as a heretic and thus deprived of mummification, Atahualpa accepted baptism and took Pizarro's christian name: Francisco. Then the Spaniards garroted Francisco Atahualpa, thirteenth Inca, and, their forces almost doubled by reinforcements, marched down the royal road to Cuzco.

Tourists were not exactly thick on the ground at Cajamarca but those who had found their way to the little town were left in no doubt as to the amount of treasure, resulting from Francisco's ultimatum. The ransom chamber they are shown is, actually, not the original which no longer exists. But, no matter, its bareness manages to convey the proportions of the treasure and bring the whole ugly incident vividly to life. A white line drawn round the walls a few inches from the ceiling marks the 'high tide' of the gold and silver accumulation.

As you look upon it, again comes the question. How did so small a force of soldiery not only defeat an immense army but attain its base and capital across vast tracks of hostile territory? But now, for the traveller between Cuzco and Cajamarca the answer had become less of an enigma.

By killing Atahualpa, the Spaniards had automatically taken sides in the civil war, ranging themselves with the Cuzco faction, that of the deposed Huascar and his followers. Thus one Inca army became allies; distrustful maybe, but at least, from the Spanish point of view, neutralised. And by virtue of their small numbers the Spaniards continued to be regarded as no more than mercenaries or as formidably-armed bandits whose accoutrements — steel swords, steel-tipped lances, fire-arms and, above all, horses — offered immeasurable advantage over Peruvians in battle.

These considerations helped to explain why Pizarro's men managed to reach Cuzco in relative safety. Many of the inhabitants of the countryside they had to cross were either allies or indifferent neutrals wanting no more than to be left alone. Only at Jauja, the halfway point, were they seriously resisted; a resistance that was painfully overcome. In a forerunner of the 'scorched earth' policy the Incas destroyed each and every suspension bridge along the line of march to prevent their advance but, with the luck of the devil, these operations took place during an unusually dry season and the rivers were low. Thus Pizarro entered Cuzco with no great difficulty on 15 November 1533, to receive a surprisingly warm welcome.

Since, to the late and vanquished Huascar's supporters, the Spaniards were no more than commercially-minded brigands whose arrival on the scene at Cajamarca was something of a godsend, they joined their ranks to regain the initiative — and the throne at Cuzco, a prize that had been denied them in battle. This fact not only adds to the explanation of the swift Spanish advance but also explains the rapture of the welcome which was aimed primarily at the accompanying Incain soldiers and, in particular, Manco Inca, Huascar's successor.

The taking of Cuzco did not, of course, complete the conquest of Peru. The continued process of conquest was delayed by fighting between various Spanish factions, who thus perpetuated the Inca civil wars by which they had initially profited. Manco Inca made an unco-operative puppet; he once came near to driving the Spaniards out of Cuzco. But the Spanish capture of the city can be taken in a real sense, however, as marking the end of the Inca era in that country and seen by some as no more than the hastening of the inevitable since the empire was in decline and beginning to break up anyway.

If the ransom chamber makes an impressive sight so does the plaza where Atahualpa was ambushed, and the stone seat set high on a hill where he is alleged to have reviewed his subjects. A mile or two away are the Inca baths — Los Banos del Inca — the naturally warm, distinctly sulphurous thermal springs where the Spaniards first encountered Atahualpa bathing his festering war wounds. Though not a shrine to the Incas of the calibre of Cuzco, the instance of history that led to their downfall can never be forgotten in Cajamarca.

Three days we allowed ourselves in this most delightful of Peruvian towns. The Hotel Sucre, not the best hostelry in town, bore a distinct similarity to an open prison, and provided us with a windowless 'suite' which comprised an annex containing a cold-water-only basin and a flush toilet that failed to flush. But it served us adequately for the cold nights and we were out exploring during the day. The first night — our stomachs distended by a repeated chicken dish — we went to bed each clutching a 50p bottle of cherry brandy which made a syrupy but sleep-producing nightcap. Thereafter we soaked in sulphur, rubber-necked the local sights, tripped not very nimbly up Santa Apolonia — the hill behind the town on which Atahualpa's seat is situated — and ate till we thought we'd never stop.

My favourite view of the town was from this hill. Cajamarca sits in a beautiful fertile valley, only a few miles wide but remarkably flat — a rare distinction in the vertical world of the Andes. It was from heights like these that Pizarro first looked down upon Atahualpa's camp. He too must have gazed contentedly upon the green meadows where scalding overflow from the Inca baths wends through lush grass to fill the valley with vapour. Today it holds cows grazing unconcernedly beneath eucalyptus groves, on ground strewn with potsherds of pre-Inca civilisations. Modern Cajamarca remains a handsome town of red roofs, fine colonial monasteries and a well-proportioned if belfry-less cathedral.

Encircled by its hills, lower and softer than elsewhere they may have been, Cajamarca provides few clues as to its past land communications. We had walked in on the royal road but where it left remained, to us, a mystery, as it did to all the citizens of Cajamarca with whom we spoke. Our researches revealed the fact that it passed through Huancabamba, 30 miles from the Ecuadoran border, reached today by a devious road of assorted surfaces designated as Highway 3. And was it not from Huancabamba that Hernando de Soto, explorer-conqueror and associate of Francisco Pizarro, glimpsed the wealth and opulence of the mysterious empire in this first Inca city he had come across? In his book, *Highway to the Sun*, Victor von Hagen relates that he had followed the old road out of Cajamarca northwards into Ecuador, 'marking its way accurately'; if so, then he must have known something we didn't; a fact that is entirely possible of course. From the vantage point of Santa Apolonia no trace of an *agger* of the road could be perceived; its route can only be surmised. We found it all a mite disappointing. From Cuzco the historic artery leaves with a whimper, picks up with a bang for a hundred miles or more from Bon Bón to Huari, fades, fluctuates, then reappears to arrive at its 700-mile point at Cajamarca with a dull thud.

Of the two of us David was the more crestfallen. For him the route of the royal road was an obsession; for me it was no more than a line, theoretical or otherwise, of a journey along the spine of the Andes. I have alluded before to this difference in approach to our Andean travels but here at Cajamarca the disparity was the most pronounced. In a way I admired his fanaticism.

Proceeding directly northwards, initially along Highway 3, might or might not have led us onto something that would have, to quote von Hagen again, enabled us to 'mark its way accurately'. But we could both discern the all too prevalent likelihood of following an invisible line bearing no tangible evidence whatsoever that the old road had come this way. We would be struggling through further mountain ranges for upwards of another 150 miles towards a border area we had been expressly forbidden to approach and for which large scale maps had been denied us. We were simply not equipped with the necessary knowledge to make the slog worthwhile. The border issue worried us not at all. I had regaled David with stories of my own disgraceful catalogue of 'border-bashing' experiences in central European and Middle-Eastern countries and he was all for adding to them had the presence of the royal road been strong enough to warrant following it directly into Ecuador. The single crossing point in that region was at La Tina, of restricted entry, and definitely not for foreigners at a time when Peru and Ecuador were at loggerheads over boundary changes. To keep within the law we should have to present ourselves to Zarumilla, beyond Tumbes, on the coastal road and it was to the coast that our eyes now turned as we studied the maps, David having made up his mind to return and explore the northerly regions at a later date*.

For us, as it had been for Pizarro and his men, Cajamarca was a watershed. For Pizarro, however, his triumph was just beginning. For us, tired, exhausted, fed up to the back teeth with each other's company and, most serious of all, dispirited by the lack of an onward trail, the project upon which we had set our hearts and minds was beginning its downward spiral towards the plughole of despair. A halfway point, a vital objective, a destination that had lain in our minds for weeks was Cajamarca, and now that it was behind us, we could raise little inspiration for continued progress.

Looking back I am of the opinion that, royal road or no royal road, we should have carried on directly northward. Even had we not been able to pick up the route, that way was where it went. Instead our new proposals were to return to the coast by public transport, regain the Pan-American Highway, move northward on it into Ecuador and at a convenient point, return inland to rejoin our original alignment. That way, we told ourselves, we

* A project which he subsequently carried out.

would see more of Peru's historical coastal cities including those with Inca-Spanish associations as well as covering another section of the route of the Inca coastal highway.

But these were excuses and, in our hearts, we knew it. The way ahead directly northwards led through more endless miles of wilderness and desolation and heartache. Suddenly we'd had enough. This time our sojourn in an urban centre had not inspired a longing to return to the wide open spaces.

My notes indicated that David and I were embroiled in another slanging match during our stay in Cajamarca. They don't say why and I'm certain the details were unimportant. Anyway it was no doubt as much my fault as his for I can be a stubborn, awkward cuss if I'm pushed the wrong way. We could both act like children — as no doubt can any human being pushed to the limits of physical and mental exhaustion — but not always did this behaviour materialise in an antagonistic fashion. In Cajamarca, as in other centres, I can recollect the many instances of us touring the bakers and cake vendors in a bid to hunt down the best bargains in sticky buns and the like, devouring them in surprising quantities on the spot. Not only were we invariably short on cash but also on sugary substances for which our bodies abnormally craved. Occasionally I felt slightly ashamed of myself; a grown man acting like a schoolboy!

Three days of relative idleness at an end, we bade a reluctant farewell to Cajamarca and left in the middle of the night aboard another of those massive high-sided Volvo trucks. This one was already full of passengers, prostrate, sleeping and uncooperative, who took none too kindly to additions to their ranks. The truck was bound for San Pedro de Loc, a town a few miles from the sea.

It was a miserably cold run. David managed to retrieve his sleeping bag from his rucksack but mine was lost to sight in darkness, buried beneath the human debris. Our direction of travel was now due west and the road, after the first ten miles, was reasonably surfaced. Temperatures warmed up with the approach to the coast and outside a small town called Pacasmayo, five miles short of San Pedro, we disembarked to spend the last hours of the night amongst the sand dunes.

Our faces turned north again, the onward journey became, as expected, a succession of uncomfortable rides and frustrating delays punctuated by argument and barter, to obtain them. A pick-up sped us to Guadalupe, a down-at-heel village inland from the ocean for here the Trans-American makes a wide swing away from the coast, leaving minor roads to serve the few seaside communities. We would soon be in the Sechura Desert — a large flat area of shifting sands — and we could feel the heat becoming more intense the nearer we got. But as with all deserts its nights were decidedly cool.

From Guadalupe we had to walk the half dozen miles to Chepen on account of nobody being willing to stop for us. It was an unpleasant six miles of walking either on the sticky tarmac or the soft sand verges. Desert-walking is hell and keeping to a lethal strip of tarmac another kind of hell. We had shed our 'winter wear' which made a heavier load on our shoulders, the hard road caused our feet to swell and the unaccustomed humidity sapped our energy so that we bathed in a sauna-like sweat. All the time we had to keep a sharp look-out for traffic coming from both ways since pedestrians in their domain were regarded as targets to be bowled over. The Pan-American highway was alive with traffic of all sorts and sizes but is of sufficient width for no more than two large trucks to pass.

At Chepen we went on strike, vowing to wait in its unsavoury outskirts until we *could* obtain a ride. The most strategic spot to get one, as every hitch-hiker knows, is a petrol station or transport café where many vehicles stop anyway. Such places have their drawbacks and that of the petrol station-cum-bar in Chepen was the unsavoury attentions of a bunch of drunks.

A Peruvian of Swedish stock rescued us in his little Saab chatting gaily to us all the way to Chiclayo, one of the liveliest of all the northern cities but not one of much history or lasting memory for the foreign visitor. We were dropped in the main shopping street and my only memory of the place is that of feeling acutely embarrassed amongst a sophisticated populace to whom we must have looked and acted like wild men from the hills.

Fighting our way onto a local bus we were deposited at

Lambayeque just eight miles further up the road. Here was the history that Chiclayo had missed out on and its narrow streets were lined with adobe houses displaying their distinctive wooden balconies and wrought iron grill-work over the windows. Here too we spent a profitable hour looking over the Brunning Museum full of pre-Inca — including Mohica and Chimu — ceramics, household implements and gold artefacts before sharing our picnic lunch with a friendly policeman within its well-kept grounds. But not even he could get us a peep into the celebrated gold display, reputed to be better than Lima's, which was closed for restoration. We were both annoyed and dismayed for assuredly here another source of Inca knowledge denied us.

A fish lorry, whose driver had the good intention of taking us to Motupe in the Desert of Sechura, unfortunately and irrevocably broke down some ten miles out of Lambayeque presenting us with the only alternative of plodding another 25 miles to that village since nothing else that came along would oblige. To counter the heat and the relentless traffic we set out on a night hike — but in vain. Crosses in the sand, like those we had seen between Chimbote and Trujillo, made sombre wayside viewing. Some were stark and simple, others ornate; even festive, but all forcibly reminded us that we were trespassing upon the domain of the automobile. We were given more prosaic reminders too. The corpses of dogs filled in the gaps between the crosses, some flung like stuffed rag-dolls on the sandy verges; others barely discernible as they had become part of the tarmac, pounded into its surface.

As we walked the countryside turned from desert to no desert, little water but sparse vegetation, then scrubby trees and bushes on hard beaten earth. Motube, or what we saw of it, produced a lorry the crew of which were reluctantly persuaded to take us to Piura. We rode on top of the cab squeezed perilously into a flimsy box-like cavity with the hot wind ever-threatening to blow us out. Occasionally the engine cut out giving excuse for us to descend and offer a helping hand pushing the vehicle over the sand-encroaching roadway.

An oasis in the hot and parched desert is Piura. This was the town founded in 1532 by the Spanish conquistadores and if it was not much of a place in that century it certainly is now. Again well inland — all the Peruvian towns along this section of coast shun the sea — Piura was entirely dependent, until recently, on the temperamental Piura river which runs through the town and is one of those that switch from a mere trickle to a raging torrent at the hint of a hailstorm. The new dam, which was being constructed at the time of our visit, was being built to top up a big reservoir to irrigate, more reliably, the long-abandoned cultivated land. That done, the town's product — high quality cotton — could be grown once again to everybody's benefit. A statue to Pizarro stands in the plaza and there are Pizarro and Cortés parks and gardens all of which offer a notion as to what side Piura's citizens supported. Of similar Spanish architectural ambience to Trujillo and equally well maintained, it played host to us for an evening. We dined on the local milk and sugar speciality — *natillas* — and spent the night under the stars on its sandy outskirts.

From Piura to Sullana is 25 miles of pure unadulterated desert, barren and sterile. We hoped we would not have to walk it all and, following a hike of some three miles out of town, our hopes were realized. An empty truck, stopping of its own accord, scooped us off the road, the driver being an amiable fellow sporting a drooping moustache and an allergy against the loneliness of the cab. Dumping our rucksacks in the buck we squeezed in beside him.

Sullana stands on a bluff over the fertile Chira valley and after the flat, airless desert, gives an impression of countryside akin to the Nile Delta even to its rows of date palms that had me dazedly wondering how Egypt had got itself into South America. We were dropped south of the town and so had to plod our way through and north of it to the large girder bridge spanning the Chira river. Here there was a police check point whose personnel, given sight of our magic letter, offered us their all, including a bottle each of fizzy lemonade. They also 'persuaded' the driver of yet another of those giant Volvo trucks to take us to Tumbes, the last town of any significance in Peru. The man was not enthusiastic but grumpily took us aboard.

As we made for Talara and the coast he gradually thawed out

and upon learning that he and I were of the same age I had him eating out of our hands. We were puzzled, however, by the slowness of his driving since such a characteristic is hardly common in Peruvian lorry driving circles, and whenever a spate of potholes appeared — which was every few yards — this reduced him to a crawl. The Pan-American Highway here was further inflicted with long sections of unsurfaced gravel across which we could have walked the faster. It eventually dawned on us that the pace was dictated by the fragility of the cargo — a fact confirmed by the revelation that the carefully-stacked plastic sacks behind us contained dynamite.

At Talara the highway resumes a love-affair with the ocean and the flat blue Pacific made exotic viewing after many weeks of vertical granite. Dry and like a moon-scape once more, the landscape began sprouting oil in the form of hard-working little 'nodding donkey' pumps dotted amongst the humpback hills. Descending one such hill in low gear we mercifully reached the bottom to have our puncture on level ground.

Changing the wheel of even so massive a vehicle as ours was no problem to a driver who must have performed the operation a hundred times before to judge from the state of his tyres. The one we removed was as smooth as a baby's head; the one we replaced it with all but transparent. On this we limped, hearts in mouth, the ten miles into Mancora there, after considerable delay, to have the original tyre vulcanised.

With Mancora we were in the province of Tumbes and a contested region that was once Ecuadoran and, according to those across the border, still should be. Police checks became, therefore, the more numerous and ferocious though of not much consequence to us beyond the frustration of the usual delays. Hugging the seashore, with police searches augmented by military searches, we came to Zorritos, there to spend the night sprawled in reasonable comfort upon the sacks of dynamite.

The village of Zorritos is renowned for its beach, one of the few reputed to be not oil-contaminated, and one which offers warm bathing. At dusk I attempted to put these claims to the test but was repelled by mosquitoes homing in from the nearby mangrove swamps.

These pests did their best to counteract the soporific effects of the waves breaking on the shore but with only partial success until, as with open-air sleeping anywhere, the dawn roused us early. Puerto Pizarro, with its rash of Pizarro motels, and San Pedro de los Incas maintained the legend of the road to its terminus, twenty miles on, at Tumbes.

Peruvian only since 1941, Tumbes was very much the frontier town. The place was swarming with soldiers, and large numbers of the first or last of this and that placards could be seen everywhere; the town's market was doing big business. But here, as indeed over the last scores of miles, few are the relics of the Inca coastal road. What remains — the dying walls of old castles we had glimpsed in the haze of desert heat or morning mist — were mostly pre-Incain. Even San Pedros de los Incas could rise only to another police check.

The end of one great Inca artery is marked by no monument in Tumbes; no poet that I know has penned an epic about it. Yet it was here, even before San Miguel, that the drama of the Spanish conquest of the Inca empire had its beginnings. As Victor von Hagen points out, the road the Spanish found outside of Tumbes was, together with the inland royal highway, the stepping stone to conquest. Never had a people so arduously made arrangements for their own downfall as did the Incas. Just as the Persians paved the way for their own defeat by the forces of Alexander the Great, so did the magnificent roads of the Incas betray them to the Spaniards.

A *tampu* called Ricaplaya lies thirteen miles south of Tumbes, its unprotected walls crumbling amongst large algarobe trees and bursts of mimosa. Had it been astride the royal road David, assuredly, would have spent hours scrutinising each stone but here we were simply in transit and off-course and our combined consciences exhibited a guilt that was almost tangible. Our eyes, however, wandered into the neighbouring territory of Ecuador, our intentions firmly tied to a resumption of a route we had lost at Cajamarca; that other highway continuing alone to the north.

South American frontiers are ferocious affairs though often their bark is worse than their bite. This had been the case of that between Bolivia and Peru all those months ago when not even a bribe or an angry word had marred the crossing. It was the same at Huaquillas, on the Ecuadoran side of the Peruvian border and for this, I am convinced it was my age that precluded any unpleasantness. We both donned spectacles to make us look the more dignified and carried our rucksacks by hand in an effort to give the impression they were suitcases. And never had I seen David act so politely. We celebrated our entry into Ecuador with an ice-cold 'coke' in a café in what is described in The *South American Handbook* as a 'seedy one-horse banana town full of touts with black briefcases.'

Aware that Ecuadoran public transport was considerably more efficient than that of Peru we took to the buses at Huaquillas, our first being a coach of a degree of comfort that had us in raptures. We now followed the southern shore of the Gulf of Guayaquil, until at a village called Puerto Bolivar we were abruptly in a swamp-infested jungle. Rarely have I seen such a sudden change of environment at a political frontier though the heat, humidity and mosquitoes remained constant. Banana groves sprouted everywhere as did luxuriant growth in bloated proportions. Machala was a city given over to the banana: its shops and markets were awash with the fruit and it was from here onwards that our staple diet switched from the potato to various sorts, sizes, shapes and colours of banana.

At Machala we turned inland and began to climb. Our destination was the city of Cuenca, back on the alignment of the royal road. The road, well-surfaced, wound through lush tropical greenery, baobab trees and timber houses raised on stilts to keep them out of land holding an *excess* of water where, a short while before, there was none at all. The soil was deep red, its fertility exciting into growth not only tall bearded trees but multi-coloured lillies, water-melons, rice and startling flowers amongst the exaggerated shrubs. In the towns and villages was an order of living that had not been apparent in Peru, some even boasting the occasional public toilet. Politically-inspired graffiti was equally prominent but this faded with the increasing distance from disputed Tumbes. People looked more prosperous, better-dressed and cleaner, and in Machala I had been surprised to see an orderly crocodile of schoolgirls, spick and span in tartan skirts and virgin-white blouses weaving through the streets.

Altitude all too soon defeated the jungle and among the foothills of distant mountain ranges we were back in a customary wilderness of heaving scenery. Lowering clouds and an angry sunset competed in the drama stakes with even our respectable bus entering into the spirit by bashing itself against a rock wall as the driver took violent action to avoid a collision with an oncoming car.

Santa Isabel, perched on its near-vertical cliff, in the dusk and Giron, a sizeable town, in darkness were the final landmarks on this ride to Cuenca, Ecuador's third largest city and one which, according to our reckoning, should have been astride or adjacent to the route of the royal road.

We arrived at midnight and it was cold again — we still wore our summer rigs. Shivering, we went in search of lodgings and were convinced it was a good omen when we found them in a Colonial building that houses an establishment labelled the Residentia de L'Inca.

8

CUENCA–CANAR–RIOBAMBA –AMBATO–QUITO

The door crashed open. From the depths of sleep I had been aware of a battering and thudding as from some distant hill and my mind was suffused with the threat of earthquake or avalanche that had come to add its quota of unpleasantness to our journey. I awoke with a start; the hills became four walls and there were three men staring down at me. For a moment I was unable to reconcile fiction with fact, then fact elbowed its way through the confusion of my mind. Ecuador. The Residencia de L'Inca... Cuenca...

Welcome to Cuenca. The man in charge didn't actually say so. Instead he flashed a cellophane card in my face. I couldn't read it but I thought I knew what it said. PIP again, or its Ecuador equivalent. I jumped out of bed, then sat down on it, aware of my nakedness.

David was already up. 'It's the criminal police,' he muttered. 'But I don't know what it's all about.'

I was ordered to stand while my rucksack was emptied of its contents on the bed. David's belongings were likewise tipped out; the items scrutinised. The twin piles of plastic bags containing what was left of my soap powder and David's foot powder were handed to the head man. They all wore civilian suits but, with their old-fashioned Homburg hats on their heads, gave off an aura of the G-men of the 1930s. In the open doorway I perceived a fourth figure, that of the Residencia proprietor, smirking but uneasy.

The senior policeman was cautiously applying minute quantities of soap flake and foot powder to his tongue and seemed not to be enjoying the flavour. The others watched enthralled, items of our property still in their hands. Expressions turned from high expectation to downright disappointment as the chief shook his head and the proprietor in the doorway slipped quietly away. Our effects were given a final combing and the raid was over, the group of visitors withdrawing without a word. I hoped they'd give its instigator hell for calling them out on an abortive drug scare.

But Cuenca had better things to offer than inquisitive policemen. Founded by the Spaniards in 1557 on the site of a native town known as Tumibamba the city has preserved its colonial air with cobblestone streets and quaint old buildings, many of them of marble. Some of the old houses around the cathedral displayed frescoed patio walls that defied their age, while the church of El Carmen boasted a portal with pairs of columns like bars of barley-sugar twisting in opposite directions, apparently the hallmark of a Spanish architect of 1680 Valencia. The cathedral, they say, took a hundred years to build and its massiveness supports this supposition, as do the multiple golden domes flashing fire in the sun.

Not that we were to see much sun in either Cuenca or Ecuador in general. The interior of the country is noted for extensive rain and the characteristic was not to let us down. It had poured the evening of our arrival, let up for a few hours in the morning as we made a preliminary tour of the town, only to descend again in earnest as we made for an afternoon treat at the sulphur baths at Banos, yet another Banos, three miles away. A Sunday market was in a frenzy of selling, the vivid colours of the stall umbrellas defying another wet and soggy morning. In all we remained four days in Cuenca and on one of them managed to locate Padre Crespi, an old bearded priest of considerable local infamy who, by founding the Crespi collection of Indian artefacts, fell foul of the authorities. We tracked him down to his confessional in a new church standing on the site of his former controversial museum which had been 'accidentally' burnt to the ground. Crowded into the little box, its curtains tightly drawn, we listened to his tale of woe and persecution as much for his satisfaction for the telling as our interest in the hearing.

What is now Ecuador was once part of the most northerly province of the Inca empire, then called the Kingdom of Quito. Throughout much of the country the Andes divide into two chains of high peaks, many of shapely volcanic cones, some still active, all snow-capped. Though the two chains are not exactly parallel, for most of their length they are only thirty or forty miles apart; well within sight of one another. Between them is a winding plateau-corridor, about 300 miles long from north to south, divided by transverse ridges into a series of shallow upland basins. Of these the southernmost, now called the Cuenca basin, is the lowest – about 8,000 feet; the northernmost, in which the city of Quito stands, is the highest – about 9,000 feet. In Inca times these areas were populated by settled peoples and, as the last to be conquered by the Incas, the province had received much attention including not only military occupation and the establishment of the benefits of Inca rule but also the bestowal of a series of royal buildings in the towns of Quito and Tumibamba. Atahualpa himself had regarded the northern provinces as the base of his power and after his capture, Spanish rumour had it that the two towns rivalled Cuzco in splendour and that their captor had stored great quantities of treasure in them.

These rumours spread far beyond the boundaries of the Inca Empire to reach the ears of one Pedro de Alvarado on occupation duty in Guatemala, who promptly raised an army of 500 men and 120 horses to effect a new conquest. They landed at Puerto Viejo (now Manta) on the Ecuadoran coast, a mistake, as it turned out, of the kind that Pizarro had made earlier in Peru. To reach the Inca royal road midway between Tumibamba (Cuenca) and Quito the new force of conquistadores had to force their way through mangrove swamps and rain forests, over high mountain passes deep with snow and against determined nonco-operation from local inhabitants on whom they inflicted a quite inexcusable brutality.

Unknown, at first, to Alvarado, a second, if smaller, army of would-be Spanish conquerors under Sebastian de Benalcazar was likewise set on a course for Quito. For Benalcazar it was a breakaway project; one made virtually on the spur of the moment and without permission from his chief, Pizarro, in Cuzco. Pizarro had sent his subordinate back to San Miguel-Piura with a consignment of loot for shipment to Panama and with orders to guard the northern approach to Peru. It was at San Miguel that Benalcazar learnt of the 'official' invasion and promptly instigated one of his own.

With no reasons for staying their hand against the Spanish enemy, such as had been the case during Pizarro's advance from Cajamarca to Cuzco, the Inca authority in the Kingdom of Quito under Quisquis could be expected to oppose the double invasion with determination and a united resistance born of the hatred of the cruel Spaniards. And this, in fact, became the case except in one instance where the natives of the Tumibamba region, the Canari, who had suffered at the hands of the conquering Incas and still resented their subjugation, contributed 3,000 fighting men and allied themselves to Benalcazar's army on his thrust towards Quito.

There is little chronicled that survives about these initial invasions of what is now Ecuador. The few fragments of eye-witness reportage come, again, from the pen of Cieza de León, the Spanish chronicler. The first important town on Benalcazar's route was Tumibamba. It was the Inca conqueror Tupac Yupanqui who had attempted to turn the place into a second Cuzco and according to Cieza:

> 'The famous buildings of Tumibamba, in the province of Canaris, are among the richest and most splendid in the whole kingdom... The temple of the Sun is built of stones very cunningly wrought, some of them being very large, coarse and black, and others resembling jasper. Some of the Indians pretend that most of the stones... have been brought from the great city of Cuzco by order of the King Huayna Capac, and of the great Tupac Inca his father, by means of strong ropes. If this be true it is a wonderful work, by reason of the great size of the stones and the lengths of the road. The doorways of many of the buildings were very handsome and brightly painted, with precious stones and emeralds let into the stone; and the interior walls of the Temple of the Sun, and of the palaces of the Incas, were lined with plates of the finest gold stamped with many figures. The roofs were of straw, so well put on that no fire would consume it, while it would endure for many

ages . . . Now these buildings of Tumibamba are in ruins, but it is easy to see how grand they once were.'

Today, in Cuenca, not even ruins remain.

Try as we did to elicit information as to the exact whereabouts of the royal road we knew once passed through or very near the city, all we could raise was the fact that little of it remained north of the town. 'Well what lies south of it?' we enquired hopefully but the shrugs in reply were equally eloquent. But fifty miles north of the town was situated Ecuador's sole major ruin, the fortress of Ingapirca, and here, surely, would be an answer to the riddle.

We made our way out of Cuenca — in the rain of course — to trudge over waterlogged grassland, trying to keep off the tarmac of the modern highway which, all too likely, *was* the exact route of the royal way. For a time we chose different paths; David to plunge off the road onto railway lines, rough tracks and open country, I to stick with the tarmac which I found drier for my feet. The ground was hilly but not exhaustingly so and we both understood that if we arrived at the subsequent town of Canar we had missed Ingapirca. In the event we were reunited before Canar to erect the tent with the advent of evening. It was still raining so we made camp in the lee of what we thought was a deserted farmhouse and only when the last peg had been rammed home into the muddy earth did the occupants emerge to invite us to utilise their farmyard. While expressing our appreciation of the offer we concluded that the interior of the tent made a better bet than did an extremely grubby cowshed. Under the penetrating gaze of four pairs of curious eyes of an age group ranging from five to fifty we cooked and consumed a disastrous meal of paraffin-impregnated packet soup, the residue of which even the dog refused. Damp and ill-tempered we retired to our sleeping bags.

A weak sun illuminated our breakfast preparations the results of which were hardly more appetising than had been our previous night's supper. David upset the porridge and I spilt the tea which, when salvaged, tasted exclusively of mud. With stomachs grumbling with discontent, and murder in our hearts we struck camp, packed away the damp gear and made tracks for Ingapirca intent upon reaching it before another nightfall come hell or — more likely — high water.

Our early departure pitched us into an incident that was to become something of a mixed blessing. Hardly had we set out along a brute of a track ankle-deep in mud when we were overtaken by a force of horsemen. They rode with wild abandon, singing at the tops of their voices and offering a romantic sight in their flying ponchos and wide-brimmed hats. Passing us in a thunder of hooves and a shower of dirty water they reined in their sweating mounts and turned to survey us. Even before anyone spoke we could see that they had been celebrating all too successfully at a local *fiesta* and the big porcelain bottles attached to their saddles confirmed it. Our nationality and destination was demanded in loud slurred voices and upon receiving the required details we were invited — no, ordered — to help ourselves to the firewater and mount the nearest horse behind its rider. This we did with some misgivings and, astride a wet horsey back I was rewarded with a mawkish kiss by my 'driver' who may have been under the delusion I was a young blonde village wench. The rum was molten fire, but this was the least of our troubles as we galloped away, David and I clinging on to whatever we could for dear life.

In this manner we made erratic progress towards Ingapirca though neither of us believed our amorous companions would actually take us to where we were going — unless it happened to be on their way. At intervals the horses were permitted to trot which, riding bareback, is the more uncomfortable gait. Our rucksacks had been taken by those not burdened by 'pillion passengers' and I occasionally glimpsed mine bouncing about on some unfortunate horse's rump. Once we slowed to a walk but this only to effect a refill of rum from the leather-bound bottles. Everyone seemed to know where they were going except us.

Cantering along a track that skirted a well-cultivated hill our group of crazed Custer's cavalry bore into a herd of grazing cows who, panic-stricken, became part of a wild charge which only came to an end at the head of the valley where the desperate animals could fan out and go their own way.

If nothing else, our scheduled arrival at the fortress complex was in advance of our expectations. We were ceremoniously dropped less than a mile from the famed ruin and it was all I could do to stand, such was the excruciating pain of seldom-used calf muscles brought into play over the period of the ride. Pressed to further draughts of rum the obligation of standing upright became increasingly difficult but the walk along a well-maintained path gradually rectified our ailments and cleared our heads.

'Ingapirca' means 'stone of the Inca' and it is certainly that. Fortress, temple, royal *tampu* and — additional to similar complexes — observatory. The squat ruin is well-preserved, with gravel paths leading to its various structures, the whole buttressed by the familiar stone which here exudes an air of importance as if it had once been a major site in the Incain hierarchy. Being Ecuador's sole remaining worthwhile souvenir of the period the imposing pile, standing firm upon an outcrop of hill, has been titivated to a well-nigh ludicrous degree though its protection is to be applauded. All around (punctuated by keep-off-the-grass notices), were excavated plots, some still under excavation while atop the main fortress block, water channels worn into the rock — something on the lines of Roman aqueducts — led out over a chasm on the north side. A most interesting piece of archaeology is Ingapirca but, to me, it lacked the evocative image of lesser ruins we had come across on lonely sites far from the hands of preservation.

It was hard to visualise that at the height of the Inca Empire such structures as these spread from the Sun temple and fortress of Purumauca in southern Chile to the Ancasmayo River in present-day Colombia. Between were the administrative centres and living complexes, storehouses, temples and fortresses as well as the simple *tampu* along the web of roads. David and I had already come across the remains of those around Cuzco, and of Limatambo, Vilcas-huamán, Bonbón, Tunsacancha, Huánuco Viejo and others. And now Ingapirca; for us almost certainly the end of the chain.

Inca architecture developed out of the rustic houses of the peasants as all great architectural styles have done throughout history. The most awe-inspiring of Inca structures — those cyclopean stone walls — are but a development of the one-room dwelling prevalent at the time. These houses, placed in a square served by a common yard, resulted in the rectangular city plan of the Incas which we had looked upon at Vilcas-huamán, Bonbón and Huánuco Viejo in particular. Inca cities had no outer walls such as the Romans erected to defend their towns. Instead each large city was built close to a hill upon which was constructed a fortress planned as a smaller copy of the city it guarded. When attacked, the people were expected to occupy it with their weapons and from there defend themselves. Not all Inca cities were exclusively their product. As the Inca conquest spread across the land and urban centres fell into their hands so the Inca builders modified the existing structures, sometimes levelling part of them and, upon them, superimposing their standard model plazas, sun temples and administrative centres. On the coast, Inca building materials would often be adobe blocks with the addition of stone for the doorways and niches for the more important edifices. Inland, as we had seen, the 'new' towns contained a larger percentage of stone buildings though, no doubt, many of the original mud dwellings of the less prosperous inhabitants had remained intact only until time and the elements wiped them away.

Yet the riddle of those massive stones continues to puzzle those who look upon Inca structures which, except where destroyed by man, have remained intact to this day and will no doubt continue to stand into the foreseeable future. The enigma of the lonely cathedrals to a lost art of construction amongst nature's magnificent contribution of the Andes remains to worry the minds of those who find their way to them. And this time there is no glib answer to the riddle as there is to that of the Spanish conquest. Some of the chambers of Ingapirca have been turned into a museum. What we saw at the time was a disappointing array of pottery with all that was of any significant interest having been removed to Quito. David and I had seen many cultural effects of the Incas in the museum of Lima and Cuzco but the very fact that these items here on show had come from this actual spot did add to their allure. Inca pottery is purely functional, well-made and of almost metallic hardness. Pottery shaping, without the potter's wheel, must have been considerably more of a skill than it is now, the method being to roll the clay into sausage form then build spirally into the projected pot, one hand feeding the sausage-shaped core, the other pressing it into shape. The result was then smoothed and moulded by a small flat disc before the ritual of drying, painting and firing. Crude though Inca pottery undoubtedly is their colouring has outlived the years and the craftsmen who made it must have possessed an eye for functional beauty.

Weaving was another skill of the Incas. Wool, until their conquests opened up the channels for trade leading to the acquisition of cotton fibre, was the only Andean material available. The wool of the alpaca, generally white but mixed with greys and natural browns, was used for wearing apparel because of its superior fineness while llama wool, coarse and greasy, was spun as fibre for heavy blankets, sacks and ropes. The vicuna, with its soft and silky coat, supplied the source for luxury weaving as practised by the Chosen Women who produced the fabulous tunics for the Lord-Inca — the kind never worn more than once. Little is known of the dyeing procedures beyond the fact that metallic substances such as copper and tin were used to give permanence to the various vegetable dyes: achiote tree pods (red), the genipa pod (black) and the seed of the avocado (blue).

There was even a foot plough or *taclla* on show of virtually similar design to the ones in use at the present time and which we had seen in operation in mid- and northern Peru. Agriculture was the soul of the Inca empire, determining everything. The Andean farmers' year was divided into two seasons: wet and dry. The land was divided fairly between the members of the *ayllu* and the fruits of the labours stored in state granaries for the use of the commune. Such storehouses invariably contained maize, *quinoa, chuno,* dried llama meat, fish, cord, hemp, wool, cotton, sandals and military arms all of which was distributed as the necessity arose. Like the modern Chinese People's Army, farmers combined their duties with soldiering — and vice versa.

The art of music was represented by a single bone flute. The musical instruments of the Incas were as limited as the variation of their dances which, like their music, was bound up with religion. Most were percussion and wind instruments, and strictly bucolic. Drums were made of a hollow log and covered either with llama or tapir hide and their sound was supplemented by tambourines, channara bells, silver bells and rattles, these last items attached to the person. Flutes and trumpets made from sea-shells formed the core of the wind instruments. To go with the music and dancing was a beverage of fermented *chicha,* quaffed in great quantities since drunkenness — in its right place — was looked upon as a normal condition for festivals.

The keeper of the small museum was a mine of information about his limited stock of artefacts but neither he nor an eccentric Virginian professor, who introduced himself to us, could identify the route of the royal road.

'It's down there,' the American pronounced, jabbing the air. He took us a hundred yards out of the fenced confines of the complex to a clearly-defined *agger* several yards wide which did, indeed, give an impression of having been an Inca highway. But its direction was all wrong though it could well have been a link road to the centre. I remembered that Victor von Hagen had reported that he too had looked upon a fragment of Inca road in 1934 when on his first expedition to South America 'From the summit of what had been an Inca fortress (Ingapirca),' he records, 'I had seen a clearly devized road, several yards wide and, bordered by a stone wall, undulating over the treeless land.' He had followed it for some miles 'until, at the edge of a canyon, it disappeared in a tangle of masonry.' The professor remained adamant that the royal road lay beneath the existing south to north highway upon which we had been the previous day; the one taking the only practical route, between the Andean mountain chain, to Quito. The guide agreed and both David and I were convinced they were right. There simply was no other route it *could* take.

The American, we learnt, was 'off the leash' — as he put it — from both his college and family; his first 'escape' in all his sixty years, so was making the most of a six-week tour. He spoke no Spanish but managed to make himself understood — at least to *his* satisfaction — in loud bursts of Virginian. With him we walked the few miles to the nearest village; the physical effort agreeably quieting him down with every footstep, though he spurned our invitation to join us for a snack of bread rolls and bananas at a cafe not very tastefully decorated with skinned corpses of guineapigs that hung from the walls and eaves.

We saw off our American friend on a bus floundering about in the quagmire of the village square and, in the fresh company of two silent youths, continued our way to the town of Canar that had given its name to the district in spite of the fact that Cuenca was by far the larger place. Pitching camp on the outskirts of the small town we succeeded in raising the tent seconds before another downpour.

Cunar, in turn, had been given its name by the natives of the surrounding region — which included Tumibamba — and, as we have seen, the Canari sided with Benalcazar's army advancing towards Quito. Cieza, the Spanish chronicler, has some flattering words to say about them:

> 'The natives of this province, called Canari, are good-looking and well grown. They wear their hair long, so much so, that by that and a circular crown of wands, as fine as those of a sieve, the Canaris may easily be known, for they wear this head-dress as a distinguishing mark... The women are very pretty, amorous, and friendly to the Spaniards. They are great labourers, for it is they who dig the land, sow the crops and reap the harvests... When any Spanish army passed through the province, the Indians at that time being obliged to supply people to carry the baggage of the Spaniards on their backs, many of these Canari sent their wives and daughters, and remained at home themselves... Some Indians say that this arises from the dearth of men and the great abundance of women owing to the cruelty of Atahualpa to the people of this province, when he entered it after having killed the captain-general of his brother Huáscar at Ambato, whose name was Atoco. They affirm that, although the men and boys came out with green boughs and palm leaves to beg for mercy, he, with a haughty air and severe voice ordered his captains to kill them all. Thus a great number of men and boys were killed, and they

say that now there are fifteen times as many women as men.'

Having irrevocably concluded that the route of the historic highway led basically along that of the modern road to Quito we could find little reason to wear ourselves out with unnecessary walking just for the sake of it. Thus we became eligible for any available forms of transportation going. Riobamba was the subsequent destination and one that held a promise of revelations, obscure but intriguing. Was it not around there that the Inca army had displayed its finest hour? Under Ruminavi, the Incas had been fighting to avenge the murder of Atahualpa and with issues no longer obscured by Spanish treachery it had become a simple case of the native armies fighting in defence of their homeland. They had no illusions about the divine status or peaceful intentions of the Spanish soldiers — they recognised them for the ruthless invaders they were. The result was that the Quitan army mounted their determined and heroic resistance climaxed by the Battle of Teocajas.

Marching north from Tumibamba, Benalcazar's men climbed the 14,000-foot pass between Canar and Riobamba to meet Ruminavi's army arrayed for battle on the chill, hail-swept uplands of *ichu* grass, swamps, mountain tarns and lichen-covered boulders saturated by mists and rain. It was over this battle-approach route too that David and I proceeded from Canar ensconsed in the caged buck of a nippy little Ford Custom van, gleaming new, behind a young driver who drove with his countryman's wild abandon.

For a few miles the road was that of the busy Pan-American Highway (now on an inland course) but we were to turn off into a land of spectacular mountain scenery and a road that fitted the environment by lacking both camber and surface. But these conditions offered no excuse for our driver to display the slightest caution or a decrease of speed and, as we skidded round corners and bounced about on a carpet of stones, I became uneasily aware of being locked within a wheeled torpedo. The impact of the larger stones hurled the vehicle bodily into the air and us from one wall of our prison to the other, a condition of travel that afforded little scope for observation of the surroundings.

I did notice, however, that, for much of the way, the winding track of the Guayaquil and Quito railway accompanied us in a kind of gyrating embrace. Its spirals matched our own and one moment it would be on the left side of the van; the next it had swung to the right. Known locally as the 'G and Q', or 'the Good and Quick', it had taken thirty-seven years to build although it is less than 300 miles long. From an altitude of over 9,000 feet at Quito, the tracks rise another 3,000 feet at Urbine and then drop to sea level at the steamy southern port of Guayaquil. The line is a favourite with tourists and is a most interesting example of railway engineering. Its greatest triumphs, the Alausi Loop and the Devil's Nose double zig-zag, lay between Sibambe and Alausi, small towns through which our road likewise led. I was to return to this intriguing stretch of railway on a later occasion*.

Back on a better road at Guamote we glimpsed the shimmering waters of Lake Colta about which considerable quantities of Inca gold and pottery were alleged to have been discovered. And then we were in Cajabamba, another Cajabamba and one that, before destruction by earthquake in 1534, was the original Riobamba. Until a large chunk of the hill above the town collapsed upon the houses below, Riobamba was as prosperous as is the new city some twelve miles to the north-east, and today all that remains is a poor, shoddy little place of ramshackle buildings continuing in decline.

It was nearby that the Battle of Teocajas took place in the month of May, 1534. The greatest pitched battle of the Conquest with 50,000 natives deployed, it was, nevertheless, an indecisive action since the Quitans failed even here to halt Benalcazar's invasion. But neither did the Spaniards succeed in destroying the Inca army in spite of repeated charges with their cavalry against which the defenders had no suitable defence. The stalemate was broken only when, under cover of darkness, the Spaniards outflanked their opponents making a long detour by way of Lake Colta and the then Riobamba back onto the royal road, north of the town.

Night had fallen before we entered the present-day Riobamba,

* See *The Great Railway Adventure* (Oxford Illustrated Press)

a considerable town of more than 75,000 inhabitants, and to our astonished and dust-stinging eyes every one of them seemed to be enthusiastically involved in either a revolution or a replay of the Battle of Teocajas. The street was full of smoke and flame and explosions. Battered but still in one piece ourselves, David and I emerged from our cage to be greeted by joyfully-flung fireworks and casually-wielded flaming torches.

The whole of the central square containing the railway station and bus depot was a seething mass of people, their shouts and laughter occasionally audible between the exploding fire-crackers. On the pavements and overflowing into the streets well-fed bonfires, fuelled by old motor tyres, illuminated the façades of houses and exploded in multiple showers of sparks as fire-works were repeatedly tossed onto the flames. Around each blaze danced, sang, laughed or lay in alcoholic stupor the residents of the district as street parties in varying stages of disintegration ignored a light drizzle and celebrated a nameless fiesta. Through the impeded streets a line of traffic attempted to pass; cars and lorries inching gingerly by each flaming pyre and thwarted by ranks of dancing dervishes galvanised into action by a sudden whim or a tune heard and recognised across a cacophony of explosions. In no mood to join the mêlée we found a flea-pit of a hotel for the night and crawled into bed to the strains of an artil-lery barrage and the sour aroma of burnt rubber.

The cacophony in the morning was of a different calibre. Its source was plainly the railway station but the sound of wheezing steam engines and shunting wagons was music to my ears — though some of the more ecstatic grunts, crashes and whistles were probably exclusive to Ecuadoran Railways. Riobamba is the Swindon of Ecuador and the headquarters of its sparse railway network so the dawn chorus was more in keeping than had been the holocaust of the night.

Usually Riobamba, we were led to believe, is a quiet dignified place; proud of its title 'Sultan of the Andes'. This morning the jubilation of the fiesta had given way to a scene of desolation and the air of a hangover. Riobamba was obviously suffering from a dose of the 'morning after'. The city stands on a flat plateau and has wide streets — now undignified depositories of half-burnt motor tyres — with ageing buildings frowning down upon the debris of debauchery.

The way to Quito led through the valley of the volcanoes and our disappointment arising from the deficiency of mementoes of the royal road was, to some extent, to be mitigated by close proximity to these sizeable peaks. Already in sight — at least on a clear day — were the giants of Sangay, Chimborazo, Carihuairazo, Altar and Tungurahua. Not the highest but certainly the most remote, explosive and dangerous was Sangay which was to occupy our attentions to the exclusion of matters Inca or anything else for a number of days.

With Quito a simple bus ride down the road we felt in need of a climactic accomplishment to our journey and 17,500-foot Sangay's smoking head only 25 direct miles south-east of where we stood offered suitable challenge in spite — or perhaps because of — its unsociable habits.

In all truth our planned attainment of this peak was no sudden whim. The mountain in a semi-permanent state of eruption, had, the previous summer, killed two British climbers and injured several others in a disaster that had made headlines in the British press. One of those injured was Richard Snailham, explorer, author and instructor of political and social studies at the Royal Military Academy, Sandhurst, whom David and I knew quite well. When told of our intentions of passing close to the mountain he had suggested — not too seriously — that we make attempts to reach it. At a lecture we had heard him give at the Royal Geographical Society we learnt of the challenge of Sangay. This is not to be found in the ascent — which is not much more than a few hours uphill grind — but in attaining its base guarded by jungle, swamp and heavy doses of the worst rainfall even Ecuador can produce. *There* lay the challenge though both of us knew in our hearts that, were we to achieve the base, we would be hard put to turn our faces from the summit in spite of the risk of an untimely eruption. The body of one of the dead climbers, Ronald Mace, had never been recovered and to this day lies on the volcano's hostile flank. Without doubt it will now have been concealed beneath a shroud of mud and lava but the idea had come to us that should we find him it would be a fitting act to offer him a decent burial while we were there.

Accordingly we went about our preparations. Two days in Riobamba gave opportunity to meet some of its leading citizens including one, Enrique Veluz Coronado, president of the Climbing Club of Chimborazo, who, from an office draped in maps, cheerfully gave us the benefit of his very considerable knowledge of the terrain. He did not mince matters. 'You'll have one hell of a hike,' he told us and we were to remember his words. The Sangay Expedition of 1976 had based their assault on Macas, reached by a small road to the east. Without transport of our own, however, we decided to make for the tiny village of Santa Rosa, further west, which would reduce the walking distance to the volcano to something like ten miles. This village, too, could be reached by a road of sorts but the snag lay in the formidable highlands between it and the mountain. To go with the road was a bus service 'of sorts' Enrique confirmed with a twinkle in his eye. He plainly knew something that we didn't.

Our second whole day in Riobamba coincided with the weekly fair distributed about the town's nine plazas. A fiesta and a fair within three days. Riobamba was not lacking in energy. But the fair was a more serious commercial undertaking and at one of the many hardware stalls — each plaza representing a different trade — we purchased a couple of serviceable machetes.

The bus we caught next morning was a respectable affair of gleaming chrome and reclining seats. Its destination was Cuenca but our dropping-off point was not many miles out of Riobamba. A side road, grandiosely asphalted to just out of sight around the corner, offered the way to Santa Rosa and thereafter we were very much on an artery of Peruvian mountain status. We carried the minimum of equipment; enough to ensure basic eating, cooking and protection from the fickle weather. Four hours of hard, unfettered walking along a track laced with hefty puddles and a great deal of mud brought us into the mountains again but these slopes were heavily wooded and overgrown with jungle-type foliage. Low-lying and dirty clouds raced overhead with urgent haste but no rain fell.

A boneshaker of a bus appeared when we least expected it, trundling erratically towards us as it attempted to avoid the larger water-filled potholes; the dense undergrowth had muffled the sound of its approach. In fits and starts it carried us the remaining distance to Santa Rosa, its complement of five silent occupants plus the two of us periodically having to disembark to push the vehicle out of the deeper water traps it had failed to negotiate. Severely attired and severely countenanced, our fellow-passengers gazed upon us without the slightest change of expression crossing their work- and weather-lined faces. Neither pleasure, curiosity nor hostility showed and our attempts at communication came to naught. The driver was of the same ilk, ignoring us completely once our fare had been collected. The longest unscheduled halt occurred when our off-side rear wheel worked itself loose and was in danger of coming off. Only as we neared Santa Rosa did the driver become garrulous, demanding an increase in fare for reasons that were beyond our understanding. But he had met his match with David and relapsed into sullen silence when he realised we wouldn't pay.

The track came to an end in a muddy clearing though of Santa Rosa there was no sign. Everyone alighted into the downpour of rain that had been waiting for this very moment and our enquiries concerning the village brought no more than unhelpful shrugs. Maybe Santa Rosa didn't exist, and if not, where were we?

Erecting a tent in driving rain is one of life's drudges I can happily do without but such conditions do encourage speed. Damp and discouraged, we crawled into our bags not even bothering about supper. The dripping trees only added to the unexplained noises of the forest as we attempted sleep.

A stiff helping of porridge — our cure for all ills — and we were away. We beat the rain but only by an hour. Shafts of hail beat diagonally down as we followed a slippery path through obscenely-bloated shrubs, banana trees and bamboo thickets and though the rain had caught up with us it was we who then caught up with its source by climbing high into the grey mist enveloping the hillside. Somewhere ahead rose the steep escarpment we presumed lay between us and Sangay, but, mercifully perhaps, we couldn't see it. Nor did we dare believe that we might now be ascending its flank. The track became narrower and less pronounced and then gave up the ghost altogether leaving us to flounder on, maintaining direction entirely by compass. Much of the vegetation was thick enough to impede progress; not halt it, and, climbing steadily, we expected the growth to thin out with altitude.

Instead it thickened. All afternoon, under a ceaseless downpour, we hacked our way through a tangle of creeper and tendril, our machete blades rising and falling powered by arms that threatened to come loose from their sockets. Soaked to the skin the exercise at least kept us warm and when we finally reached the top of the ridge we had the only slightly less dismal task of hacking our way down the other side.

In every tale of tropical adventure the hero is certain sooner or later to 'cut his way through the forest'. It is a perfect phrase, full-flavoured and romantic, suggesting in half a dozen brief words a picture of indomitable men whirling polished axes in a dim green light, while gigantic trees topple off their roots like corn before the reaper. As a confirmed reader of such tales I had promised myself a glamorous time spitting on my hands and striking lustily about me whilst the bright chips flew; but after the manner of anticipation it was rather different.

The barrier was not solid timber, but a network of parasitic growths that linked the trees in a confused trailing mass that was adhesive and irritating. It was not unlike cutting one's way through a strong elastic spider's web, the strands of which bore an almost unlimited strain, but yielded quickly enough to a knife. Yet this was hardly jungle of Amazonian proportions though near enough as far as we were concerned.

At intervals in the dense mass we came to unaccountable clearings of low bush, where for a while we could sheathe our machetes and push our way through springy branches that lashed out at us and poked us, or rope-weed that grabbed at our ankles. Then the morass would engulf us once more.

The one satisfaction I gained from these frustrating, exhausting days in the semi-jungle was that, unaccountably, I had become the leader. Devoid of Inca lore or relics and in an environment plainly more alien to him than me, David was content to follow my guidance and footsteps, stumbling, sliding and cursing at my heels like an ill-tempered dog. Yet I had very little experience of tropical jungle; only the East African variety which is of a very different texture.

With less confidence than I pretended I directed our footfalls into endless black bogs and swamps through which we waded, sometimes up to our knees. Our rate of progress was the slow-motion step of a man on the moon; not because of the depth of the slime, but because of the gluey mud beneath our boots. Even with the help of a stout stick acting as a third leg it was hellishly hard going.

Dusk found us physically and mentally drained. Even while we raised the tent and prepared a hot supper the night descended; a condition only a degree or two darker than it had been all day. The rain had diminished to a sulky drizzle which permitted the production of a watery stew thickened by improperly-drained rice.

Next morning we returned to the onslaught in a fit of new-found optimism. A night's sleep, a bellyful of stew and oatmeal, and we were ready to break through the foliage belt we told ourselves with a confidence that drained away all too swiftly. And by mid-day we had indeed reached level ground but the water-logged terrain only encouraged the undergrowth to grow thicker and more resilient. Now, with every yard of fresh progress we had to cross a slimy sea into which we sank repeatedly up to our knees. Above and around us a new storm of rain hissed from a sky we were unable to see.

In spite of worsening conditions the going was considerably better than it had been the previous day: the omnipresent mud was not so adhesive and the undergrowth less thick. We became disorientated several times; maintaining a straight line in a jungle and bog is the very devil, and our route became something of a circuitous one, frequently directed by an imagined or actual lightening of a patch of sky seen through the jungle skein ahead. On these occasions our compass would pull us back into line to the accompaniment of a sarcastic comment from David who was better at reading a compass than I.

The afternoon offered a setback. If the bog had become less sticky the undergrowth decided to redress the balance and thicken up again. For hours on end our way led through virgin jungle — there is no other description for it — which had to be physically cut back to enable us to make the slightest headway. The rain continued to pour down but it made little difference since, even when it stopped, the greenery drenched us as we passed by. Every few minutes we collapsed on heaps of rotting vegetation, to catch our breath and to allow tired arms a rest. Both of us were covered in bruises, scratches and insect bites and I was suffering from another bout of diarrhoea. David's teeth were eternally chattering and we began to wonder about the symptoms of pneumonia. Just before our third jungle night we found ourselves amongst another plantation of giant tubers, distant relations of the potato family, called *sachapelma,* but decided to tackle them next morning when we would feel fresher.

Ravenous but unable to get the stove to work we ate most of our supper raw. But sleep and blessed oblivion came all too easily as, wet through, we clung to each other for warmth.

The new day was to become 'The Day of the *Sachapelmas'* — the day when we had to tackle these most evil of plants. By comparison, triffids would have been friendly daisies. Through the curtain of these ten-foot prickly stalks capped by enormous swollen leaves resembling grotesque rhubarb we hacked our way leaving a train of debris in our wake. The one saving grace was that this debris was visible for quite a distance and, while we could see it, we knew we were moving in a straight line. Six hours we took to battle through the plantation and, the deed accomplished, there was still no light at the end of the tunnel.

With every pause for breath I had watched the grey streaks of mist penetrating the stunted trees blotting out any tell-tale signs of sunshine. Sometimes a slight brightening of the murk had me believing the impossible but throughout the day the outline of the foliage merged imperceptibly from black to deep purple but never to a distinguishable colour like green. It was all indescribably depressing and came a moment when we both arrived at the inevitable conclusion that we'd had enough. We were attempting the impossible. Whole expeditions equipped with guides, porters, mules and transport had been used by previous visitors to, and climbers of, Sangay and here we were, the two of us, hopelessly unprepared as usual, trying to do it on our own. We knew, only too well, that Sangay was inaccessible, incendiary and well-nigh inviolate. The mountain, sometimes called 'the flaming terror of the Andes', had, moreover, a well-deserved reputation for being a killer — and we didn't even have such rudimentary apparatus as helmets or anti-fume masks. And *was* it so easy to climb once its base had been reached? At 17,496 feet its Fujiyama-like shape, almost the perfect cone, must surely offer more than an afternoon's slog? The local Indians, Jivaroes of head-shrinking fame, live in dread of it mainly on account of the evil spirits reputed to live in the crater. Our fear lay not so much with the spirits as the volcano's explosive habits. A climber of any of the more traditional volcanoes like Kratatoka, Vesuvius or Etna could count himself extremely lucky if he fell victim to an eruption yet a climber on Sangay should count himself fortunate if he did not. No, maybe the bogs, the rain and the *sachapelmas* were trying to tell us something . . . if so we were listening at last.

And so voicing a variety of excuses we abandoned the fight and squelched our way back towards firmer terrain conscious of the fact that Sangay might well have been just yards away laughing at our amateurish efforts. We finally consoled ourselves with the notion that the Sangay project was no more than a side-show anyway but I have to admit that I would have given much to have even seen the legendary and dangerous mountain from close quarters.

Another jungle night and it was then no more than a case of following our trail of debris back through the tangle leading towards the path to the mystical Santa Rosa. We held little hope of catching another bus to the main road and resigned ourselves to a prolonged hike but, together with a distinct improvement in the weather, our luck started to change. An ancient lorry, loaded with timber, emerged, dodging about the track like a drunken sailor, its cab full of laughing men who invited us to hop up behind. Astride a wet log we returned, thankfully, to Riobamba.

Alas, our preoccupation with volcanoes was not to be concluded so easily. While crossing the main square of the town to re-book into our squalid hotel we met Willi. Willi, I should point out, was a 29-year old Bavarian and a mountaineer of some repute. He'd come all this way, he explained in tones of pure tragedy, to climb Chimborazo and could find nobody who would accompany him to the summit of the 21,000-foot volcano. Had it been the Alps it would have been a different matter; certain safety measures could be taken and there were services that could be relied upon to safeguard a lone climber. But here in the Andes... Willi's hands traced a pattern of hopelessness and despair. He looked at us anticipatingly, but more at David than me.

'No way...' I began with feeling but then I noticed that my partner was not at all adverse to the idea. That David was out for a climax to our journey I could understand but a 21,000-foot mountain — 3,500 feet higher than Sangay — seemed to be stretching the point a little.

To entangle us deeper into both his web and his debt Willi invited us to share his Riobamba accommodation. This was no more than the bare floor of a rat-infested office he had managed to borrow for the night but it was no worse than our hotel room and, more to the point, saved a hotel bill. David and I discussed the matter at length that evening while recuperating from our ordeal. Willi had discretely withdrawn. 'Of course, at *your* age I can't blame you for wanting to opt out,' came David's cruel reply following my repeated expressions of disapproval — and at once I capitulated. Uneasily I cast my vote with the majority — even if only to prove there was life in the old dog yet...

Attempting to console myself in the knowledge that Chimborazo was at least a *dormant* volcano and that, from its flank or peak, we should see Sangay I allowed myself to be fitted out with the *de rigueur* equipment of mountain climbing. Enrique Velez again became our adviser and provided the fiendish tools of ice-axes, crampons, rope and goggles pronounced necessary for scaling heights. But I defeated him when it came to the loan of the proper footwear, my size eleven feet obstinately refusing to cram into any boot of his stock. His largest crampons, however, appeared to nestle snugly beneath my canvas-topped jungle boots and this settled the matter. Enrique then proceeded to frighten the life out of me by declaring in all seriousness that, because of the equatorial bulge, the summit was the point on the world's surface furthest from the centre of the earth and that only experienced mountaineers should attempt the ascent. 'We *were* all competent climbers of course?' he asked and my utterances to the contrary were painfully kicked into silence by my companions.

Loaded down with additional gear we set out by bus in the morning for Ambato, a step further along the valley of the volcanoes and, happily, another step nearer Quito. Suddenly the capital of Ecuador and the chief goal of the journey seemed a desirable place to be.

Ambato is described as the Indian version of The Garden of Eden and, though I wouldn't put it quite like that, it does manage a certain grace. Much was destroyed in the 1949 earthquake but it has risen again to become the sixth largest city in the country. This is where, during the first battle of the civil war in Inca times — when Atahualpa routed the Southerners — he took terrible vengeance, ordering his commanders to kill most of the town's male citizens even though they had come to surrender. Such atrocities as this help to explain the numerous defections by the native tribes to the side of the Spanish conquerors. For me, my mind on more prosaic matters, Ambato was the town closest to Chimborazo, spawning a bus service that led past the base of the mountain. In the plaza we alighted from our Riobamba bus amongst a squad of lady labourers wielding pick-axes with the aplomb of men.

If I have to be labelled anything I am a walker, a trekker, a cautious scrambler but decidedly not a climber. My feet are for the more or less perpendicular terrain of this earth; not the vertical. In North Africa I pushed myself up 14,000-foot Toubkel because it was there when I was. In East Africa I lived for a miserable week on the snow-bound slopes of Mount Kenya at 17,000 feet looking for the source of a river. In the Himalayas the only way out of a defile I'd got myself into was over an 18,000-foot pass. But these were scramblers' ascents, the sort of thing a trekker has to take in his stride. Now I was being confronted with Chimborazo, one of the highest peaks in South America.

In the Indian language the name means 'Mountain of Snow' and even Alexander von Humbolt failed to reach the summit in 1802 when it was thought to be the highest mountain in the world. Chimborazo was finally conquered by Edward Whymper in 1880 and today it is climbed fairly frequently — though not, I declare, by many 53-year olds in gym shoes.

Humbolt was not the only famed climber who was beaten by the mountain; one Joseph Dieudonné Boussingault made a second attempt that also failed. With two companions, Humbolt reached a height of 19,290 feet before an impassable ravine halted the trio in their tracks. The ravine was alleged to be 400 feet deep and 60 feet wide and accounts of the climb contain such entries as 'there was no means of getting round the cleft . . . the softness of the snowy mass prohibited such an attempt . . .' and, worst of all, 'the mountaineers . . . suffered nausea, giddiness and blood exuded from their lips and gums.'

Boussingault's effort, in 1831, failed equally spectacularly. His party suffered similar torments to Humbolt's 'extreme fatigue from the want of consistency in the snowy soil, which gave way continually under our feet, and in which we sank sometimes up to our waists. We were convinced of the impossibility of proceeding.' On their second attempt they exceeded the height reached by Humbolt by a few hundred feet — but it was not until 1880 that Whymper and his two Swiss guides finally conquered Chimborazo.

Almost as though there had been a scheduled connection we caught a local bus that purported to pass by the village of Pogyo, the closest point by the road to Chimborazo. The road is the one to Guaranda and, for those who want to follow my footsteps, the distance from Ambato police station to Pogyo (sometimes called Poggios to confuse the issue still further) is exactly 50 kilometres. The route to the base of the great volcano is spectacular in the extreme, replete with raging torrents surging under open-sided bridges over which the bus speeds with inches to spare. Having missed the five straw huts that we didn't realise *was* Pogyo, we were finally dropped at a village some distance ahead. Alighting from the vehicle, Chimborazo, hiding its head, looked deceptively close.

Our fellow passengers had added to my unease by loudly proclaiming that we were attempting to climb the mountain at positively the wrong time of year. They said we'd get lost in the fog and looking at the ugly cloud that smothered the peak I could well see their point. Already Enrique had stressed the vital importance of reaching the one and only refuge hut at 16,000 feet by nightfall and his warning took on a more ominous ring with the excited declarations from our companions that failure to reach it in time spelt certain death from exposure. A group of moustachioed men graphically slid the flat of their hands across their throats in a cheerless message of farewell.

But Enrique had tempered his warnings with more comforting facts. From Pogyo to the hut was but a three-hour walk, he'd said, and a trail led to the top of a knoll from which a compass sighting of 120 degrees would indicate the *refugio.* The trail was subsequently supposed to become easier to locate across more ridges and a broad plain of volcanic debris before climbing steeply again to the glacier-filled valley at the head of which the all-important hut was situated. Fine, but we were not at Pogyo.

However, lo and behold, a faint trail led up the side of an embankment and seemingly in the right direction. Arms of lava soil, cheerful with gaunt springy thickets and vivid splashes of alpine flowers, pushed down to meet us before the track disappeared into a confusion of volcanic rocks and scree made the more treacherous by isolated patches of snow. It was cold and the cold increased as we toiled uneasily upwards, Willi repeatedly referring to his compass. For a time the way ahead was clear but, around mid-afternoon, the grey cloud descended to obliterate everything in an icy embrace, being pushed steadily across the face of the mountain by a rising wind. The realization struck home that we were lost so we fanned out like beaters at a partridge shoot attempting to locate a non-existent track or, better still, an elusive cabin through the occasional and momentary breaks in the mist. Our shouts echoed dismally; dismembered voices not of triumph or fear but simply attempting to maintain contact.

Willi's altitude meter told us that we were at 17,000 feet; too high above the level of the refuge so our eyes began to search the murk below. My breath was turning to agonising pants and my movements were limited to bursts of a dozen or so footsteps that were accomplished only with every ounce of strength I possessed. David too was surprisingly distressed having not yet found his second wind but Willi, born and bred in the Bavarian Alps, was hopping about like a mountain goat.

Above us a local peak emerged from the mist and, perhaps because it was the only ground visible in the clear light of day, we made for it, climbing and scrambling in our different manners but with a certain universal sense of desperation.

My feet were already cold; my socks saturated. Underfoot the ground was solid snow and ice hiding sharp lava rock underneath. One minute all was grey nothing; the next the cloud had parted and through the rent appeared a wondrous sight.

Far below, the valley of the volcanoes was hidden by the grey blanket through which we had pushed our way. Protruding from it were the peaks of other volcanoes and mountains. Directly to the south east was 16,000-foot Altar and, behind, less distinct but recognizable, was a cone that could only have been Sangay. Their snow-capped crowns were tinted an amazing blood-red which turned deeper with every second as the sunset matured and faded. The spectacle had me dumbfounded and eclipsed for a few moments the dread that was welling within me.

With the dying of the sun came a terrible cold and hastily we scrabbled to a lip of level rock clear of snow. Here we held council, consumed some food and wriggled, fully dressed and booted, into our sleeping bags to prepare for our onward transition to the 'Great Beyond'. 'It's absolutely imperative you reach the hut by nightfall,' I remembered, and saw again the throat-cutting motion of the bus passengers. Childhood recollections of Captain Oates going out into the arctic blizzard to die assailed me and I began searching for a piece of paper on which to scribble my last will and testament, unable to remember whether I had made out a will at home. 'Get in close. Hug together like bears,' commanded Willi. 'We must generate all the warmth we can.' The German was firmly in control and I, for one, had no objections. He was the expert at this game and had got us into this situation. Now it was up to him to get us out or at least ensure our demise was as painless as possible. I snuggled close to the others, trying not to think about wet boots and socks and death. Above, the myriad stars made a heavenly ceiling and I felt no real cold. All in all it seemed not a bad way to go.

I awoke with a bursting bladder and what appeared to be a fever. For a fraction of a second I thought I'd arrived at the wrong place. I wriggled from the cocoon of bodies and straightway felt the biting wind. But what startled me most was that I was sweating like a pig. My movement had woken the others and gradually we all inched away to lessen the heat our combined bodies had generated. It was only the agony of a distended bladder that held me awake until dawn.

Daylight showed the *refugio* beneath us. Blue sky above, white mountain flank below and the wooden octagonal structure we had been searching for was painted brilliant orange and stood out like a sore thumb. We rose rather sheepishly and I don't think I was the only one who surreptitiously screwed up and disposed of a piece of paper.

Thereafter things went more or less according to plan. We spent the new day between bouts of cooking and eating in the filthy little refuge which we cleaned out as best we could. Around it was a mess of discarded tins and food wrappers going back to about the time of Edward Whymper. The name of the hut was 'Fabian Zurita' and, whoever he was, I wished he'd come and clean his place up. I am told that a second refuge cabin has since been constructed.

Chimborazo is a mountain that tests the physical stamina rather than the technical ability of the climber. There are three main obstacles to its ascent: one geological, one geographical, and one psychological.

The first difficulty is to locate a breach in a 500-foot wall of sheer rock barring the path to the twin summits. This great rampart, known as the 'Red Walls', arises with startling grandeur at a height of 18,700 feet. Above it, a further 300 feet of snow and ice weld together into a slippery collar studded by a vast portcullis of 100-foot icicles. It was this obstacle that finally beat Boussingault.

But this is not all. Above this hazard there arises the second obstacle – a huge crevasse that extends for hundreds of yards at the 20,000-foot mark. It proved too daunting for a number of early climbing expeditions; one of them led by the German scientist Hans Meyer.

The third pitfall is that occasioned by human limits of endurance and the appalling strain of having to battle for considerable distances through soft snow – and this without oxygen and at altitudes approaching 22,000 feet.

By the grace of God I was not aware of these hazards that lay in wait; nor, I think, was Willi. That or else he prudently kept quiet about them. Had we known I don't think any of us would have raised the nerve to challenge such a formidable range of deterrents.

To attain the summit and return to the refuge before nightfall it was necessary to set out by three o'clock in the morning. We returned to our sleeping bags with the coming of darkness and spent a sleepless night warding off the friendly mountain rats who emerged from the floorboards to investigate their visitors, sample the wares in their 'larder' and nibble their hair and ears. Willi, in true Teutonic fashion, murdered a couple with his ice-axe as an example to the others but it did little good. I am usually a reliable alarm clock when it comes to an early rising but, in this instance, I was prepared to let things slide. It was therefore Willi who chivvied us out of bed at one o'clock. We laboriously melted some snow to make tea and donned strange items of apparel before setting off at three. Outside was pitch darkness but the wind was low and the cold, therefore, not so painful. Our early breakfast of stale rat-nibbled rolls and packet soup had not been appetizing but Willi, exerting his mountaineering authority once more, forced us to get it down. 'Food is warmth and it'll give you strength,' he intoned.

Though the dawn was nowhere to be seen a feeble moon lit up the snow to dilute the darkness. We made slow progress up steep escarpments of lava rock and across black scree frozen solid in a cement of ice. Ten paces. Stop. Ten paces. Stop. It was the best I could do. Every now and again I retched, my head between my knees. We rested at ever more frequent intervals in spite of the cold that crept through our layers of clothing. Willi and David, with youth on their side, always remained ahead of me so that their halts commenced before I could reach them, a state of affairs which coaxed me into paroxysms of effort to catch up and so obtain my full entitlement of rest. Two steps up. One slip back. Stop. Ten paces. Stop.

We reached the glacier at 17,500 feet and clumsily affixed our crampons. I had never worn such implements before but found them no problem beyond the fact that they repeatedly parted company with my soft boots to slide impishly down the glacier with me limping and cursing in hot pursuit. The corrugated ice surface cracked and groaned ominously putting the fear of God into me. Willi tried to be reassuring. 'It's safe I'm sure,' he observed. 'Bending ice is safe ice,' a rejoinder that might have been encouraging for an afternoon's skating on the village pond.

I never thought I would get off that glacier. Even Willi showed signs of exhaustion as we stepped onto soft snow into which my boots sank to dislodge my crampons the faster. Dawn had broken and we had not even noticed it. The wind rose to cut through our layers of long-johns, multiple socks and gauntlets and through our goggles we perceived a grey world instead of a black one. My hair and beard had turned me into a caricature of Jack Frost.

Beneath the overhang of cliffs that were the 'Red Walls' we ate some biscuits and chocolate. The cold was so great it had even me rearing to go. We circled the base of the great bulwark with long icicle daggers pointing down on our heads and swung once more upwards. The soft snow turned to hard snow hiding deep gashes of ice. Willi unslung his nylon rope and attached it to the three of us. This is where I really let the side down I thought but, heavy slog though it was, I had found my second — or was it third — wind and made reasonable progress behind David.

The breach in the walls was easier to find than expected. Fortunately I was not to know that Edward Whymper had written into his report the warning, 'Thus far and no farther a man may go who is not a mountaineer'. In my blissful ignorance I was about to become a trespasser into the realm of the elite few as we started up the steep slope of frozen snow punctuated by outcrops of slippery, ice-coated rock. We progressed slowly partly on account of the necessity for extreme caution on the climb up and out of the 'Red Walls', and also because the laggard at the end of the rope could move no faster even had all the hounds of hell been snapping at his ankles.

The nausea that had slowed my footsteps on the glacier returned with a vengeance. This time it was more than exhaustion. I had been sick earlier but now the malady had me by the throat causing me to retch uncontrollably and bringing me to a halt every few seconds. Yet the symptoms were not those described by Sebastian Snow who attained Chimborazo's summit, together with an Ecuadoran, in more recent years. He called it *soroche;* it had them shivering from head to foot and very nearly defeated both of them. With me, as long as I could rest frequently, I was able to continue. But, as it is with all climbers of this mountain, we were working against the clock and the time-bomb that would end our lives if darkness overtook us was ticking away remorselessly. And certainly we would not survive a second night on a bare mountain above 20,000 feet.

It was this knowledge that pushed me to the limits of my endurance. That and not wanting to be a drag on the others. I even managed to keep pace with them — much to David's surprise — for, at times, I had the uncharitable feeling that he was utilising my slow rate of climb to hide his own stupefying exhaustion. The broken ice steps led to a steep incline of virgin white stretching away towards the open sky.

The gradient steepened as we scrambled, staggered, shuffled towards its crest, our heels and toe-caps kicking for holds. Twice I was hauled bodily forward by Willi as he found a ledge from which he could turn and encourage his hopelessly inadequate charges. All feeling had left my hands and feet, and movement became no more than a mechanical reaction to each new set of circumstances and obstacles. I think if Willi had designated a jump into oblivion I would have obediently leaped without a thought of the consequences.

Willi's altimeter recorded an altitude of 19,650 feet but the revelation meant nothing to me. My brain simply refused to function. Only my eyes saw — but failed to convey to my mind — the great crevasse that appeared ahead to bar the way.

We approached with extreme caution and, keeping away from

the treacherous edge, tried to gauge its depth for ourselves. It certainly was in excess of fifty feet in width but the depth of this snow and ice ravine was anybody's guess. Working our way along the fissure we discovered to our joy that it narrowed and before many yards had become no more than a crack a few feet wide — but still of unimaginable depth. Why earlier champions of the peak had not come upon this narrowing process we shall never know. Maybe some volcanic action over the years had closed the gap?

Willi selected a spot that he considered a satisfactory crossing point and, thrusting his ice-axe into the snow, inched away on the anchored rope to as close to the rim as he dared. Satisfied that the gap was leapable even if he had to trust to providence that the landing point would hold he turned to us and nodded. 'Let's go,' he shouted in a voice that seemed to lack conviction. He regained his ice-axe while David and I played out a few more yards of rope.

Gingerly Willi stole to the very edge of the crevasse knowing he was treading upon the forbidden path of an overhang which might crumble into powder any moment. Bunching himself, he leapt.

He landed safely with a foot to spare. The rope tautened, pulling him backwards towards the lip and feverishly we played out more to allow him to scramble away. He turned again to give a 'thumbs up' signal and then it was our turn.

David, utilising Willi's footprints, repeated the German's every movement and without a second's hesitation jumped and landed easily on the other side. He scrambled to Willi's side.

My turn. I too put every effort into undertaking a carbon copy of my two companions' actions while inwardly blessing the good Lord for having favoured me with a good long-jumping record at my school forty years before. Then I too hurled myself towards the opposite overhang, landed clumsily and started to fall back. The rope tautened, bit into my flesh and I was hauled forward to safety. We were across and we were alive.

The snow grew softer, deeper and whiter. Chimborazo's southern summit — the Whymper summit as it is sometimes called — was only a snow-slog of a few hundred yards away. We forged on, each footfall involving a struggle to remove a leg from two feet of clinging snow, a determination driving us forward and raising reserves of energy I thought no human frame could muster.

Attaining the top of the ridge a wind of intense ferocity rose to sear the flesh of the exposed portions of our faces. Frozen flecks of snow stung my ears and the bitter cold numbed my limbs that were inadequately covered. The snow grew deeper, as our struggle to free our legs got more difficult. Maybe the efforts of combating the trapping of our feet served to hold the cold at bay before it could overwhelm and paralyse us. I don't know. All that my mind would register was the necessity to conquer the mountain even though it was proving to be a hell on earth. Nothing else — nothing at all — mattered. Life itself had suddenly become subservient to the one aim of putting myself on that summit. Never before had I experienced such strength of purpose for so small a reason and I hope I shall never again for it is a kind of madness; a spasm of insanity that turns the famed champions of geography into an elite of men.

At any rate the spasm took me to the southern summit in company with my two colleagues. Less than fifty yards separated us from the western peak; the true summit of Chimborazo. Time was inexorably ticking away but all rational thought had been cast aside.

We made for the final ridge in a line abreast of each other, still roped together but no longer working as a team. The snow rose to our thighs; sometimes to our waists so that, at times, we were crawling, lying flat on the snow and paddling; anything to avoid having to make a downward thrust on a leg that would only be trapped in a freezing cast. The wind rose to a shrieking crescendo, alternately howling and moaning; a kind of maniacal laughing at our dying threshings in the snow.

I have never used an ice-axe before or since but the one I wielded inexpertly that day on Chimborazo — reaching out to sink the blade into virgin snow banks and hauling myself bodily forward towards it — taught me a new method of motivation. Gradually, painfully it narrowed the gap until Willi, David and I merged together in a struggling mass, abruptly joining the wind in mad laughter that was now a song of triumph. Unable to stand on the peak I could only sit on it.

Sanity returned and Willi estimated that our endeavours had been carried out in only a little more time than the Chimborazo climbing manual allows; eight hours from 'Fabian Zurita'. But there was no time to spare if we were to return to it in one piece.

The way down to the base of the 'Red Walls' made an anti-climax; to me the happiest non-event of our Andean journeyings. Willi brought his disciplinary measures to bear and bade us exercise the greatest care on the downward course which involved less effort but was the more dangerous. Still roped, we returned across the great crevasse and beyond, David and I slavishly using Willi's prints to avoid other deep cracks which may have lain in wait for us, their danger hidden by snow.

Atop the 'Red Walls' the sun shone brilliantly to give the whole landscape a Christmas card effect. It cheered me up no end. Every twelfth step or so one of my crampons would remain behind under the snow from where it had to be retrieved and refastened until there came a point when I gave up and slung them both round my neck.

Cloud obscured the view below, as it had from the summit, and I did not like the look of the wisps of mist rising from the base of the mountain. I was eager to return to less spectacular altitudes, preferably around sea-level. The moment of triumph had receded leaving in its wake the confirmed conviction that mountaineering is not for me under any circumstances whatever.

Faster than we came up we came down. In the refuge hut we cooked a substantial dinner but fell asleep waiting for it to boil. If the friendly rats paraded upon our prostrate forms we neither felt them or cared. We slept the sleep of the dead men we were supposed to have been and, in the morning, we came down off the mountain.

Our return to Ambato was hastened by the lucky intervention of a lorry. In the back was a load of chaff, a pig and ten humans. The chaff got into my eyes, the pig was sick over my boots and, along with the rest of the humans, I lay on the floor to avoid being seen at the police checkpoint in the suburbs of the city.

There is, apparently, an Ambato bye-law forbidding lifts on lorries.

Next day we completed the odyssey to Quito within the confines of a luxury coach. It seemed a mite incongruous. Above us, lost in cloud, were the peaks of Catopaxi and Tungurahua but I'd had my fill of volcanoes. The road was assuredly that of the route of the royal road but it lay under tarmac and was now called the Pan-American Highway. Only Incain ghosts might have noticed our inconspicuous entry into Quito – but I doubt it.

9

QUITO–IBARRA–SAN LORENZO –POPAYAN–CALI–BOGOTA

Quito, assuredly, is the most pleasant of all the Andean capitals. Few cities in the world have a setting to match its three-mile high situation encircled by mountains that are higher still, the nearest peak being that of the slumbering, 15,700-foot Pichincha. For rain-swept Ecuador, the climate is rapturous; akin to that of an English spring.

Never in any town can there have been such noisy church bells. Not even in Cuzco. They began at five in the morning, their clatter slowly building up to a crescendo around seven though their call to prayer mostly went unheeded. It was as if the good citizens of Quito were deaf — as indeed they well might have been after a lifetime of bells tolling in their ears.

The main plaza of the city is a less pronounced centre than is the one in Cuzco — my mind had fastened upon the notion of comparing the cities at each end of the royal road — but is more pleasing to the eye. From one viewpoint I could drink in the vision of the cathedral with its arcades, the square laid out with flower beds and clipped trees, and many tiled domes and campaniles rich in the promise of their golden interiors. There would seem at a glance to be as many churches as there are in Salzburg; and this at nearly ten thousand feet and only a dozen or so miles south of the equator.

Quito has a more ecclesiastical character than Cuzco and this not only because of its profusion of churches. Except for its exterior there is little either of the Incas or the conquistadores to be seen, even though it was the northern Inca capital. Instead much of the Jesuit, the Franciscan, and the Dominican exudes from the grandiose interiors of its edifices.

But of Inca involvement in the Ecuadoran capital's growth there is no doubt. Although Quito and its environs were not fully part of that empire until 1492, the Incas constructed their usual urban centres — which were far in advance of anything Europe was doing at the same date. It was in full operation and 'beautifully wrought' even within fifty years of its Inca conquest.

Modern Quito extends northward into a luxuriant plain; it has wide avenues, parks, embassies and villas of elegant proportions. But the city's charm lies in the old section where its cobbled streets are deep and winding. Its heart is the Plaza Independencia, dominated by a cathedral of grey stone porticos and green tile cupolas. The government palace is a severe colonial structure made a little less gaunt by palace guards in fairy-tale uniforms.

Quito, of course, is an Inca city if refounded by Sebastián de Benalcázar in 1534 so that the architectural talents of both civilisations have, across the years, contributed to the magnificence of this, the third highest capital on earth (the second is Lhasa). Of the two small Spanish armies that advanced northwards to take this prize of conquest it was Benalcázar's force who finally entered the city, beating his rival Alvarado and his men. Another army that advanced upon Quito, of course, was the Inca force of Quisquis nearing the end of their year-long withdrawal from Cuzco and now retreating from its recent chosen battleground of Teocajas. Had Quisquis arrived earlier and established contact with Ruminavi and his Quito defenders the former's defeat could still have ended in an Inca triumph with the Spanish invasion forestalled at the gates of the capital. As it was, his men, weary and disheartened, mutinied, disposed of their leader and dispersed to their homes. A determined counter-attack by Ruminavi's army nearly succeeded but was eventually repulsed by the city's new occupiers and his soldiers forced to flee again. In ruins, its treasure carried away by the withdrawing Inca, Quito became irrefutably Spanish.

The Spanish chronicler, Cieza de Leon, passed through the city fifteen years after its conquest and his description of the region remains today as good as any:

> 'Quito is under the equinoctial line, indeed only seven leagues distant from it. The surrounding country appears to be sterile, but in reality is very fertile, and all kinds of cattle are bred on

it plentifully, besides other provisions, corn and pulse, fruit and birds. The country is very pleasant, and particularly resembles Spain in its pastures and climate, for the summer begins in April, and lasts until November, and, though it is cold, the land is no more injured by it than in Spain...

'In the plains they reap a great quantity of wheat and barley, so that there is a plentiful supply of provisions in the province, and in time it will yield all the fruits of our Spain, for even now they begin to grow some of them. The natives are in general more gentle and better disposed, and have fewer vices than any of those we have passed, and indeed than all Indians of the greater part of Peru... They are a people of middle height, and very hard workers. They live in the same way as the people of the Kings Yncas, except that they are not so clever, seeing that they were conquered by them, and now live by the rules which were ordered to be observed by the Yncas. For in ancient times they were, like their neighbours, badly dressed and without industry in the erection of buildings'.

The Spanish conquistadores initially were not very satisfied with their prize for Quito had been systematically evacuated and burnt. Ruminavi had removed all the treasure and a reputed four thousand women. But later settlers found the region to be not without advantages. The Kingdom of Quito never rivalled central and southern Peru as a fount of silver and gold; but it was prosperous and productive and clearly, in Spanish eyes as de León makes clear, a pleasant place to live.

David and I, based upon the Hotel Grand Casino — another misnomer if there ever was one — spent nearly a week in the Ecuadoran capital finding plenty to do and see in the city's mixture of streets. From its history-minded citizens as well as its museums and libraries we learnt of the final years of the Inca civilisation; how, after their swift defeat by the Spaniards, they waged a guerrilla war for more than thirty-five years, right up to the death of the last Lord-Inca, Tupac Amaru. Speedily they had learnt to defend themselves against canon, mastered the art of using captured firearms, and gained the ability to ride and control horses. Operating out of their new capital, Vilcapamba, they made their presence felt in no uncertain manner.

As a one-time soldier myself I was interested in the manner of the Incas' undoubted ability to wage war. Until the Spaniards arrived no force in the Andes could stem the tide of their advance to conquer. By all accounts the violence of their onslaught was awesome. Following the defeat of the opposition there was wholesale slaughter on the field of battle and then a ceremonial slaughter later. Inca warriors were decorated — not by medals but by paint — and their captive foes, if any remained alive, were taken to be humiliated before the sun temples. Heads were removed from the more ferocious of the enemy and made into drinking cups or, alternatively, their bodies were stuffed and turned into caricatures; sometimes their stomachs were made into drums which were beaten prior to subsequent battle. Their own conquest by an equally ferocious invader must have been a considerable shock.

Quito, as a city, has benefitted from capture by the Spaniards, for unlike Lima, (already in existence before they came), it blossomed into the fine capital it has become under Spanish influence. Shortly after his capture of it Sebastian de Benalcazar, in the presence of his soldiers and 206 of the remaining inhabitants, set up a municipal council and declared it open for the business of reconstruction. He planned Quito as a typical Spanish city with streets running north and south, east and west from the central square as they do today.

Though the goal of our project, Quito was not our final destination. This lay far to the north — the city of Bogota, capital of neighbouring Colombia — from where we would be flying home some eighteen days hence. We were aware that, for some of the way, we should be following the direction of the royal road extension into Colombia but, whilst the fact offered satisfaction, we had no serious notions of investigating it. Instead we intended travelling gently northward indulging ourselves in what pleasures and places of interest materialised. But we had reckoned without an incident in Quito's sophisticated Amazonas Street on our last day in the city.

In short I was robbed. It was one of those cleverly-organised pick-pocketing operations wherein one villain occupies your attention and, from the cover of a jostling crowd, the finger man — or 'dip' — lifts your wallet. The dipping in this instance took place on a crowded bus. I should have known better, of course, for I have been the mug in similar goings-on in Kabul and the middle of the Baluchistan Desert. My passport and the remainder of our travel cheques reposed sweatily against my tummy, but my aeroplane ticket, credit cards and all our combined currencies were in my buttoned jacket pocket.

I knew my wallet had flown very few seconds after it had been lifted and, together, David and I made ourselves very unpopular indeed by yelling to the driver to stop, denying exit to all those wishing to alight and dragging aboard a reluctant policeman on point duty who felt impelled to line everyone up against the bus sides to be searched with their hands over their heads. Meanwhile the two villains, who had escaped before the hullabaloo, simply melted into the horrifying traffic pandemonium resulting from the now uncontrolled intersection.

It was all a waste of effort, of course, and alone once more, we totted up our surviving wealth. Bogota was a thousand miles away and, because our homeward flight booking had already been fixed, we had eighteen days still to kill. Between us we had less than a dollar a day to maintain our existence — and Colombia was going to be more expensive than Ecuador.

I suppose we could have gone to the British Embassy and thrown ourselves at the feet of the second secretary or whatever broke travellers do in such circumstances. But a kind of pride kept us from this course of action. After all we had *some* money — enough for basic fodder — and wasn't there a challenge here?

The first thing to do was to get out of Quito. Capitals are expensive luxuries. Hotel accommodation of any description was going to be out for the next fortnight and more, yet there was no hurry to reach Colombian territory since not only were prices higher there, but the country had an unsavoury reputation for violence against back-packing visitors with time on their hands.

Initially it was ENFE, the Ecuadoran Railway, that came to the rescue, providing free transportation following representations I made to their public relations department in their modest Quito offices. Wasn't I, as a travel writer and journalist from

Ingleterra, in a unique position to tell the world of the efficiency and technical achievements of the Ecuadoran railway system? the PRO looked at me in some surprise, uncertain as to whether I was pulling his leg, but fortunately finally deciding I wasn't. He then issued us with two first-class seat passes valid between the capital and San Lorenzo on the coast. We thanked him profusely and asked for the latest edition of the timetable, trying not to bat an eyelid when we noticed its date as 1923.

The one drawback to utilising trains for our continuing journey was that only as far as Ibarra, no more than fifty miles ahead, did the tracks lead to where we wanted to go. Thereafter they swung north-west, almost paralleling the Colombian border, to end up at the Pacific. But the seaside seemed a sensible place for two down-and-outs to idle away a few days. With warm balmy nights and soft sand beaches who needed expensive items like hotels?

We felt the wrench of leaving Quito as we waited at its miniscule station for our train. I, for one, had fallen under the spell of this city of hills from whence you can look down upon an array of churches, each one more beautiful than the next. Nor are they drowned in a sea of concrete as they are in the next capital we were to see. Here in Quito they still raise their heads knowingly above everything transitory.

And the air that blows down is fresh and exhilarating from the mountains. Quito is famous for its ozone, for even though virtually astride the equator one is 8,000 feet above the heat and so living in a perpetual spring. This is a city where contemplative men should settle — a city where communication with the earth has not yet been lost through contact with asphalt. More than any capital I know it belongs to its people.

The train that bore us away was a little one-class railcar, nippy but noisy. The *South American Handbook* points out that the rail journey to Ibarra takes over twice as long as does the road journey and 'cannot be recommended for comfort or scenic beauty'. With time on our hands the slowness of the train mattered not at all and since the road too ran through some of the driest, dustiest, most barren land in the Ecuadoran Andes before attaining the rich irrigated farmlands beyond, the choice was marginal. There was a brief stop at Cayambe and we debated the notion of making an excursion to see the Inca ruins of Rumicucho at San Antonio but this was a two-hour drive from Cayambe and an impractical proposition for two destitute gringoes. However the more localised attractions of Otavalo pulled us off the train.

Once away from the undeniable pull of Quito my heart felt the lighter. Whatever happened next I was going to enjoy the onward journey. No longer were we tied to a fixed route or bound by a course of action with but a single purpose. Our mission was behind us. Quito had been part of that mission. Now we had escaped and if fate had intervened to complicate the last section of our journey then I, for one, had few qualms.

David was not able to share my optimism. For him the mission had not been the unqualified success he had wished it to be. Large stretches of the royal road had remained concealed from his eyes and, from the agonizing viewpoint of hindsight, he perceived the actions we should have taken but didn't. Not even his conquest of Chimborazo would compensate. Now came the uncertainties of a different sort of survival game.

For the first time in months I found myself in command of our destiny. It was I making the suggestions, planning our movements and leading our execution of them. The transition was not immediate nor total and it graduated to a situation of equality that I had never experienced with David before. Suddenly the disparity of our ages and temperaments mattered not at all. Our relationship had at last found a tranquility that not even the abrasive Andes had been able to conjure.

In Quito they had said that it would be a great mistake to miss the markets in Otavalo. We could hardly afford to buy anything but at least they would enable us to go 'window'-shopping. The Indians of Otavalo are unique. Their skin is lighter than that of their brothers and they are far more conscientious; a double factor that gave the region a serene atmosphere, almost tangible, from the moment of our arrival. Here the youngsters run after you in the streets not to show contempt or lewd curiosity but for the mere pleasure of being able to talk to a foreigner. Even the smallest children waddle out of doors of white thatched houses to lisp 'Dónde va?'.

Inside, the father sits at an ancient loom and the mother keeps her spinning wheel turning to prevent the strands from slipping, while the little girl on the floor nibbles a sugar cane. You will find here the finest homespuns with English patterns from designs brought back by their richer countrymen who have been to Europe.

The Indians from Otavalo, however, produce the noblest cloths for themselves, weaving the thick meshes by hand. The blue poncho worn on Sunday to market is three times as heavy as is the loom cloth and in his dark overmantle the head of the family looks like a great Lord-Inca. His wife however is less impressively-attired, at least to European eyes. She wears a hat with a broad curling brim below which a bright-coloured kerchief hangs down over the shoulders.

Our pleasure at finding ourselves in such serene and friendly countryside had obviously been shared by those who had gone before. On the subject, Cieza de Leon's chronicles made interesting reading.

> 'There are many warm valleys where fruit trees and pulses are cultivated all the year round. There are also vineyards in these valleys, but as the cultivation has only lately commenced, I can only mention the hope that they will yield; but they already have large orange and lime trees. The pulses of Spain yield abundantly, and all other provisions may be had that man requires. There is also a kind of spice, which we call cinnamon, brought from the forests to the eastward. It is a fruit, or kind of flower, which grows on the very large cinnamon trees, and there is nothing in Spain that can be compared to it, unless it be an acorn, but it is of a reddish colour inclined to black and much larger and rounder. The taste is very pleasant, like that of real cinnamon, and it is only eaten after it has been pounded, for, if it is stewed like real cinnamon, it loses the strength of its flavour. It makes a warm cordial, as I can affirm from experience, for the natives trade with it, and use it in their illnesses, particularly for pains in the bowels and stomach. They take it as a drink.
>
> They have great store of cotton, which they make into cloth

for their dresses, and also for paying tribute. In the neighbourhood of the city of Quito there are many flocks of what we call sheep, but they are more like camels . . . of provisions, besides maize, there are two other products which form the principal food of these Indians. One is called potato, and is a kind of earth nut, which, after it has been boiled, is as tender as a cooked chestnut, but it has no more skin than a truffle, and it grows under the earth in the same way. This root produces a plant exactly like a poppy. The other food is very good, and is called *guinea.* The leaf is like a moorish rush (amaranth?) and the plant grows almost to the height of a man, forming a very small seed, sometimes white and at others reddish. Of these seeds they make a drink, and also eat them cooked, as we do rice.'

There being only one train a day between Quito and Ibarra we spent the night in Otavalo though aware that we could have probably obtained a lift to Ibarra which was only some ten miles distant. But what held us in the colourful little market town was the invitation to stay by a family. Their adobe house was simple in the extreme as was the bean-stew they insisted upon us sharing with them, but, for sleep, we had the benefit of one of those massive home-spun creations into which to snuggle. We could offer no payment but pressed upon the lady of the house a three-colour ballpoint pen the couple plainly coveted. Of the market there was no sign since we were a day late.

By all accounts Ibarra sounded an equally-pleasant township, situated, as it is, midway between Quito and the Colombian frontier. And with our arrival there in the same little railcar we discovered it was as pleasant as its reputation made it out to be.

It is neatly ringed by a volcano and a mountain range and possesses a nearby lake where Atahualpa is supposed to have drowned his Indian captives. We spent the first of two nights on the floor of the stationmaster's office with strident bells and telephones ringing unanswered all around us though, again, there was only one scheduled train a day passing through. In the morning the station staff arrived, stepped over us and began their duties taking our prostrate forms entirely for granted. For breakfast we consumed half a pint of rum donated by the office staff and a cut loaf that had been supplied the previous evening by a grocer and Jehova Witness. He had engaged us in a bible study discussion when we had gone into his shop to enquire the price of biscuits and, being surrounded by mouth-watering goodies, we listened hopefully. The loaf of bread had materialised but even our pretended biblical enthusiasm failed to produce the seven fishes of the parable.

Aware that our usage of the Ibarra railway facilities as a doss-house might be construed as an inconvenience if we dallied there a third night we took to the trains again. But notions of sleeping cars and plush first-class compartments were eclipsed by first sight of Ecuadoran Rail's little monster called an *autocarril* that was reserved for this lesser section of their network. Basically it is a vehicle that started life as a common-o'garden lorry or bus to end it on flanged wheels and a fixed course. Depending upon whether the particular vehicle was a one-time bus or a lorry went the variation in comfort and since the distance to San Lorenzo is nearly two hundred miles this distinction is important.

Our train was a Ford and, for the first half of the journey, was of the lorry variety. Though our ticket stipulated reserved seats, there weren't any seats. The cope bulged with humanity, chickens, bags of flour and a nanny goat. We were classed as 'mixed goods' and the definition was correct. In a tunnel we ran out of petrol and it was the nanny goat this time that was sick over my sandals. A raging river cuts the line in two — literally — by the simple expedient of having swept away the bridge some years before, thus necessitating the crossing — by no more than four passengers at a time — of a temporary rope structure that sways dramatically, to the second train waiting the other side.

The second train was an old bus, equally full, though I managed part of a seat. Two landslides that required passenger participation for the clearing, followed by a waterfall that falls directly onto the train (necessitating firmly-closed windows), and we swept into San Lorenzo and its steaming jungle. But the soft beaches of our fevered imagination turned out to be mangrove swamps and the balmy night disintegrated into a tropical downpour. We spent the night in the ticket office of San Lorenzo

Main being eaten alive by mosquitoes and in the morning returned, thankfully, to Ibarra.

Now we were impatient to see Colombia — in spite of the pitfalls — so we progressed due north again, toting for rides. A co-operative police detachment put us up in their honeymoon suite (the cleanest cell) in a police station, and a village restaurant was persuaded to let us extend our simple evening meal — and only meal of the day — into an all-night sitting on the floor. At the border the Ecuadoran customs forgot to ask us for the compulsory exit tax of fifty *sucres* and — as we had no intention of reminding them — we won ourselves a blow-out at the last restaurant in Ecuador.

Inside Colombian territory we were asked for proof of our solvency and a valid ticket for anywhere outside of the country. With our finances at a farcically low ebb and my air ticket lost we put our faith in the ambassadorial letter now two countries 'invalidated'. Dazzled by the array of seals the officer omitted to notice my thumb was covering the 'Lima' in the notepaper heading and so presumed the document to have emanated from Bogota. We got through.

Hitch-hiking in Colombia, they told us, was a dangerous game. Kidnapping, robbery, murder was, it appeared, all too prevalent. But the bus fares had rocketed to well beyond our means so we risked the hell and damnation of the open road. Our modes of transportation varied from a truck of manure and a lorry load of school-children to a smart Toyota Land Cruiser of the Colombian Water Corporation. Respective drivers were co-operative, sympathetic and charming and one took us home for a guinea-pig high tea. We lived to tell the tale.

In Popayan, learning that an English artist who played the bagpipes was living there, we hunted him down. The man who came to the door seemed very un-English to me and appeared more interested in Buddhism. He gave us a meal nevertheless and it was only when I enquired about his paintings that we discovered we had called at the wrong house. Peter's was next door. Reorientated we ran Peter the painter to earth to subsequently remain with him and his Colombian wife for three days.

Peter Walton lived in a bare house on the edge of the town

which is the provincial capital of the district of Cauca. Popayan, founded by Benalcazar in 1536, is to Colombia what Weimar is to Germany, or Burgos is to Spain, a place of monasteries, cloisters of pure Spanish classic architecture and clean wide streets shaded from a warm unoppressive sun by handsome white buildings. Its gems formed many a subject for Peter's palette and ever-active brush and some of his Popayan paintings, interspersed with Dorset landscapes, are on permanent display in the tourist office on Carrera Street – or they were before the cruel earthquake struck the town in 1983.

There were reasons for the bareness of the house. One was that Peter was as bankrupt as we were, the other because, were it even modestly furnished, the neighbours would steal everything. Peter was popular with the neighbours though he was well aware that many were nothing less than 'banditos'. And that's how it is in Colombia; even in a respectable community like Popayan where many an aristocratic family have their roots.

There are four classes of people in Colombia; the aristocracy, the middle and working classes and those that are forced to steal to exist. There is a perpetual if undeclared war going on in the country. Occasionally it boils over into a full-scale civil conflict like 'The Violence', as it was called, between Liberals and Conservatives from 1948 to 1958 when 200,000 people died. But usually it simmers quietly with unreported guerilla actions taking place in the remote hills and mountains. Robbery with violence is a common occurrence, especially in Bogota, and the industrial city of Cali where many a foreign traveller – who is singled out for attention – has a tale of woe to tell.

Violence is not the only scourge in Colombia. Infant mortality too is very high. Because of poor housing conditions, lack of proper water supplies and sanitation, malnutrition and inadequate medical services, health is an acute problem. Venereal diseases are widely spread and leprosy has not been completely stamped out. Typhus, nutritional goitre and scurvy are common while an ever-higher increase in the population only worsens the situation. But these are national problems. Peter had some of his own.

There are 398 Indian tribes in the country. Nana, Peter's wife, originated from one of them though her Indian blood was diluted with that of Spanish ancestry. She had her first child when she was thirteen and the father's family had done the right thing by bringing up the boy. Peter was married previously and had a boy of his own now boarded at a school in Popayan. For Nana, Colombia was her native home and her country. And, physically, it is a very beautiful country indeed. Peter loved it too but its problems were intruding into his life. Nana had no papers; officially she was a non-person. To become a citizen she would require 5,000 pesos (then about £100) in legal fees; it might as well have been a million so far as she and Peter were concerned. And papers are required to leave Colombia, even temporarily. Peter had papers and *could* leave — if he could afford the air fare. But to leave the country without Nana and his new baby daughter Clary was out of the question. Thus the prospect of a transfer to Britain was a mixed one aggravated by the question of how Nana would or could settle in an environment so utterly different to that to which she was accustomed.

Colombia is no welfare state. If little Clary Sol Fernandez became ill there is no National Health Service to take care of her. Peter had only to succumb to a police check without his papers and he could be press-ganged into the army — or worse. Already DAS, the Colombian Security Police, had planted drugs in his empty house and only a hefty bribe — Peter's every peso at the time — kept him out of a prison that provides no food other than what is allowed in from relatives of inmates. He had also experienced unbelievable difficulties even when his papers *were* in order. Not surprisingly he had become something of a paranoic though insisting that the worst was over and that he was fast becoming accepted by both his 'bandito' fellow-citizens and officialdom.

David and I were taken to see a child relative of his in the local reform school. I had been primed with stories of savage beatings and was prepared for the worst. A policeman stalking the perimeter fence cradling a sub-machine gun only served to sharpen my expectations but inside the stark but not heinous buildings I was able to speak to the boy entirely without supervision. The food? Quite good; he was quick to answer my query. Even my own son has never praised *his* school fare. I gave the boy a few pesos and he straightway ran off to purchase some sweets at an invisible tuckshop. Did he have regular lessons, I asked thinking of allegations I had heard of the inmates carrying out no other activity outside their capacity as industrial slaves. 'Of course,' he replied, puzzled at my question. It was his turn now. 'Got any pot?' he enquired with an automatic glance over his shoulder. 'We're short of it here.' Pot was what he was 'in' for; running the stuff. Everybody smokes and denies it in Colombia.

The boy was Peter's son, and this was his 'boarding school'. Negotiations were under way for his transfer to a school in Britain since his 'crime' was hardly the blackest in the book. But it seemed that the British Foreign Office in the guise of the consul at Cali, more than the Colombian authorities, was dragging his feet*. Association with teenage 'banditos' leads to bad habits which could be rectified in a British crammer. Thus arose another problem for Peter. With a son in Britain where would his loyalties lie?

Nana lived in a fairy-tale world of her own, gathering wild flowers to decorate her jet black hair. Peter was hardly less impractical though I did hear him scold her once for buying sweets with their few pesos which could have gone on bread. His pictures found few buyers which meant his income was next to nothing though he had ideas of utilising the bagpipes to commercial advantage when they arrived by post from his aunt in London.

Thus the four of us — and little Clary — survived over the duration of our stay on an uninspiring diet composed of the results of mixing the last of our soup powder together with stale bread and *oca,* adding water and heating it on the Walton electric ring. But in spite of the inadequacies of the cuisine it was a happy three days during which we explored Popayan and its surrounding countryside and, as mentioned, visited the delinquent son.

On our last morning in Popayan we were serenaded by the neighbours to the accompaniment of a guitar and I was to see at

* I hear that the boy is now back in Britain.

first hand how accustomed — indeed appreciative — they had become of the strange gringo in their midst. God knows what they'd make of him when Aunt Martha in Camberwell sends him his bagpipes . . .

Such had been the frugality of our living that David and I had managed to save enough money to take the bus to Cali. We could even have raised the fare to go right through to Bogota but there arose the question of survival in the Colombian capital while awaiting departure of the flight home. However since the explaining and replacement of a lost flight ticket was likely to take a day or two we would of necessity have to spend some time in the city.

The bus was full but, again, we managed a seat amongst a clientele of hairy men and women who eyed our persons with a certain relish that was disconcerting. Colombia's reputation had not been lost upon us and already David had been relieved of his pocket-book while in Popayan. Henceforth we had unpacked our machetes to display their ferocious blades in an effort to dissuade any further attentions. The trouble now was that they became simply further items likely to be 'nicked' the instant we put them down.

The journey to Cali lasted only three hours before we were pitched out into the bus station; invariably a notorious establishment in violence-prone cities and Cali's in particular. Hastily we made our way into the city centre not quite sure what we intended to do there.

Cali is the third largest city in Colombia but despite its size, it has not forgotten that it was once the heart of a colonial ranching economy and it has the grace of all cities built along rivers. This particular river is the Cauca running through a fertile valley endowed with sugar plantations, rice paddies and cotton fields. Again Benalcazar — his statue stands impressively in the central square — was involved in its birth in 1536.

Benalcazar had thus penetrated the northern extremes of the Inca empire and, together with the exploits of Almago in the south, it marked the end of a chapter and the beginning of a transition in the regions they traversed from discovery to conquest, to quarrelling over the spoils, and eventually to a settled colonial administration. Lured by further expectations of riches in the north Benalcazar, having established his administration in Quito, moved hopefully north with not only the idea of further conquests in mind but of putting distance between himself and Pizarro. Late in 1537, Francisco Pizarro, suspecting that Benalcazar was developing ideas above his station, sent Lorenzo de Aldana and a force of horsemen in pursuit with instructions to arrest Benalcazar and bring him back but, because of his quarry's depredations, he failed to catch up. So, driving a herd of pigs before him as a living food stock, foraging for grain and potatoes, and fighting with those who disputed his passage, Benalcazar moved on. He passed through Popayan and into the fertile Neiva valley on the upper Magdalena arriving eventually at the Cali river to be forestalled by his own countrymen coming down from fresh conquests in the north.

All the settled territories of the Andes were difficult of access and none more so than the highland regions of what is now Colombia (the Spaniards called it New Granada). The Pacific coast is uninviting; it is laced with mangrove swamps and forests, and the rivers are difficult to navigate. Thus, after some initial attempts, no other Spanish explorers felt tempted to enter the country by that route. Inland, Colombia is extraordinarily rugged, even by Andean standards. East-west travel is almost impossible; even today nearly all the roads and the few railway lines run north and south. Of the three major cordilleras that form this section of the Andes, the central and the southern are the most awesome, containing many high peaks. Amongst them is the plateau of Cundinamarca, 'Land of the Condor', and it was here that the north-bound and south-bound streams of Spanish exploration met in 1537. And with this meeting began the decline of the new conquest as Spanish factions began squabbling among themselves and with other European intruders. Thus the Incas and, in turn, the conquistadores pass into history on an all too familiar note of human frailty.

The physical obstacles to travel in this part of the world triggered, for us, the idea of attempting to repeat the success of our approach to the railway authority in Quito and we made for the station in Cali though our optimism decreased when we perceived its diminutiveness and lack of stature. Industrial city though it was, Cali put small store in its rail communications.

There was not even a railway administration office in evidence so, remembering an incident in my life when I had cadged a free ride on a passenger train between Basra and Baghdad, we went in search of the stationmaster. We found him — or his deputy — drinking coffee in a poky little office full of acrid tobacco smoke.

The ensuing interview, with David as spokesman, started badly. 'There is no passenger service from this station,' we were told firmly but I had my eyes on a number of freight trains lined up on adjacent tracks. 'Surely one of those will be going to Bogota sometime?' we suggested, pushing the subject a little.

'Yes,' agreed the man, showing the first signs of a not-inexcusable impatience, 'no doubt so but that's not to say . . .'

We placed the ambassadorial letter and my press card under his nose while David trotted out our sob-story; laying it on for all it was worth. It ended with us being offered coffee, a wagon in which to sleep and free transit to the Colombian capital 'sometime during tomorrow morning'.

The brake wagon that became our bed-chamber for the night was hardly *Wagon-Lit* either but bare boards were hardly strangers to us. We were able to lock ourselves in against the marauders of the darkness and, around mid-morning next day, we jerked into motion. Through heavily-louvred windows we glimpsed a lush green countryside of gorges and semi-tropical forest.

Though it rarely halted the train was painfully slow. However another night on board was a blessing in disguise since it precluded the possibility of being stranded in an unsalubrious district of Bogota in the middle of the night. There being no corridor we were not disturbed. All the same, by the time we clanked into the capital we had had enough. Our food intake since Popayan had been no more than some bread and cheese, both long past their prime, so our appetites were huge. Near the station we satisfied them at a dubious but inexpensive café, blowing some of our precious pesos on repeated helpings of bacon and eggs.

Replenished, we trudged through poverty-stricken back streets our eyes alert for ambushes and gentlemen with flick knives. I noticed elderly women sitting in the gutters and wondered why they should be doing so until I saw the stream of urine issuing out from the base of their voluminous skirts.

Bogota, another product of the Spanish conquest, is a capital of over five million at a height of 8,661 feet which puts it fourth in the capital city altitude stakes. Unlike Quito it has no pretence to beauty or illusion about its far from satisfactory climate. A contributor to the *South American Handbook* effuses thus: '... Shrouded often in the clouds of the high plateau, drenched often in rain, cursed with a climate that has no seasons, it is scarcely an exhilarating spot'. But though a big brute of a city sprouting skyscrapers and spawning asphyxiating traffic fumes it is saved from downright ugliness by a backdrop of mountains, green with trees, rising almost straight from the eastern section of the town.

Perhaps I'm being unfair to Bogota for our opinions of it were possibly coloured by exhaustion and an entry to the city not made under the happiest of circumstances. Its notoriety, too was not to be ignored. 'Armed attacks on pedestrians are common,' warns the handbook. 'Gangs of up to six or eight men with knives often attack small groups of tourists and do not hesitate to use their weapons for even small amounts of money. Under state-of-siege legislation police may shoot and kill a suspect during any narcotics operation and it will be automatically classified as self-defence.' Can you wonder at our wariness.

Within forty years the population has grown from 325,000 to well over four million and the building work that went into housing it has been nothing short of maniacal with high-rise buildings, vibrant slums, elegant mansions and endless housing estates growing up and outwards at a pace rarely seen elsewhere. What is left of old Bogota has to be searched for; colonial buildings, museums — including the unique Musco del Oro (The Gold Museum) — and attractive Spanish churches are often hidden, always overshadowed by concrete mountains.

Civilization came to this area long before the arrival of Europeans. Originally the valley in which Bogota stands had been covered with the waters of a lake which disappeared leaving a rich soil that supported the farming communities of the Chibcha

Indians, some of the most skilful craftsmen of early South America.

The Chibchas' fame as goldsmiths spread far and wide and by the time it reached the lowlands, had become another version of the legend of El Dorado. It was in pursuit of this legend that Gonzalo Jimenez de Queseda set out to duplicate the prowess of Francisco Pizarro and though his Spanish army lost half its men en route across the cruel terrain the ragged survivors finally stumbled upon the lake bed, beat the Chibchas in battle and founded Bogota. The story is worth telling if only for the fact that the city was one of few in New Granada that was *not* founded by Benalcazar.

Though bereft of the architectural skills of Benalcazar, de Quesada planned well. At the hands of artisans from Spain Bogota blossomed and the results of this workmanship are visible today in the architecture, together with that of subsequent colonialists. Still growing, its current planners have to deal with a jumble of narrow colonial streets running parallel to four-lane thoroughfares and glass-sheathed skyscrapers rising beside one-storey shacks.

All this David and I took in during our enforced sojourn in the city but our immediate destination was the offices of British Caledonian Airways in Carrera 10, one of the central streets. Its staff were somewhat taken aback by the sudden appearance of two none-too-clean 'desperados' brandishing naked machetes but managed to recover their poise. Our explanations of our plight made, telex messages to Gatwick Airport put in hand, we turned to leave and ran straight into an acquaintance of mine.

Captain Adrian Goldsack, attired in perfectly-creased service dress complete with a brilliantly-polished sam browne, stood rooted to the spot as he gazed at the apparition before him that appeared to be claiming his friendship. To be honest I did not know him well but his presence was going to be the answer to a maiden's prayer if I had anything to do with it.

It materialised that he was deputy-leader of the British Amazonas Expedition recently arrived in Bogota prior to the undertaking of an ecological, archaeological and medical survey of the Amazon Basin. Furthermore he was in charge of their base situated in a sumptuous district of the city. The unfortunate Adrian saw how my mind was working the moment he released this information but his subsequent evasions and excuses were useless. I clung to him like a leech and eventually — and with no great fervour — he accepted us as a pair of undesirable guests. In all fairness it must be said that we had put him in a difficult position since the expedition funds and facilities were, understandably, limited.

Not wishing to take advantage of this lucky turn of events we delayed until evening before setting off to locate and descend upon the house and straightaway came under the kindly jurisdiction of the gracious Bridget Saunders, wife of the expedition leader, Captain John Saunders, who wholeheartedly and unreservedly made us welcome.

Thus, sleeping upon sofas that, to us, offered the pinnacle of luxury, and sharing military rations that might have been described as dull by some standards though certainly not ours, we marked time in the Colombian capital. My air ticket was replaced and it became simply a case of waiting for our scheduled departure.

I cannot say I enjoyed those last days in Bogota. Not only were we gate-crashers into someone else's expedition but this one was just beginning and ours was ending. It was a melancholy state of affairs and quite time we went home.

So, following a third of a year of tortuous, ground-hugging travelling over the rugged terrain of four Andean countries, we took to the air. The flight from Bogota's El Dorado Airport to Caracas, Venezuela's capital, was no more than a few hours, yet the distance was more than we had trudged for those sometimes heartbreaking months. The big Boeing 747 was almost empty and the cabin staff must have chalked us up as their scruffiest and hungriest passengers. If so they showed no disapproval of our dishevelled appearance and loaded us down with airline goodies. On the long haul across the ocean we succumbed to the deepest slumber.

I was still worth a dollar when I turned into my front door. And in the sum of my experience of the Andean territories of South America as well as my new-found knowledge of the Inca realm I looked upon myself as a very wealthy man indeed.

Glossary

Agger: The faint markings of a former road.
Ayllu: A combine. Communally held land.
Cabuya: A fleshy-leafed plant from which Inca bridge cables were woven.
Camino: Lorry (Spanish).
Cana: A local rum.
Chaca: A bridge.
Charqui: Sun-dried meat.
Chasqui: Postal runner or courier of Inca times.
Chicha: A mildly intoxicating, thick, malt-smelling beverage (formerly *Aka).*
Chuno: Dehydrated potato.
Coca: A low tropical bush the leaves of which contain cocaine.
Collectivo: A private taxi.
Cordillera: A mountain range.
Curaca: A local Inca judge or governor.
Estancia: A ranch. (Spanish)
Hacienda: A large farm (Spanish)
Ichú: Andean bunch grass.
Isnu: A fort-like edifice.
Jefe, El: Spanish word for 'Chief'.
Jivaro: Ecuadoran Indians of one-time head-shrinking fame.
Lomo: A popular dish containing meat and vegetable.
Manana: Tomorrow (Spanish).
Manzanilla: A dried herb.
Muera: Death (Spanish).
Natillas: A sugar speciality of Puira, Peru.
Oca: A tuberous plant similar to the potato.
O'kla: Rudely-made roadside hut of Inca days.
Olloco: A peppery variety of potato.
Oro: Gold (Spanish).

Pisco: A Peruvian brandy.
Puna: High treeless savannah. Bleak tableland found in the Andes.
Quechua: The Peruvian Indian language.
Quinoa: A pig-weed, member of the goosefoot family, a tall reddish stalk with edible seeds.
Soles: Peruvian denomination of currency.
Taclla: A foot plough.
Tampu: An inn, shelter and storehouse built by the Incas alongside the highway.
Topo: A woman's shawl held in place by an ornamental pin.
Viva: Life (Spanish).
Yacolla: A woman's cape garment made from alpaca wool.

Bibliography

Brooks, John, *South American Handbook* (Trade & Travel Publications)
Fodor, Eugene, *Fodor's Guide to South America* (Hodder & Stoughton)
Hagen, Victor von, *Highway of the Sun* (Gollancz)
Hagen, Victor von, *Realm of the Incas* (New American Library)
Hemming, John, *Conquest of the Incas* (MacMillan)
Moore, JH, *Tears of the Sun God* (Faber)
Parry, JH, *The Discovery of South America* (Elek)
Prestcott, WH, *History of the Conquest of Peru* (Weidenfeld & Nicolson)
Snow, Sebastian, *The Rucksack Man* (Hodder & Stoughton)
Snow, Sebastian, *Half A Dozen of the Other* (Hodder & Stoughton)
Bradt, Hilary and George, *Backpacking and Trekking in Peru and Bolivia* (Bradt Enterprises)
Byford-Jones, W, *Four Faces of Peru* (Robert Hale)